the g.i. diet

Menopause

clinic

Also by Rick Gallop

The G.I. Diet
Living the G.I. Diet
The G.I. Diet Guide to Shopping and Eating Out
The Family G.I. Diet
The G.I. Diet Cookbook
The G.I. Diet Clinic
The G.I. Diet Express

the g.i. diet
Menopause
clinic

RICK GALLOP

RANDOM HOUSE CANADA

Random House Canada and colophon are trademarks

www.randomhouse.ca

Library and Archives Canada Cataloguing in Publication

Gallop, Rick
　　The G.I. diet menopause clinic / Rick Gallop.

Includes index.

ISBN 978-0-307-35708-3

1. Menopause—Diet therapy—Recipes.　2. Menopause—Nutritional aspects.
3. Middle-aged women—Health and hygiene.　4. Glycemic index.　I. Title.

RG186.G34 2009　　　　　　　618.1'750654　　　　　　　C2008-904125-9

Printed and bound in Canada

10 9 8 7 6 5 4 3 2 1

To my wife, Dr. Ruth Gallop,
whose insights into women's emotions and behaviours
during menopause proved invaluable in the development
of both the e-clinic and this book.

Contents

Introduction

Menopause seems to make it more difficult to lose the weight—the losses are so slow it is disheartening ... this time I want to do it for my health—my first granddaughter is not yet one and I want to make sure I am around to dance at her wedding and not dead from heart or stroke problems. Lynn

I have tried over the counter diet pills, Weight Watchers, Atkins, eating once a day, and all to no avail ... Over the years pounds kept creeping back on and now I feel horrible about myself. I always failed at sticking to the diets because I would get hungry. But, after thought, I know I did, and do, a lot of emotional eating. Lonely? Hurt? Depressed? Find the chocolate or snacks. Janice

I am a lifetime member of Weight Watchers but the last two times (after menopause began) I wasn't able to lose weight (only 5 lbs) ... My resolve diminishes when there is no visual success and eventually I return to dessert. Sharon

This all gets very discouraging, especially when your hormones are all over the place with menopause. I know I'm not in my twenties anymore (nor do I want to be and weighing what I did back then!), but I do want to remain healthy and active. Heather

I tried WW again but found the point system difficult. [On] South Beach and Atkins I again lost weight but [I] was grumpy, miserable, sluggish and just couldn't stick with it due to lack of carbs. Roxanne

These comments were made by participants in a menopausal e-clinic I recently conducted before they commenced the program. If their struggles sound familiar, then this book is for you.

Menopause and post-menopause can be a challenging time of life for women and their husbands/partners. It is a time of not only physical change, but also empty nests and aging parents. Metabolism slows and hormonal storms play havoc with daily lives. Many are at the peak of demanding careers, which only adds to the stress. And, if that wasn't enough, for many women the most significant outcome is a gain in weight and girth—the dreaded middle-aged spread. It doesn't have to be this way. There is something you can do right now to regain your figure, increase your energy, improve your health, and, in many cases, reduce those hot flashes and other menopausal symptoms. Just read on.

This book is based on the experiences of a group of forty menopausal or post-menopausal women who volunteered to participate in a thirteen-week G.I. Diet Menopausal e-clinic.

The e-clinic was based on the *G.I. Diet*, which I originally wrote back in 2002 based on my personal struggle to lose weight when I was president of the Heart and Stroke Foundation of Ontario. The diet I developed is based on the principles of the glycemic index, or G.I., which measures the rate at which the body digests a wide range of foods. Foods with a low G.I. rating digest more slowly while those with a higher G.I. rating digest more quickly. Low G.I., slow-digesting foods are more satiating, which means they leave you feeling fuller for a longer time. That way, you eat less without going hungry, which is the most important criterion for any successful diet. Going hungry is the principle reason people stop their diets.

Low–G.I. foods, such as fruits and vegetables, whole grains, pasta, and low-fat dairy products, coupled with lean protein and "best" fats, provide an balanced and nutritious way to eat.

To keep it simple, the G.I. Diet has colour-coded all foods into three traffic-light colours. You will never have to count calories or points, or weigh and measure food again.

Since the original *G.I. Diet* book hit shelves, I've heard from tens of thousands of people who are thrilled with their weight loss on the program. But as well as hearing about successes, I also heard a lot about readers' challenges and frustrations. Many women were coming to the G.I. Diet after a long string of other attempts to manage their weight, having tried every diet under the sun and still failing time and time again. Compounding women's struggles were the hormonal storms brought on by menopause and weight gain and middle-age spread.

The dilemma I faced was that my books are, by their nature, a monologue or a one-way communication: I discuss the diet, tell the readers what to do, and that's it—end of story. But these women needed not a monologue—but a dialogue. I had gained some valuable experience in building an interactive experience with readers in an earlier e-clinic to help "big people" with serious weight problems. We were able to communicate with each other as they were going through the process of trying to lose weight.

That experience provided me with a template for an e-clinic designed specifically for menopausal or post-menopausal women. The concept was simple: Start with the already user-friendly G.I. Diet, and make it even *more* user-friendly by leading participants in detail through the critical first thirteen weeks. During this time, participants were coached on the multiple components of the program: how to handle crises such as falling off the wagon or getting stuck on a weight plateau; and, most importantly, how to stay motivated—even in the face of unexpected weight gain or cravings for fattening foods. Sticking to the plan was made even easier with complete meal plans covering every meal—and snack—of every day, accompanied by recipes and shopping lists.

In addition, we shared together our day-to-day challenges and discussed solutions as a group. This was weekly communication: I sent to the group a newsletter addressing a particular concern commonly faced by people on the G.I. Diet. In return, once a week each participant sent me her weight and measurements, and a weekly diary illustrating any questions or concerns encountered over the course of the clinic. I reviewed and highlighted some of the issues raised and incorporated them into my weekly electronic newsletters.

Though hundreds of people applied for the e-clinic, I could choose only forty to participate. Amazingly, over 90 percent of the group completed the thirteen-week program.

This book is a reproduction of the e-clinic that I conducted with those forty participants. You'll share the same experiences they did: the same menus, the same advice, most likely the same kinds of highs and lows, and—ultimately—the same success.

How to Use This Book

In **Part 1**, I explain the principles of health and nutrition, the basics of successful weight loss, and the way the G.I. Diet works. It's not complicated at all: all foods are traffic-light colour coded:

Red-light—foods to avoid.
Yellow-light—foods that you should use occasionally.
Green-light—foods you can eat freely.

Also included is information on how to make sensible decisions when shopping, cooking, or reading a food label.

Because knowledge of nutrition and the mechanics of weight loss are critical to your success, I recommend that you read **Part 1** closely before moving on, and refer back to it constantly over the course of your clinic. With a complete understanding of what is happening in your body while you are on the G.I. Diet, you will greatly enhance your chances of success. Don't worry—this isn't rocket science. This is everyday information that's sensible and easy to follow.

Part 2 is the heart of the matter. Here you'll find the thirteen-week *G.I. Diet Menopause Clinic* broken down into week-by-week chapters. Each chapter deals with a different core aspect of success on the G.I. Diet—matters such as behaviour change, staying motivated, and how to keep your diet intact when eating out, as well as issues pertaining to menopause.

As this book is primarily concerned with weight loss, we do not propose to make this a primer on menopause. However, should you require additional material about menopause, I have found the U.S. National Institute of Health to be a good source as it contains the most latest information—and more importantly—information that can be understood by the non-medical reader. You can reach the Institute at: www.nlm.nih.gov/medlineplus/tutorials/menopauseintroduction/htm/index.htm.

I will show you diet's role in post-menopausal gain in weight and girth, as well as in other related menopausal symptoms such as hot flashes, sleep deprivation, mood swings, and lack of energy. So whether you are currently going through menopause or are still struggling with the after-effects, the *G.I. Diet Menopause Clinic* will help you regain your waistline and energy levels, and improve your health. My discussion of each topic is accompanied by what the participants of the original e-clinic had to say about these subjects as well as their own experiences, along with my responses to them.

Each week I include a recent reader's success story—a motivational minute—from the thousands of letters I received, so you can see how the G.I. Diet worked for them, as well as the lessons they learned. I believe you will find these successes most motivating.

The weekly sequence is laid out in an intentional order that loosely maps the experiences you'll have over the course of three months on the G.I. Diet. Week 1, for instance, is "Getting Started", along with an introduction to menopause and weight gain; while Week 9 is "Keeping Motivated".

However, the clinic is not rigid! If you find yourself having difficulties eating outside your home, reread or skip forward to the appropriate chapter. Of particular note is Week 10, "Celebrations: Holidays and Entertaining," which addresses those days and celebrations when we often find it difficult to stick to our healthy eating habits. Of course, visit the advice and recommendations for this week when a holiday or celebration comes up on your calendar—move it up a few weeks, or push it back, as necessary.

Each week also includes a detailed meal plan (three daily meals, plus snacks), along with an accompanying grocery list that provides all you need to make the week's worth of food. These meal plans are both optional and flexible. While some people who prefer a fully structured program might follow each day to the letter, others might prefer to plan their own green-light meals and snacks, using the meal plan only as a guide. Diary space is provided for you to record your measurements and your observations or comments on your weekly experience with the diet and your changing lifestyle.

Part 3 deals with life after the first thirteen weeks, both for those who have reached their target weight, and those who still have some way to go. This section outlines Phase II of the G.I. Diet, reintroducing some yellow-light treats, and modifying your diet as you approach your target weight, and advice on eating in order to maintain your new healthy weight for the rest of your life.

At the end of the thirteen weeks of my original e-clinic, the e-clinic members were offered an extension to the program consisting of nine monthly e-mail newsletters—rounding out their experience to a full year. Everyone in the group elected to participate.

Once you've made it through the thirteen weeks outlined in this book, you are invited to sign on for these additional nine monthly e-mail newsletters, which will provide you with support, the latest news on green-light products and dishes, and further recipes and tips. An on-line Green-Light Discussion Forum is also available. I also invite you to submit your own monthly diary and measurements in response to these letters—an ongoing e-clinic of your very own! See page 225 for more information on this program.

Part 4 lists over seventy delicious recipes divided by meal type—virtually all the recipes you'll need in order to make the dishes suggested in each week's meal plan. The recipes are green-light, low-G.I., and (best of all) delicious— you'll know you've made the right choice of diet when you try the recipe for Pecan Brownies!

The recipes are followed by a comprehensive breakdown of common foods and ingredients, categorizing the contents into the three traffic-light colours— red, yellow and green. It's a handy reference for times when your palate wanders from the meals and recipes indicated elsewhere in the book. Copy it and take it with you when eating out, especially in the first month of the program when you are making adjustments to your eating habits. Whether you are menopausal or post-menopausal, and whether this is your first introduction to the G.I. Diet program, or you are an old hand looking for a new approach, I'm confident that this clinic will help you lose weight permanently. This is not so much a diet as a new way of eating that allows you to lose weight without going hungry or feeling deprived. The traffic-light colour coding of foods keeps it simple so you'll never have to count another calorie. And, finally, it's a balanced, nutritious diet that will help you reduce the risk of major diseases and live a longer and more active life.

PART I

The G.I. Diet

CHAPTER ONE

The Truth about Carbs, Fats and Protein

It's just about impossible to live in this country and not know that we are in the midst of an "obesity epidemic." If you watch television, listen to the radio, read the newspaper or simply notice the magazine headlines at the supermarket checkout, you can't help but be aware that nearly 56 percent of Canadians are overweight and that our obesity rate has doubled over the past twenty years. Everyone seems to have an explanation for our collective weight crisis: some hold the fast-food industry responsible; others blame our sedentary lifestyle. Some maintain we are eating too much fat; others say we are eating too many carbohydrates. So what's the truth?

Well, all of these reasons are part of the answer. But if you reduce the problem to its physiological cause, it's actually quite simple: we're consuming more calories than we're expending, and the resulting surplus is stored around our waists, hips and thighs as fat. There's no mystery here. But to understand why we are consuming more calories, we need to get back to basics and look at the three fundamental elements of our diet: carbohydrates, fats and protein. We need to understand the role these components play in the digestive system and how they work together—whether we're in the process of getting fat or thin.

We'll start with carbohydrates, since the popularity of low-carbohydrate diets like the Atkins program has made them a hot topic and given them a bad rap. Carbohydrates have been so much in the news over the past few years that a new word—"carbs"—has entered the language. Though they've been blamed for all our weight problems, their role in weight control has really been misunderstood.

Carbohydrates

Carbohydrates are a necessary part of a healthy diet. They are rich in fibre, vitamins and minerals, including antioxidants, which we now know play an important role in the prevention of heart disease and cancer. Carbohydrates are also the primary source of energy for our bodies. They are found in grains, vegetables, fruits, legumes (beans) and dairy products.

Here is how carbs work: when you eat an orange or a bagel, your body digests the carbohydrates in the food and turns them into glucose, which provides you with energy. The glucose dissolves in your bloodstream and then travels to the parts of your body that use energy, such as your muscles and brain. So carbs are critical to everyone's health. When managing weight, however, it is important to realize that not all carbs are created equal.

Some carbohydrates break down into glucose in the digestive system at a slow and steady rate, gradually releasing their nutrients and keeping us feeling full and satisfied. Others break down rapidly, spiking our glucose levels and then disappearing quickly, leaving us feeling hungry again. For example, cornflakes and old-fashioned, large-flake oatmeal are both carbohydrates, but we all know the difference between eating a bowl of oatmeal for breakfast and eating a bowl of cornflakes. The oatmeal stays with you—it "sticks to your ribs," as my mother used to say—whereas your stomach starts rumbling an hour after eating the cornflakes, pushing you toward your next snack or meal. Throughout the course of a day, if you are eating carbs that break down rapidly, like cornflakes, as opposed to those that break down slowly, you will be eating more and, as a result, will begin to put on weight. If, however, you start eating carbs that break down slowly, like old-fashioned oatmeal, you will eat less and begin to lose weight. Selecting the right type of carb is key to achieving your optimum energy and weight. But how do you know which carbohydrate is the right type and which isn't?

Well, the first clue is the amount of processing that the food has undergone. The more a food is processed beyond its natural, fibrous state, the less processing your body has to do to digest it. The quicker you digest the food, the sooner you feel hungry again. This helps explain why the number of Canadian adults who are overweight has surged over the last fifty years. A hundred years ago, most of the food people ate came straight from the farm to the dinner table. Lack of refrigeration and scant knowledge of food chemistry meant that most food remained in its original state. However, advances in science, along with the migration of many women out of the kitchen and into the workforce, led to a revolution in prepared foods geared to speed and simplicity of preparation. The giant food companies—Kraft, Kellogg's, Del Monte, Nestlé, etc.—were born. We happily began spending more money for the convenience of prepared, processed, packaged, canned, frozen and bottled food. The Kraft Dinner era had begun.

It was during this period that the miller's traditional wind and water mills were replaced with high-speed steel rolling mills, which stripped away most of the key nutrients, including the bran, fibre and wheat germ (which could spoil), to produce a talcum-like powder: today's white flour. This fine white flour is the basic ingredient for most of our breads and cereals, as well as for baked goods and snacks such as cookies, muffins, crackers and pretzels. Walk through any supermarket and you will be surrounded by towering stacks of these flour-based processed products. And we're eating more and more of these foods; over the past three decades our consumption of grain has increased by 50 percent. Our bodies are paying the price for this radical change in eating habits.

The second clue in determining whether a carbohydrate is the right type is the amount of fibre it contains. Fibre, in simple terms, provides low-calorie filler. It does double duty, in fact: it literally fills up your stomach, so you feel satiated; and your body takes much longer to break it down, so it stays with you longer and slows the digestive process. There are two forms of fibre: soluble and insoluble. Soluble fibre is found in carbs such as oatmeal, beans, barley and citrus fruits, and has been shown to lower blood cholesterol levels. Insoluble fibre is important for normal bowel function and is typically found in whole wheat breads and cereals, and most vegetables.

There are two other important components that inhibit the rapid breakdown of food in our digestive system, and they are fats and protein. Let's look at fats first.

Fats

Fat, like fibre, acts as a brake in the digestive process. When combined with other foods, fat becomes a barrier to digestive juices. It also signals the brain that you are satisfied and do not require more food. Does this mean that we should eat all the fat we want? Definitely not!

Though fat is essential for a nutritious diet, containing various key elements that are crucial to the digestive process, cell development and overall health, it also contains twice the number of calories per gram as carbohydrates and protein. If you decide to "just add peanut butter" to your otherwise disciplined regime, it doesn't take much of it—two tablespoons—to spike your total calorie count. As well, once you eat fat, your body is a genius at hanging onto it and refusing to let it go. This is because fat is how the body stores reserve supplies of energy, usually around the waist, hips and thighs. Fat is money in the bank as far as the body is concerned—a rainy-day investment for when you have to call up extra energy. This clever system originally helped our ancestors survive during periods of famine. The problem today is that we don't live with cycles of feast and famine—it's more like feast, and then feast again! But the body's eagerness for fat continues, along with its reluctance to give it up.

This is why losing weight is so difficult: your body does everything it can to persuade you to eat more fat. How? Through fat's capacity to make things taste good. So it's not just you who thinks that juicy steaks, chocolate cake and rich ice cream taste better than a bean sprout. That's the fat content of cake and steak talking.

Sorry to say, there's no getting around it: if you want to lose weight, you have to watch your fat consumption. In addition, you need to be concerned about the type of fats you eat; many fats are harmful to your health. There are four types of fat: the best, the good, the bad and the really ugly. The "really ugly" fats are potentially the most dangerous, and they lurk in many of our most popular snack foods. They are vegetable oils that have been heat-treated to make them thicken—the trans fats you've been hearing so much about in the media. They raise the amount of LDL, or bad, cholesterol in our bodies while lowering the amount of HDL, or good, cholesterol, which protects us from heart disease. As a result, they boost our cholesterol levels, which thickens our arteries and causes heart attack and stroke. So avoid using trans fats, such as vegetable shortening and hard margarine, and avoid packaged snack foods, baked goods, crackers and cereals that contain them. (You can spot them by checking labels for "hydrogenated" or "partially hydrogenated" oils.)

The "bad" fats are called saturated fats and almost always come from animal sources. Butter, cheese and meat are all high in saturated fats. There are a couple of others you should be aware of too: coconut oil and palm oil are two vegetable oils that are saturated and, because they are cheap, they are used in many snack foods, especially cookies. Saturated fats, such as butter or cheese, are solid at room temperature. They elevate your risk of heart disease and Alzheimer's. The evidence is also growing that many cancers, including colon, prostate and breast cancer, are associated with diets high in saturated fats.

The "good" fats are the polyunsaturated ones, and they are cholesterol free. Most vegetable oils, such as corn and sunflower, fall into this category. What you really should be eating, however, are the "best" fats, the monounsaturated fats, which actually promote good health. These are the fats found in olives, almonds, and canola and olive oils. Monounsaturated fats have a beneficial effect on cholesterol and are good for your heart. This is one reason the incidence of heart disease is low in Mediterranean countries, where olive oil is a staple. Although fancy olive oil is expensive, you can enjoy the same health benefits from less costly supermarket brands.

Another highly beneficial oil that falls into the "best" category is omega-3, a fatty acid found in deep-sea fish, such as salmon, mackerel, albacore tuna and herring, as well as in lake trout, walnuts, and flaxseed and canola oils. Some brands of eggs and liquid eggs also contain omega-3, which can help lower cholesterol and protect cardiovascular health.

So the "best" and "good" fats are an important part of a healthy diet and also help slow digestion. Still, they're fat and they pack a lot of calories. Over twice as many calories per gram as carbohydrates or protein. We have to be careful, then, to limit our intake of polyunsaturated fats when trying to lose weight.

Since protein also acts as a brake in the digestive process, let's look at it in more detail.

Protein

Protein is an absolutely essential part of your diet. In fact, you are already half protein: 50 percent of your dry body weight is made up of muscles, organs, skin and hair, all forms of protein. We need this element to build and repair body tissues, and it figures in nearly all metabolic reactions. Protein is also a critical brain food, providing amino acids for the neurotransmitters that relay messages to the brain. This is why it's not a good idea to skip breakfast on the morning of a big meeting or exam. The "brain fog" people experience on some diets is likely the result of diminished protein. Protein is literally food for thought.

The main sources of dietary protein come from animals: meat, seafood, dairy and eggs. Vegetable sources include beans and soy-based products such as tofu. Unfortunately, protein sources such as red meat and full-fat dairy products are also high in "bad," or saturated, fats, which are harmful to your health. It is important that we get our protein from sources that are low in saturated fats, such as lean meats, skinless poultry, seafood, low-fat dairy products, cholesterol-reduced liquid eggs, and tofu and other soy products. One exceptional source of protein is the humble bean. Beans are a perfect food, really: they're high in protein and fibre, and low in saturated fat. No wonder so many of the world's cuisines have found myriad wonderful ways to cook beans. North Americans need to become more bean savvy. Nuts are another excellent source of protein and are relatively low in fat—as long as you don't eat a whole bowlful.

Protein is much more effective than carbohydrates or fat at satisfying hunger. It will make you feel fuller longer, which is why you should try to incorporate some protein into every meal and snack. This will help keep you on the ball and feeling satisfied.

Now that we know how carbohydrates, fats and protein work in the digestive system, let's use the science to discover how to take off the extra pounds.

TO SUM UP

- Eat carbohydrates that have not been highly processed and that do not contain highly processed ingredients.
- Eat less fat overall and look for low-fat alternatives to your current food choices.
- Eat only monounsaturated and polyunsaturated fats.
- Include some protein in all your meals and snacks.
- Eat only low-fat protein, preferably from both animal and vegetable sources.

CHAPTER TWO

The Secret to Easy, Permanent Weight Loss

The "G.I." in G.I. Diet stands for glycemic index, which is the basis of this diet—and the only scientific phrase you'll need to know. The glycemic index is the secret to reducing calories and losing weight without going hungry. It measures the speed at which carbohydrates break down in our digestive system and turn into glucose, the body's main source of energy or fuel.

The glycemic index was developed by Dr. David Jenkins, a professor of nutritional sciences at the University of Toronto, when he was researching the impact of different carbohydrates on the blood sugar, or glucose, level of diabetics. He found that certain carbohydrates broke down quickly and flooded the bloodstream with sugar, but others broke down more slowly, only marginally increasing blood sugar levels. The faster a food breaks down, the higher its rating on the glycemic index, which sets sugar at 100 and scores all other foods against that number. These findings were important to diabetics, who could then use the index to identify low-G.I., slow-release foods that would help control their blood sugar levels. At right are some examples of the G.I. ratings of a range of popular foods.

Examples of G.I. Ratings			
High G.I.		**Low G.I.**	
Baguette	95	Orange	44
Cornflakes	84	All-Bran	43
Rice cake	82	Oatmeal	42
Doughnut	76	Spaghetti	41
Bagel	72	Apple	38
Cereal bar	72	Beans	31
Biscuit	69	Plain yogurt	25

What do these G.I. ratings have to do with the numbers on your bathroom scale? Well, it turns out that low–G.I., slow-release foods have a significant impact on our ability to lose weight. As I have explained, when we eat the wrong type of carb, a high–G.I. food, the body quickly digests it and releases a flood of sugar (glucose) into the bloodstream. This gives us a short-term high, but the sugar is just as quickly absorbed by the body, leaving us with a post-sugar slump. We feel lethargic and start looking for our next sugar fix. A fast-food lunch of a double cheeseburger, fries and a Coke delivers a short-term burst of energy, but by mid-afternoon we start feeling tired, sluggish and hungry. That's when we reach for "just one" brownie or bag of potato chips. These high–G.I. foods deliver the rush we want and then let us down again. The roller-coaster ride is a hard cycle to break. But a high–G.I. diet will make you feel hungry more often, so you end up eating more and gaining more weight.

Let's look at the other end of the G.I. index. Low–G.I. foods, such as fruits, vegetables, whole grains, pasta, beans and low-fat dairy products, take longer to digest, deliver a steady supply of sugar to our bloodstream and leave us feeling fuller for a longer time. Consequently, we eat less. It also helps that these foods are lower in calories. As a result, we consume less food and fewer calories, without going hungry or feeling unsatisfied.

The key player in this process of energy storage and retrieval is insulin, a hormone secreted by the pancreas. Insulin does two things very well. First, it regulates the amount of sugar (glucose) in our bloodstream, removing the excess and storing it as glycogen for immediate use by our muscles, or putting it into storage as fat. Second, insulin acts as a security guard at the fat gates, reluctantly giving up its reserves. This evolutionary feature is a throwback to the days when our ancestors were hunter-gatherers, habitually experiencing times of feast or famine. When food was in abundance, the body stored its surplus as fat to tide it over the inevitable days of famine.

A few years ago, I was on vacation in a remote part of central Mexico, visiting the Copper Canyon, which, incredibly, is larger and deeper than the Grand Canyon in Arizona. A tribe of Tarahumara Indians still resides there. Until recently, these indigenous peoples typically put on 30 pounds during the summer and fall, when the crops, particularly corn, were plentiful. Then, over the course of the winter, when food became scarce, they lost these 30 pounds. Insulin was the champion in this process, both helping to accumulate fat and then guarding its depletion.

Of course, food is now readily available to us at the nearest twenty-four-hour supermarket. But our bodies still function very much as they did in the earliest days. When we eat a high–G.I. food, our pancreas releases insulin to reduce the glucose level in our blood, which, if left unchecked, would lead to hyperglycemia. If we aren't using all that energy at the moment, the glucose is stored as fat. Soon we become hungry again. Our body can either draw on our reserves of fat and laboriously convert them back to sugar, or it can look for more food. Since giving up extra fat is the body's last choice—who knows when that supply might come in handy?—our body would rather send us to the fridge than work to convert fat back to sugar. This helped our survival back in the old days, but it gets in the way of weight loss now.

Blood sugar levels are also influenced by hormonal changes. Your period, pregnancy and menopause all create hormonal swings that cause blood sugar levels to fluctuate. This is a principal trigger for weight gain in women, as well as changes in mood—PMS is a classic example. With menopause, these hormonal changes are more extreme and long lasting. They result in not only weight gain and mood swings, but also other menopausal symptoms such as interrupted sleep patterns and hot flashes. Stabilizing your blood sugar levels will go a long way to help manage these symptoms, and the G.I. Diet can help.

So our goal is to limit the amount of insulin in our system by avoiding high–G.I. foods, which stimulate its production, and instead choosing low–G.I. foods, which keep the supply of sugar in our bloodstream consistent. Slow-release, low–G.I. carbohydrates help curb your appetite by leaving you feeling fuller for a longer period of time. When you combine them with lean protein and the best fats, which help slow the digestive process, you have the magic combination that will allow you to lose weight without going hungry.

Translated into real food, what does this mean? Well, for dinner you could have a grilled chicken breast, boiled new potatoes, a side salad of romaine lettuce and red pepper dressed with a bit of olive oil and lemon juice, and some asparagus if you feel like it. The trick is to stick with foods that have a low G.I., are low in fat and are low-ish in calories. This sounds—and is, in fact—quite complex. It might seem to you as though I'm breaking my promise of an easy weight-loss plan. But don't worry: I've done all the calculations, measurements and math for you, and sorted the foods you like to eat into one of three categories based on the colours of the traffic light. On pages 317–326, you will find the Complete G.I. Diet Food Guide, which has a list of foods in a red column, a list in a yellow column and a list in a green column. Here's how the colour-coded categories work:

Red-Light Foods

The foods in the red column are to be avoided. They are high–G.I., higher-calorie foods that will make it impossible for you to lose weight.

Yellow-Light Foods

The foods in the yellow column are mid-range G.I. foods that should be treated with caution. They should be avoided when you are trying to lose weight, but once you've slimmed down to your ideal weight, you can begin to enjoy yellow-light foods from time to time.

Green-Light Foods

The green column lists foods that are low–G.I., low in fat and lower in calories. These are the foods that will allow you to lose weight. Don't expect them to be tasteless and boring! There are many delicious and satisfying choices that will make you feel as though you aren't even on a diet.

If you're a veteran of the low-carbohydrate craze, you'll be surprised to find potatoes and rice in the green-light column, but they are fine as long as they are the right type. Baked potatoes and french fries have a high G.I., while boiled new potatoes have a lower G.I. The short-grain, glutinous rice served in Chinese and Thai restaurants is high–G.I., while long-grain, brown, basmati and wild rice are low. Pasta is also a green-light food—as long as it is cooked only until al dente (with some firmness to the bite). Any processing of food, including cooking, increases a food's G.I., since heat breaks down starch capsules and fibre, giving your digestive juices a head start. This is why you should never overcook vegetables; instead, steam them or boil them in a small amount of water just until they are tender. This way, they will retain their vitamins and other nutrients, and their G.I. rating will remain low.

While eating green-light foods is really the core of the G.I. Diet, there are a few more things you'll need to know to follow the program. Let's discuss these in the next chapter.

TO SUM UP

- Low–G.I. foods take longer to digest, so you feel satiated longer.
- The key to losing weight is to eat low–G.I., low-calorie foods—in other words, foods from the green-light column of the Complete G.I. Diet Food Guide.

CHAPTER THREE

The G.I. Diet Essentials

The G.I. Diet consists of two phases. For those with a more serious weight problem, an additional Preliminary Phase has been added. The Preliminary Phase and Phase I are the dramatic parts of the G.I. Diet—the period when those extra unwanted pounds come off! During these stages, you'll focus on eating foods that are low–G.I. and also low in fat and sugar—the foods in the green-light column of the Complete G.I. Diet Food Guide on pages 317–326. Yes, this means a farewell to bagels and a fond adieu to Häagen-Dazs. But it doesn't mean you won't have a multitude of delicious foods to choose from. Once you've slimmed down to your ideal weight, you enter Phase II, the maintenance phase of the program, which is the way you will eat for the rest of your life.

To decide whether you will be starting with the Preliminary Phase or Phase I, you will need to find out your body mass index (BMI), which is a measurement of how much body fat you are carrying relative to your height.

Your BMI

While the BMI gives a relatively accurate measure of body fat, it applies only to people who are twenty to sixty-five years of age. It isn't valid for children, pregnant or nursing women, the elderly or heavily muscled athletes. For the rest of us, however, it is the only accepted international standard for weight.

You can calculate your BMI from the table on pages 28–29 by running your finger down the left vertical column of the table until you reach your height. Then run your finger across that row until you find the number that is closest to your weight. The bold number at the top of that column is your BMI.

If your BMI falls between 19 and 24, your weight is within the acceptable norm and is considered healthy. Anything between 25 and 29 is considered overweight; if you're 30 or over, you are officially obese. **If your BMI is 32 or under**, I recommend you begin with Phase I of the program. If it's over 32, then start with the Preliminary Phase.

Frame Size

You will note that the BMI tables have a broad range of weights in each of the weight categories—healthy weight (BMI 19–24), overweight (BMI 25–29) and obese (BMI 30 and over). A 5'5" woman, for instance, has a healthy weight range from 114 pounds (BMI 19) to 144 pounds (BMI 24). The reason for this broad range is primarily to allow for variances in people's different frame sizes.

People with small frames should have a healthy weight in the bottom third of the range while those with large frames, in the top third; (i.e., small frame, BMI 19–21; medium frame, BMI 21–22; large frame, BMI 23–24).

To calculate which size frame you fit into, here is a guide for women based on your wrist measurement. The measurement should be taken with a tape measure at the narrowest point on your wrist.

WRIST SIZE IN INCHES	HEIGHT UNDER 5'2"	HEIGHT 5'2"–5'5"	HEIGHT OVER 5'5"
Under 5.50	S	S	S
5.50–5.75	M	S	S
5.75–6.00	L	S	S
6.00–6.25	L	M	S
6.25–6.50	L	L	M
Over 6.50	L	L	L

Key:
S = Small frame
M = Medium frame
L = Large frame
Source: National Library of Medicine

So Diane, who is 5'7" and has a wrist measurement of 6.0 inches, will have a small frame. Her healthy weight will therefore be between 121 and 127 pounds (BMI 19–20). Jennifer, on the other hand, who is also 5'7", has a wrist measurement of 6.6 inches and therefore has a large frame. Jennifer's healthy weight, by comparison, will range from 146 to 153 pounds (BMI 23–24) or 25 pounds more than Diane's.

Incidentally, if your husband/partner is 5'5" or more and wants in on the act, then his measurements are simply:

Wrist under 6.5 inches = small frame

Wrist 6.5–7.5 inches = medium frame

Wrist over 7.5 inches = large frame

The Preliminary Phase and Phase I

To determine whether to begin with the Preliminary Phase or with Phase I, take a look at the BMI chart. If your BMI is 32 or under, I recommend you begin with Phase I of the program. If your BMI is over 32, start with the Preliminary Phase. The Preliminary Phase is in effect, a "step-in" plan that helps reduce any initial hunger pangs caused by a sudden drop in calories that people with a significant weight problem sometimes experience.

The Preliminary Phase lasts as long as you continue to weigh more than 32 on the BMI chart. So it is important that you recalculate your BMI when you weigh yourself every week. If you feel that you can manage without the Preliminary Phase, please feel free to go straight to Phase I. About half of the original e-clinic members with a BMI of over 32 elected to do this without significant difficulty.

Now that you know whether you'll be starting with the Preliminary Phase or Phase I, it's time to get into the details: what to eat, how much and how often.

What Do I Eat?

As you know, during the Preliminary Phase and Phase I, you will be sticking to the foods listed in the green-light column of the Complete G.I. Diet Food Guide on pages 317–326. To get a breakdown of your green-light choices for each meal, turn to pages 30–32 (breakfast), 35–37 (lunch), 39–41 (dinner) and 45 (snacks).

How Much Do I Eat?

Remember, this is not a starvation diet—far from it. Going hungry is simply not necessary for weight loss; in fact, it's something to be resolutely avoided! Hunger is the absolute death knell for any weight-loss program. If you are hungry for a sustained period of time, your body will feel that it hasn't received enough fuel to meet its needs and will slow the rate at which it burns calories, making it even harder to lose those extra pounds. So never leave your digestive system with nothing to do. If your digestive system is busy processing food and steadily supplying energy to your brain, not only will your metabolism keep firing at a steady rate, but also you won't be looking for high-calorie snacks. This is why you can, for the most part, eat as much green-light food as you want on the G.I. Diet.

In Phase I, you should be eating three meals and three snacks every day. And in the Preliminary Phase, you should be eating three meals and four snacks every day. The reason I recommend an extra snack in the Preliminary Phase is that someone with a larger body requires more calories just to keep functioning on a daily basis than someone who is lighter. This is also why I suggest larger serving sizes for some green-light foods in the Preliminary Phase than in Phase I. Although I generally do not restrict quantities of green-light foods—within reason (five heads of cabbage is a bit extreme)—there are a few exceptions, which I outline below. (Except where indicated, a serving size is per meal, not per day.)

Portions

Each meal and snack should contain, if possible, a combination of green-light protein, carbohydrates—especially vegetables and fruit—and fats. An easy way to visualize portion size is to divide your plate into three sections (see illustration below). Half the

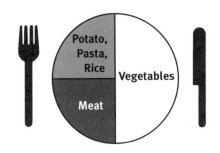

plate should be filled with vegetables; one-quarter should contain protein, such as lean meat, poultry, seafood, eggs, tofu or legumes; and the last quarter should contain a green-light serving of rice, pasta or potatoes.

When Do I Eat?

Try to eat regularly throughout the day. If you skimp on breakfast and lunch, you will probably be starving by dinner and end up piling on the food. Have one snack mid-morning, another mid-afternoon and the last before bed. In the Preliminary Phase, the fourth snack can be eaten later in the afternoon if you usually have a late dinner, or during the evening if you generally have an early dinner. It's really up to you—have the extra snack at the time of day when you feel you most need it. The idea is to keep your digestive system happily busy so you won't start craving those red-light snacks.

Green-Light Servings

GREEN-LIGHT FOOD	PRELIMINARY PHASE (BMI OF 33 OR MORE)	PHASE I (BMI OF 32 OR LESS)
Crispbreads (with high fibre, e.g., Wasa Fibre)	3 crispbreads	2 crispbreads
Green-light breads (which have at least 2$\frac{1}{2}$ to 3 grams of fibre per slice)	2 slices per day	1 slice per day
Green-light cereals	$\frac{2}{3}$ cup	$\frac{1}{2}$ cup
Green-light nuts	12 to 15	8 to 10
Margarine (non-hydrogenated, light)	3 teaspoons	2 teaspoons
Meat, fish, poultry	6 ounces	4 ounces (about the size of a pack of cards)
Olive/canola oil	1 $\frac{1}{2}$ teaspoons	1 teaspoon
Olives	6 to 8	4 to 5
Pasta	1 cup cooked	$\frac{3}{4}$ cup cooked
Potatoes (new or small, boiled)	4 to 5	2 to 3
Rice (basmati, brown, long-grain)	$\frac{3}{4}$ cup cooked	$\frac{2}{3}$ cup cooked

BODY MASS

	NORMAL						OVERWEIGHT					OBESE	
BMI	19	20	21	22	23	24	25	26	27	28	29	30	31
HEIGHT	WEIGHT (POUNDS)												
4'10"	91	96	100	105	110	115	119	124	129	134	138	143	148
4'11"	94	99	104	109	114	119	124	128	133	138	143	148	153
5'0"	97	102	107	112	118	123	128	133	138	143	148	153	158
5'1"	100	106	111	116	122	127	132	137	143	148	153	158	164
5'2"	104	109	115	120	126	131	136	142	147	153	158	164	169
5'3"	107	113	118	124	130	135	141	146	152	158	163	169	175
5'4"	110	116	122	128	134	140	145	151	157	163	169	174	180
5'5"	114	120	126	132	138	144	150	156	162	168	174	180	186
5'6"	118	124	130	136	142	148	155	161	167	173	179	186	192
5'7"	121	127	134	140	146	153	159	166	172	178	185	191	198
5'8"	125	131	138	144	151	158	164	171	177	184	190	197	203
5'9"	128	135	142	149	155	162	169	176	182	189	196	203	209
5'10"	132	139	146	153	160	167	174	181	188	195	202	209	216
5'11"	136	143	150	157	165	172	179	186	193	200	208	215	222
6'0"	140	147	154	162	169	177	184	191	199	206	213	221	228
6'1"	144	151	159	166	174	182	189	197	204	212	219	227	235
6'2"	148	155	163	171	179	186	194	202	210	218	225	233	241
6'3"	152	160	168	176	184	192	200	208	216	224	232	240	248
6'4"	156	164	172	180	189	197	205	213	221	230	238	246	254

Source: U.S. National Heart, Lung and Blood Institute

INDEX (BMI)

OBESE   **EXTREMELY OBESE**

32	33	34	35	36	37	38	39	40	41	42	43	44	45
WEIGHT (POUNDS)													
153	158	162	167	172	177	181	186	191	196	201	205	210	215
158	163	168	173	178	183	188	193	198	203	208	212	217	222
163	168	174	179	184	189	194	199	204	209	215	220	225	230
169	174	180	185	190	195	201	206	211	217	222	227	232	238
175	180	186	191	196	202	207	213	218	224	229	235	240	246
180	186	191	197	203	208	214	220	225	231	237	242	248	254
186	192	197	204	209	215	221	227	232	238	244	250	256	262
192	198	204	210	216	222	228	234	240	246	252	258	264	270
198	204	210	216	223	229	235	241	247	253	260	266	272	278
204	211	217	223	230	236	242	249	255	261	268	274	280	287
210	216	223	230	236	243	249	256	262	269	276	282	289	295
216	223	230	236	243	250	257	263	270	277	284	291	297	304
222	229	236	243	250	257	264	271	278	285	292	299	306	313
229	236	243	250	257	265	272	279	286	293	301	308	315	322
235	242	250	258	265	272	279	287	294	302	309	316	324	331
242	250	257	265	272	280	288	295	302	310	318	325	333	340
249	256	264	272	280	287	295	303	311	319	326	334	342	350
256	264	272	279	287	295	303	311	319	327	335	343	351	359
263	271	279	287	295	304	312	320	328	336	344	353	361	369

Meal Basics

Because the green-light way of eating is most likely new to you, you're probably wondering what to eat instead of that bagel with cream cheese for breakfast, that hamburger for lunch, and those tortilla chips and salsa for a snack. On the following pages I'll go over your various green-light options for each of the main meals and snacks of your daily G.I. program. Let's start with breakfast.

Breakfast

I know you've been told that breakfast is the most important meal of the day, and it's actually true. It's the first thing you eat after your night-long "fast" of twelve hours or more, and it launches you into your workday. Eating a healthy breakfast will help you avoid the need to grab a coffee and Danish as soon as you hit the office, and will make you feel satisfied and energetic. Eating breakfast every day doesn't mean you have to set the alarm any earlier. If you have time to read the paper or feed the cat, you have time to prepare and eat a green-light breakfast.

The following chart lists typical breakfast foods in the colour-coded categories. To ensure you have a balanced breakfast, include some green-light carbohydrates, protein and fat. For a complete list of foods, see the Complete G.I. Diet Food Guide on pages 317–326.

Let's take a closer look at some of the usual breakfast choices.

PROTEIN			
Meat and Eggs	Regular bacon Sausages Whole regular eggs	Turkey bacon Whole omega-3 eggs	Back bacon Lean ham Liquid eggs/egg whites
Dairy	Cheese Cottage cheese (whole or 2%) Cream	Cream cheese (light) Milk (1%) Sour cream (light)	Buttermilk Cottage/cream cheese or sour cream (1% or fat-free)

Dairy	Milk (whole or 2%) Sour cream Yogurt (whole or 2%)	Yogurt (low-fat with sugar)	Extra low-fat cheese Fruit yogurt (fat-free with sweetener) Milk (skim) Soy milk (plain, low-fat)

CARBOHYDRATES

Cereals	All cold cereals except those listed as yellow- or green-light Granola Muesli (commercial)	Kashi Go Lean Kashi Go Lean Crunch Kashi Good Friends Shredded Wheat Bran	All-Bran Bran Buds Fibre First Oat Bran Porridge (old-fashioned rolled oats) Red River
Breads/Grains	Bagels Baguette Cookies Doughnuts Muffins Pancakes/Waffles White bread	Crispbreads (with fibre)* Whole-grain breads*	100% stone-ground whole wheat bread* Crispbreads (high fibre, e.g., Wasa Fibre)* Green-light muffins (see pp. 301–303) Whole-grain, high-fibre breads (min. 3 g fibre per slice)*
Fruits * Limit serving size (see page 27). ** For baking, it is OK to use a modest amount of dried apricots or cranberries.	Applesauce containing sugar Canned fruit in syrup Melons	Apricots (fresh and dried)** Bananas Fruit cocktail in juice	Apples Berries Cherries Grapefruit

Fruits	Most dried fruit	Kiwi	Grapes
		Mango	Oranges
		Papaya	Peaches
		Pineapple	Plums
Juices	Fruit drinks	Apple (unsweetened)	Eat the fruit rather than drink its juice
	Prune		
	Sweetened juices	Grapefruit (unsweetened)	
	Watermelon		
		Orange (unsweetened)	
		Pear (unsweetened)	
Vegetables	French fries		Most vegetables
	Hash browns		
FATS			
	Butter	Most nuts	Almonds*
	Hard margarine	Natural nut butters	Canola oil*
	Peanut butter (regular and light)	Peanut butter (100% peanuts)	Hazelnuts*
			Olive oil*
	Tropical oils	Soft margarine (non-hydrogenated)	Soft margarine (non-hydrogenated, light)*
	Vegetable shortening	Vegetable oils	

* Limit serving size (see page 27).

Coffee and Tea

OK, this is the toughest one. The trouble with coffee is caffeine. It's not a health problem in itself, but it does stimulate the production of insulin. That's part of the "buzz" we get from coffee. But insulin reduces blood sugar levels, which then increases your appetite. Have you ever ordered a venti from Starbucks and then felt positively shaky an hour later? That's your blood sugar hitting bottom. You cure it by eating a bagel—which isn't helpful when you're trying to lose weight. So in Phase I, try to cut out caffeine altogether. As unpleasant as it may be, caffeine withdrawal will end in a day or two. Cut down gradually: go from a medium coffee to a small; then try a half-caffeinated, half-decaf blend. Then limit yourself to decaffeinated coffee—some brands taste as good as the real thing.

Even better, switch to tea. It has only about one-third of the caffeine that coffee has, and black tea and green tea have health benefits as well: they're rich in antioxidants, and beneficial for heart health and reducing the risk of dementia. Green tea is also considered an anti-carcinogen. (My ninety-eight-year-old mother and her tea-drinking cronies are living proof!) Herbal teas, such as peppermint, chamomile and other blends, are fine too, as long as they contain no caffeine.

If no coffee is going to be a deal breaker, then go ahead, have one cup a day—but not a double espresso. If you take milk and sugar, make it skim milk and a sweetener such as Splenda.

Cereals

Another toughie. Most cold cereals contain hidden or not-so-hidden sugars, and are therefore red-light. Green-light cereals are high in fibre; they have at least **10 grams per serving**. All right, they're not a lot of fun by themselves, but you can liven them up with fresh, canned or frozen fruits, a few nuts and some fruit yogurt (fat-free, with sweetener).

My personal favourite cereal is good old-fashioned oatmeal—not the instant type that comes in packets but the large-flake, slow-cooking kind. (They're starting to serve it in the smartest hotels now.) Large-flake oatmeal is not only low–G.I., but also low calorie and has been shown to lower cholesterol. Yes, you have to cook it, but it takes only about three minutes or so in the microwave, and not much longer for one portion on the stovetop. Dress it up with yogurt, sliced almonds, berries or unsweetened applesauce. It's also just fine with nothing but milk on it.

I probably receive more e-mails about people's delight at rediscovering oatmeal than about any other food or meal. Give it a try.

Toast

Go ahead, but have no more than one slice per meal. Make sure your bread has at least 3 grams of fibre per slice. (Note: Some bread labels quote a two-slice serving, which should equal 6 grams per serving.) The best choice is 100% stone-ground whole wheat bread, which has a coarser grind and therefore a lower G.I. White bread, cracked wheat or anything else made with white flour is red-light.

Butter and Jams

Butter is out. It's very high in saturated fat, and despite the protestations of the dairy industry, it's not good for your health or waistline. Yes, it does make things taste good—that's what fat does best. But you can still enjoy any one of a variety of light non-hydrogenated soft margarines, if you use only a teaspoon or so.

When buying fruit spreads, look for the "extra fruit/no sugar added" varieties. Fruit, not sugar, should be the first ingredient listed. These varieties taste great and don't have the calories of the usual commercial jams. Although I rarely plug brands, the President's Choice Blue Menu jams are a good buy.

Dairy

Low-fat dairy products are an ideal green-light choice and an excellent source of protein. I have a glass of skim milk every morning. I admit that skim didn't taste great at first, but I weaned myself off 2% by switching to 1% before moving on to skim. Now 2% tastes like cream!

Fat-free yogurt with sugar substitute instead of sugar is ideal for breakfast, dessert or a snack, either by itself or added to fruits or cereals. Low-fat cottage cheese is also a top-rated green-light source of protein. Or you can make a low-fat soft cheese spread by letting yogurt drain in cheesecloth overnight in the refrigerator.

Regular full-fat dairy products, including whole milk and cream, cheese and butter, are loaded with saturated fat and should be avoided completely.

Eggs

Use liquid eggs, such as Naturegg Break Free or Omega Pro. They are lower in saturated fat and cholesterol than regular eggs, and they make wonderful omelettes. Otherwise, use egg whites. If you're eating a hotel breakfast, in most cases the kitchen is happy to make omelettes with egg whites only.

Bacon

Bacon is red-light because of its high saturated-fat content. However, there are tasty green-light alternatives—such as Canadian back bacon, and lean ham—that make great BLTs.

Lunch

Lunch is usually the most problematic meal for my readers because they tend to eat it outside the home and in a hurry. Bringing your lunch to work is the easiest way to ensure you eat green-light. And there are other advantages to brown-bagging it, besides avoiding the temptation of a red-light lunch: it's cheaper, and it gives you downtime at your desk to read or catch up on paperwork. However, it's a good idea to actually get away from your desk altogether so you can be more mindful of what you are eating—rather than trying to work and eat at the same time. If you can get away from your desk for half an hour or so, try taking your lunch outside and adding a little exercise to your day. Here are the ground rules for making that brown bag a green-light bag. For a complete list of foods, see the Complete G.I. Diet Food Guide on pages 317–326.

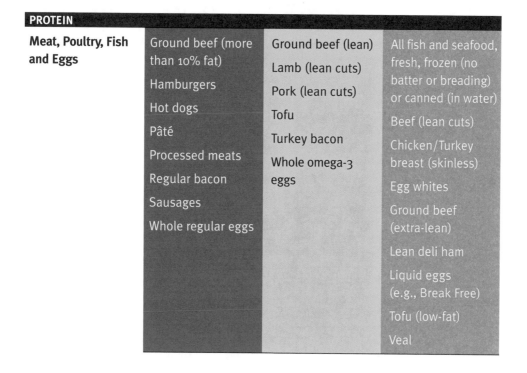

PROTEIN			
Meat, Poultry, Fish and Eggs	Ground beef (more than 10% fat)	Ground beef (lean)	All fish and seafood, fresh, frozen (no batter or breading) or canned (in water)
	Hamburgers	Lamb (lean cuts)	
	Hot dogs	Pork (lean cuts)	
	Pâté	Tofu	Beef (lean cuts)
	Processed meats	Turkey bacon	Chicken/Turkey breast (skinless)
	Regular bacon	Whole omega-3 eggs	
	Sausages		Egg whites
	Whole regular eggs		Ground beef (extra-lean)
			Lean deli ham
			Liquid eggs (e.g., Break Free)
			Tofu (low-fat)
			Veal

CARBOHYDRATES

Breads/Grains			
Bagels	Crispbreads (with fibre, e.g., Ryvita High Fibre)	100% stone-ground whole wheat bread*	
Baguette/Croissants	Pita (whole wheat)	Crispbreads (high fibre, e.g., Wasa Fibre)*	
Croutons	Tortillas (whole wheat)	Pasta (fettuccine, spaghetti, penne, vermicelli, linguine, macaroni)*	
Cake/Cookies	Whole-grain breads*		
Hamburger/Hot dog buns		Quinoa	
Macaroni and cheese		Rice (basmati, wild, brown, long-grain)*	
Muffins/Doughnuts		Whole-grain, high-fibre breads (min. 3 g fibre per slice)*	
Noodles (canned or instant)			
Pancakes/Waffles			
Pasta filled with cheese or meat			
Pizza			
Rice (short-grain, white, instant)			

Fruits/Vegetables			
Broad beans	Apricots	Apples	Cabbage
French fries	Artichokes	Arugula	Carrots
Melons	Bananas	Asparagus	Cauliflower
Most dried fruit	Beets	Avocado*	Celery
Parsnips	Corn	Beans (green/wax)	Cherries
Potatoes (mashed or baked)	Kiwi	Bell peppers	Cucumbers
Rutabaga	Mangoes	Blackberries	Eggplant
	Papaya	Blueberries	Grapefruit
	Pineapple	Broccoli	Grapes
	Potatoes (boiled)	Brussels sprouts	Leeks
	Squash		Lemons
			Lettuce

* Limit serving size (see page 27).

Fruits/Vegetables

	(Red)	(Yellow)	(Green)
Fruits/Vegetables		Sweet potatoes Yams	Mushrooms Olives* Onions Oranges (all varieties) Peaches Pears Peas Peppers (hot) Pickles · Plums Potatoes (new or small) Radishes Raspberries Snow peas Spinach Strawberries Tomatoes Zucchini
FATS	Butter Hard margarine Mayonnaise Peanut butter (regular, light) Salad dressings (regular) Tropical oils	Mayonnaise (light) Most nuts Peanut butter (100% peanuts) Salad dressings (light) Soft margarine (non-hydrogenated)	Almonds* Canola oil* Mayonnaise (fat-free) Olive oil* Salad dressings (low-fat, low-sugar) Soft margarine (non-hydrogenated, light)*
SOUPS	All cream-based soups Canned black bean Canned green pea Canned puréed vegetable Canned split pea	Canned chicken noodle Canned lentil Canned tomato	Chunky bean and vegetable soups (e.g., Campbell's Healthy Request, Healthy Choice) Homemade soups with green-light ingredients

* Limit serving size (see page 27).

Sandwiches

Sandwiches are a lunchtime staple, and it's no wonder: they're portable and easy to make, and they offer endless variety. They can also be a dietary disaster, but if you follow the suggestions below, you can keep your sandwiches green-light.

- Always use 100% stone-ground whole wheat or high-fibre whole-grain bread (min. 3 grams of fibre per slice).
- Sandwiches should be served open-faced. Either pack components separately and assemble just before eating or make your sandwich with a "lettuce lining" that helps keep the bread from getting soggy.
- Include at least three vegetables, such as lettuce, tomato, red or green bell pepper, cucumber, sprouts or onion.
- Instead of spreading the bread with butter or margarine, use mustard or hummus.
- Add up to 4 ounces of cooked lean meat or fish: roast beef, turkey, shrimp or salmon.
- If you make tuna or chicken salad, use low-fat mayonnaise or low-fat salad dressing and celery.
- Mix canned salmon with malt vinegar or fresh lemon.

Salads

Preparing salads may seem more labour intensive than making sandwiches, but it doesn't have to be. Invest in a variety of reusable plastic containers so you can bring individual-sized salads to work. Keep a supply of green-light vinaigrette on hand, and wash greens ahead of time and store in paper towels in plastic bags. You'll find that salads are a creative way to use up leftovers with a minimum of fuss.

Dinner

Dinner is traditionally the main meal of the day, and the one where we may have a tendency to overeat. We usually have more time for eating at the end of the day, and we generally feel fatigued as well, which encourages us to consume more. But since we will probably be spending the evening relaxing before going to bed, rather than being active, it is important that we don't overdo it. For a complete list of foods, see the Complete G.I. Diet Food Guide on pages 317–326.

Protein

No dinner is complete without protein. Whether it is in the form of meat, poultry, seafood, beans or tofu, it should cover no more than one-quarter of your plate. A serving size should be 4 ounces,* which is roughly the size of the palm of your hand.

PROTEIN			
Meat, Poultry, Fish and Eggs	Breaded fish and seafood Fish canned in oil Ground beef (more than 10% fat) Hamburgers Hot dogs Processed meats Sausages Sushi Whole regular eggs	Ground beef (lean) Lamb (lean cuts) Pork (lean cuts) Whole omega-3 eggs	All fish and seafood (not breaded or canned in oil) Beef (lean cuts) Chicken breast (skinless) Egg whites Ground beef (extra lean) Lean deli ham Liquid eggs Turkey breast (skinless) Veal
Dairy	Cheese Cottage cheese (whole or 2%) Milk (whole or 2%) Sour cream Yogurt (whole or 2%)	Cheese (light) Milk (1%) Sour cream (light) Yogurt (low-fat)	Cheese (fat-free) Cottage cheese/ sour cream (1% or fat-free) Fruit yogurt (fat-free with sweetener) Milk (skim) Soy milk (low-fat)

* For Preliminary Phase servings see page 27.

	Red	Yellow	Green	
Breads/Grains	Bagels Baguette/Croissants Cake/Cookies Macaroni and cheese Muffins/Doughnuts Noodles (canned or instant) Pasta filled with cheese or meat Pizza Rice (short-grain, white, instant) Tortillas	Pita (whole wheat) Whole-grain breads*	100% stone-ground whole wheat bread* Pasta (fettuccine, spaghetti, penne, vermicelli, linguine, macaroni)* Quinoa Rice (basmati, wild, brown, long-grain)* Whole-grain, high-fibre breads (min. 3 g fibre per slice)*	
Fruits/ Vegetables	Broad beans French fries Melons Most dried fruit Parsnips Potatoes (mashed or baked)	Apricots Bananas Beets Corn Kiwi Mangoes Papaya Pineapple Pomegranates Potatoes (boiled) Squash Sweet potatoes Yams	Apples Arugula Asparagus Avocado* Beans (green/wax) Bell peppers Blueberries Blackberries Broccoli Brussels sprouts Cabbage Carrots Cauliflower	Celery Cherries Cucumbers Eggplant Grapefruit Grapes Leeks Lemons Lettuce Mushrooms Olives* Onions Oranges (all varieties) Peaches

* Limit serving size (see page 27).

Fruits/Vegetables

		Pears, Peas, Peppers (hot), Pickles, Plums, Potatoes (boiled new), Radishes, Raspberries, Snow peas, Spinach, Strawberries, Tomatoes, Zucchini

FATS

Butter	Corn oil	Almonds*
Hard margarine	Mayonnaise (light)	Canola oil*
Mayonnaise	Most nuts	Hazelnuts
Peanut butter (regular, light)	Salad dressings (light)	Mayonnaise (fat-free)
Salad dressings (regular)	Soft margarine (non-hydrogenated)	Olive oil*
Tropical oils	Vegetable oils	Pistachios*
Vegetable shortening	Walnuts	Salad dressings (low-fat, low sugar)
		Soft margarine (non-hydrogenated, light)

SOUPS

All cream-based soups	Canned chicken noodle	Chunky bean and vegetable soups (e.g., Campbell's Healthy Request, Healthy Choice)
Canned black bean	Canned lentil	Homemade soups with green-light ingredients
Canned green pea	Canned tomato	
Canned puréed vegetable		
Canned split pea		

* Limit serving size (see page 27).

Red Meat

Though most red meat does contain saturated fat, there are ways to minimize it:

- Buy only low-fat meats such as top round beef. For hamburgers or spaghetti sauces, buy extra-lean ground beef. Veal and pork tenderloin are low in fat, too. As for juicy steaks, well, they are juicy because of the fat in them, so they're not a good choice.
- Trim any visible fat from the meat. Even a quarter inch of fat can double the total amount of fat in the meat.
- Broiling or grilling allows the excess fat from the meat to drain off. (Try one of those George Foreman–style fat-draining electric grills.)
- For stovetop cooking, use a non-stick pan with a little vegetable oil spray rather than oil. The spray goes further.

Poultry

Skinless chicken and turkey breast are excellent green-light choices. In the yellow-light category are skinless thighs, wings and legs, which are higher in fat.

Seafood

This is always a good green-light choice. Although certain cold-water fish, such as salmon and cod, have a relatively high oil content, this oil is omega-3 and is beneficial to your heart health. Shrimp and squid are fine, too, as long as they aren't breaded or battered. Fish and chips, alas, is out.

Beans (Legumes)

If you don't think you're into beans, it's time to re-evaluate! Beans are such an excellent source of so many good things: fibre, low-fat protein and "good" carbs that deliver nutrients while taking their time going through the digestive system. And they are a snap to incorporate into salads and soups to up the protein quotient. Chickpeas, lentils, navy beans, black beans, kidney beans—there's a bean for every day of the week. But watch out for canned pork and beans, which is high in sugar and fat, and avoid canned bean soups, which are processed to the point where their overall G.I. rating is too high. Homemade bean soups, however, are an excellent choice.

You will find several delicious recipes using beans in the recipes section of this book.

Tofu

You don't have to be a vegetarian to enjoy tofu, which is low in saturated fat and an excellent source of protein. While tofu is not necessarily a thriller on its own, it takes on the flavours of whatever seasonings and sauces it is cooked with. Seasoned tofu scrambles, for instance, are a good substitute for scrambled eggs. Choose soft tofu, which has up to one-third less fat than the firm variety.

Textured Vegetable Protein (TVP)

This is not a new device for pre-recording TV shows! TVP is a soy alternative to meat that looks a lot like ground beef, and can be used in the same ways—in lasagna, chili, stir-fries and spaghetti sauce. It's quite tasty and delivers the texture of meat. Our middle son, a vegetarian who has since left the nest, put us on to this versatile product.

Potatoes, Pasta, Rice

These carbohydrates should cover only one-quarter of the plate. Remember, with potatoes your first choice is boiled small new potatoes. Most other choices, especially baked potatoes or french fries, are red-light. Sweet potatoes are a good lower–G.I. food, but since they tend to come in larger sizes, I suggest you save them for Phase II.

Your serving of pasta should be no more than 3/4 cup cooked*—just until al dente. If you have rice, make it 2/3 cup cooked basmati, wild, brown or long-grain rice.

---

* For Preliminary Phase servings see p. 27.

Vegetables

Here you can put the measuring cup away. Eat as many vegetables and as much salad as you like; they should be the backbone of your meal. Always include at least two vegetables, and remember to cook them just until tender-crisp. Experiment with something you've never had before. Baby bok choy is delicious grilled, and rapini, a dark green vegetable that looks like broccoli with more leaves, is a nice change. The dark, curly green vegetables such as kale are full of good things, including folic acid.

Greens such as mesclun or baby spinach come conveniently pre-washed in bags. Frozen bags of mixed vegetables are also convenient and inexpensive; you can even toss the veggies into a saucepan, add tomato juice with a dollop of salsa and you have a quick vegetable soup.

Dessert

Yes, dessert is part of the G.I. Diet—at least, the kind of dessert that is green-light and good for you. This includes most fruits, and low-fat dairy products, such as yogurt and ice cream sweetened with sugar substitute rather than sugar. You can also try silken or dessert tofu but watch the serving size (maximum of $1/2$ cup). All my books have recipes for delicious green-light desserts.

Snacks

Keep your digestive system busy and your energy up with between-meal snacks—four a day during the Preliminary Phase and three a day during Phase I.

Try to eat balanced snacks that include a bit of protein and carbohydrates; for example, a piece of fruit with a few nuts, or cottage cheese with celery sticks.

A convenient snack for when you're on the go is half a nutrition bar. Be careful when choosing one: most are full of cereal and sugar. The ones to look for have 20 to 30 grams of carbohydrates, 12 to 15 grams of protein and 5 grams of fat. Balance and ZonePerfect bars are two examples.

Keep in mind that many snacks and desserts labelled "low-fat" or "sugar-free" aren't necessarily green-light. Sugar-free instant puddings and "low-fat" muffins are still high–G.I. because they contain highly processed grains.

Bagels	Bananas	Almonds**
Candy	Dark chocolate (70% cocoa)	Applesauce (unsweetened)
Cookies		
Crackers	Ice cream (low-fat)	Canned peaches/pears in juice or water
Doughnuts	Most nuts	
Flavoured gelatin (all varieties)	Popcorn (air popped)	Cottage cheese (1% or fat-free)
French fries		Extra-low-fat cheese (e.g., Laughing Cow Light, Boursin Light)
Ice cream		
Muffins (commercial)		Fruit yogurt (fat-free with sweetener)
Popcorn (regular)		Hazelnuts**
Potato chips		Homemade green-light snacks (see pages 300–305)
Pretzels		
Pudding		Ice cream (low-fat and no added sugar, e.g., Breyers Premium Fat-Free, Nestlé Legend)
Raisins		
Rice cakes		
Sorbet		
Tortilla chips		Most fresh fruit
Trail mix		Most fresh vegetables
White bread		Nutrition bars*
		Pickles
		Pumpkin seeds
		Sugar-free hard candies
		Sunflower seeds

* 180–225 calorie bars, e.g., ZonePerfect or Balance Bars; 1/2 bar per serving.

** Limit serving size (see page 27).

What Do I Drink?

Because liquids don't trip our satiety mechanisms, it's a waste to take in calories through them. Also, many beverages are high in calories. Juice, for example, is a processed product, and has a much higher G.I. than the fruit or vegetable it is made from. A glass of orange juice contains nearly two and a half times the calories of a fresh orange! So eat the fruit or vegetable rather than drink its juice. That way you'll get all the benefits of its nutrients and fibre while consuming fewer calories.

As well, stay away from any beverage that contains added sugar or caffeine. As I explained earlier, caffeine stimulates insulin, which leads to us feeling hungry. So no coffee or soft drinks containing caffeine in Phase I.

That said, fluids are an important part of any diet (I'm sure you're all familiar with the eight-glasses-a-day prescription). The following are your best greenlight choices:

Water

The cheapest, easiest and best thing to drink is plain water. Seventy percent of our body consists of water, which is needed for digestion, circulation, regulation of body temperature, lubrication of joints and healthy skin. We can live for months without food, but we can survive only a few days without water.

Don't feel you have to drink eight glasses of water a day in addition to other beverages. Milk, tea and soft drinks all contribute to the eight-glasses-a-day recommendation. But do try to drink a glass of water *before* each meal—it will help you feel fuller so that you don't overeat. Add a slice of lemon or lime for flavour if you dislike plain water.

Skim Milk

After a skeptical start, I've grown to really enjoy skim milk, and I like to drink it with breakfast and lunch, which tend to be a little short on protein. Skim milk is an ideal green-light food.

Soft Drinks

If you're used to drinking soft drinks, you can still enjoy the sugar- and caffeine-free diet ones. People often treat regular soft drinks and fruit juices as non-foods, but this is how extra calories slip by us.

Tea

Although black and green teas do contain caffeine, the amount is only about one-third of that of coffee. Tea has health benefits as well. Black and green teas contain antioxidant properties that help protect against heart disease and Alzheimer's. In fact, tea has more flavonoids (antioxidants) than any vegetable tested. Two cups of black or green tea have the same amount of antioxidants as 7 cups of orange juice or 28 cups of apple juice.

So tea in moderation is fine—minus the sugar and cream, of course. Try some new varieties: Darjeeling, Earl Grey, English Breakfast or spicy chai (with sugar substitute). Herbal teas, as long as they are caffeine-free, are also a green-light option, though they lack the flavonoids. Iced tea is acceptable if it's sugar-free.

Alcohol

Alcohol is generally a disaster for any weight-loss program. It puts your blood sugar on a roller coaster: you go up and feel great, then come down and feel like having another drink, or eating the whole bowl of peanuts. Alcohol also contains a lot of calories. So in Phase I, put away the corkscrew and the ice cube tray.

Now that you know how the G.I. Diet works, it's time to get ready to start. In the next chapter, I'll outline the steps for launching you into the program.

TO SUM UP
- In the Preliminary Phase and Phase I, eat only green-light foods.
- Eat three balanced meals plus four snacks a day in the Preliminary Phase and three balanced meals plus three snacks in Phase I.
- Pay attention to portion size: palm of your hand for protein, and a quarter plate for pasta, potatoes or rice. Use common sense and eat moderate amounts.
- Drink plenty of fluids, including an 8-ounce glass of water with meals and snacks (but no caffeine or alcohol).

CHAPTER FOUR

Before You Start

The G.I. Diet it not so much a diet as a completely new and permanent way of eating. This is without question the most important message in this book. Unfortunately, most people view diets as a short-term change in eating habits that are ditched once weight-loss targets have been achieved. They then revert to their old dietary habits and, not suprisingly, they are soon back at their original weight, or worse.

The G.I. Diet is the way you will eat for the rest of your life. The one constant refrain I received from the tens of thousands of successful readers is that this is a new way of eating that has become a permanent part of their lives.

Your motivation to lose weight is high, and with the G.I. Diet you now have the action plan that will help you make those unwanted pounds disappear. Still, to be successful you will have to make some significant changes in your life, and the better prepared you are, the better equipped you will be to handle any challenges that may arise. The following six steps will get you off to the best possible start.

1. Go see your doctor.

Before starting any major change in your eating patterns, check with your doctor to see if you have any health concerns that could affect your weight-loss plans. As you lose weight, your health will certainly improve, and it will be wonderfully motivating to learn that your blood glucose levels have improved or that your blood pressure has gone down. It may even be possible to change any medications you might be taking for weight-related conditions such as diabetes or high blood pressure.

2. Assess whether it's the right time to start.

Are you in the middle of a job change? A major house renovation or move? Is it the week before Christmas or before the cruise you've been planning for a year? Then it's probably not the best time to start a new way of eating. Some life events will make it harder—or even impossible—for you to give the program the attention it needs or to stick with it. Choose a period when your life is relatively stable and when you have time to learn new eating habits—not when your stress levels are even higher than usual. If your enthusiasm for a new slim you is high and the timing is right, then there's no better moment than the present!

3. Set your weight-loss target.

It's important to have a healthy, realistic weight-loss target in mind before starting the program. A good place to start is the BMI table on pages 28–29, not the glossy pages of a fashion or fitness magazine. Being too thin or too heavy is not good. Your health is at risk if your BMI is below 18.5 or above 25. Remember, the BMI tables are only a guide.

The other measurement you should concern yourself with is your waist measurement, which is an even better predictor of the state of your health than your weight. Abdominal fat is more than just a weight problem. Recent research has shown that abdominal fat acts almost like a separate organ in the body, except this "organ" is a destructive one that releases harmful proteins and free fatty acids, increasing your risk of life-threatening conditions, especially heart disease.

If you are female and have a waist measurement of 35 inches or more, or are male with a waist measurement of over 37 inches, you are at risk of endangering your health. Women with a measurement of 37 inches or more, and men with a measurement over 40 inches are at serious risk of heart disease, stroke, cancer and diabetes.

So I have your attention now! Make sure that you measure correctly: put a tape measure around your waist just above navel level till it fits snugly, without cutting into your flesh. Do not adopt the walking-down-the-beach-sucking-in-your-stomach stance. Just stand naturally. There's no point in trying to fudge the numbers, because the only person you're kidding is yourself.

Now that you know your BMI and waist measurement, you can set your weight-loss target and know roughly how long it will take you to reach that goal. When you lose weight in a healthy way, you can expect to lose about one pound per week. I say "about" because most people do not lose weight at a fixed and steady rate. The usual pattern is to lose more at the start of the diet, when you are losing mostly water weight, followed by a series of drops and plateaus. The closer you get to your target weight, the slower your weight loss will be. If you are planning to lose up to 20 percent of your body weight—for example, if you weigh 150 pounds and want to lose 30 pounds—assume this will take you thirty weeks, one pound per week. If you have more than 20 percent to shed, the good news is that you will lose at a faster rate. This is simply because your larger body weight requires more calories just to keep operating than someone who is lighter. Still, be prepared for measured results—it took you a while to put on those extra pounds and it will take some time to lose them. Be patient and know that once that weight is gone, it will be gone forever as you keep it off in Phase II of the program.

Although I recommend recording your progress, please don't get obsessed with numbers on the scale. Many people find themselves losing inches before they register any weight loss. Clothes start feeling a little looser, and before you know it you are down a dress size or getting into your old jeans. Soon you'll probably have to buy new clothes. My readers often tell me I should have warned them about the extra cost of refurbishing their closet!

4. Give your kitchen a green-light makeover.

Take a look in your fridge—what do you see? Two jars of mayonnaise, some leftover cheddar and a lot of sugar-laden condiments in jars? Now open the cupboards: what's the cookie and cracker situation? Now is the time to do an honest evaluation of what you tend to keep on hand. Consult the Complete G.I. Diet Food Guide (pages 317–326) and throw out anything that's in the red-light column.

Be ruthless. If you always have chips on hand, you will eat them. If you keep Goldfish crackers around "for the kids," you can be sure that they won't be the only ones snacking on them. Give the unopened food items and cans to your skinny neighbours or local food bank.

5. Eat before you shop.

You know what happens when you drop by the supermarket on your way home from work, famished—before you know it you've bought the biggest tray of cannelloni ever made. The worst mistake you can make is to go shopping on an empty stomach. You'll only be tempted to fill your cart with high–G.I., sugar-rich foods.

6. Shop green-light.

For those of you who prefer a day-by-day guide to your planning, for each week of the G.I. Diet Menopause Clinic in Part II, I provide a complete meal and snack plan and a grocery list. If you'd rather not follow the plan, go back and consult Chapter 3 to get some ideas of what you'd like to have for breakfast, lunch, dinner and snacks during your first week on the G.I. Diet; have a look at the Complete G.I. Diet Food Guide on pages 317–326; and peruse the recipe section of this book, *The G.I. Diet Cookbook*, or any of my other books. Write a shopping list and head out to the supermarket. Your first few green-light shopping trips will require a bit more time and attention than usual, as you familiarize yourself with green-light eating and meal planning. But don't worry: before long your new shopping and eating habits will become second nature.

Since it would be impossible to include every brand available in today's enormous supermarkets in the Complete G.I. Diet Food Guide, I've listed categories of food rather than individual brands, except in cases where clarification is needed, or where there is an especially useful product available. This means that you will have to pay some attention to food labels when comparing brands.

How to Read a Food Label

When reading a food label, there are six factors to consider when making the best green-light choice:

Serving Size

Is the serving size realistic, or has the manufacturer lowered it to make the calories and fat levels look better than the competition's? When comparing brands, ensure that you are comparing the same serving size.

Calories

The product with the least amount of calories is obviously the best choice. Some products flagged as "low-fat" still have plenty of calories, so don't be fooled by the diet-friendly slogans. Calories are calories, whether they come from fat or sugar.

Fat

Look at the amount of fat, which is often expressed as a percentage, say 2 percent (good) or 20 percent (forget it). Then check to see what sort of fat it is. You want foods that are low-fat, with minimal or no saturated fats and trans fats. Remember that trans fats are often called "hydrogenated oils" or "partially hydrogenated oils."

Fibre

Foods with lots of fibre have a low G.I., so this is an important component. When comparing brands, choose the one with higher fibre.

Sugar

Choose products that are low in sugar. Again, watch for products advertised as "low-fat." Companies will sometimes quietly bump up the sugar content to make up for any perceived loss of taste. This often happens with yogurts and cereals.

Sugars are sometimes listed as dextrose, glucose, fructose or sucrose; regardless of the form, it's sugar.

Sodium

Sodium (salt) increases water retention, which doesn't help when you are trying to lose weight. It also contributes to premenstrual bloating in women and is a factor in hypertension (high blood pressure). Combine high blood pressure with excess weight and you move up to the front of the risk line for heart disease and stroke. Low-sodium products are therefore preferable.

The Recommended Dietary Allowance (RDA) for sodium is 2,500 mg, but this is generally regarded as too high. The U.S. National Academy of Science's new recommendation of 1,500 mg makes more sense. Since the average North American consumption of sodium per person per day is over 3,000 mg, it goes without saying that most of us could stand to cut back. However, if you have a BMI over 30 and have any blood pressure, circulation or heart problems, you need to be even more vigilant about seeking out low-sodium brands. Canned foods such as soups are often very high in sodium, as are many fast foods and processed foods.

You've talked to your doctor, decided there's no better time than the present to lose weight and get healthy, set your weight-loss target, cleared your kitchen of fat-building foods, and restocked your pantry with delicious green-light choices. Now all you have to do is eat green-light meals and snacks each day and you're well on your way to your new trim self. In the next section, you'll find a week-by-week guide to all the challenges and issues that will come up as you follow the G.I. Diet for the first thirteen weeks. By the end of it you will know everything there is to know to achieve your weight-loss dreams, and you'll have lost a significant amount of weight along the way!

TO SUM UP

The six steps to get you launched into the G.I. Diet are:

1. Go see your doctor.
2. Assess whether it's the right time to start.
3. Set your weight-loss target.
4. Give your kitchen a green-light makeover.
5. Eat before you shop.
6. Shop green-light.

PART II

The G.I. Diet Menopause Clinic

Week 1

Getting Started

Welcome to the G.I. Diet Menopause Clinic. You are starting out on one of the biggest and most important adventures of your life. This is a journey that is truly life changing as you will have the opportunity to remodel your body and increase your energy levels as well make the changes that come with menopause a positive experience.

Target Weight

The first thing I would like you to do is fill in your current measurements below as well as your target weight, so that you have a baseline with which to compare your progress and a place to remind yourself of your ultimate weight-loss goal. There is nothing more motivating than recording your success so I will be asking you to write down your weight and waist and hip measurements at the end of each week. Be sure to measure yourself at the same time of the day each week since a meal or even a bowel movement can make a difference of a pound or two at a time when every pound counts! An ideal time is first thing in the morning, before breakfast.

Talking of scales, it is important that you are able to have an accurate measure of your weight. Many of you are probably using scales you have had around for years. Chances are they are the analog type (either with a pointer or a rotating disk). Over time, the springs in these types of scales stretch and become wildly inaccurate. Do yourself a favour and purchase a digital scale. They can be bought for well under $50.

Current Weight: _____

Current Waist: _____

Current Hips: _____

Target Weight: _____

A few words about setting your weight target. The international standard for weight measurement is the Body Mass Index or BMI. Measure your BMI on the BMI table. The ideal BMI range is 19–24. (For a more detailed rundown on where you might fit in this range, see Frame Size, page 24)

However, it is important that you've set **your** goals. Everyone has different motivations for losing weight and neither I nor the BMI tables can do this for you. So set your target weight goals and write them on the previous page.

Remember, you are starting on a journey. Don't expect miracles. The weight will come off.

For those with a BMI of over 30 who may feel overwhelmed by the task ahead, you do have one advantage over your skinnier compatriots in that you will lose weight at a faster rate.

You are starting on a new way of eating that will be your way of eating for the rest of your life. Congratulations for making the decision to take control. Enjoy the ride!

Menopause and Weight Gain

Now, here are a few basic facts about menopause and how it can have an impact upon your weight. Besides genetics, it is hormonal changes that occur during a woman's life cycle that are the principal trigger for weight gain. Principal hormonal changes take place in adolescence, pregnancy and menopause. All of you have experienced adolescence and the associated weight gain from the rounding out of hips, breasts and thighs. The resulting body image and associated weight consciousness was for many the beginning of a lifetime struggle. Next, many of you experienced the major hormonal shifts of pregnancy with its inevitable weight gain. The final hormonal shift takes places during menopause, where again many women feel its effects.

This may come as a surprise, but the link between menopause and weight gain is not clearly understood. There are several reasonable theories, but nothing conclusive to date. However, we do know why women's traditional "pear" shape, with weight distribution around the bottom, hips and thighs, shifts to the more prevalent male "apple" shape with the middle (read beer belly!) carrying the weight. This is because the female hormone, estrogen, was responsible for the development of your female shape during adolescence. During menopause estrogen production in your ovaries drops, so your body shape redistributes and you accumulate more fat around your abdomen. It's this increase in abdominal fat that has serious implications for your health, especially heart disease, stroke and diabetes.

The likely causes of weight gain during menopause are a combination of both hormonal and age-related factors. Here's what we do know:

- **Estrogen/progesterone:** Both estrogen and progesterone hormones become depleted during menopause and this interferes with appetite control. In one research program, some HRT (hormone therapy replacement) users showed less weight gain and less redistribution of weight, though those prone to weight gain did not appear to benefit.
- **Metabolism:** This is the rate at which your body burns calories. During and post-menopause your metabolic rate drops. So if you burn calories more slowly then you need fewer calories. This change in metabolic rate is partly due to the natural aging process. Remember, burning fewer calories without reducing your calorie input inevitably leads to weight gain.
- **Muscle mass:** Muscles are the body's largest calorie consumers and we start losing muscle mass from the age of 20. This muscle loss really accelerates during post-menopause (for men it's post 60 years) which means again you're burning fewer calories and therefore putting on the pounds if you haven't adjusted your calorie consumption.
- **Physical activity:** As we approach our fifties (average North American menopause age is 51 years) many of us become less active. Child rearing and its associated activity are largely over. Exercise becomes more of an effort and we become more conscious of the wear and tear on our bodies along with the inevitable aches and pains. Less exercise means fewer calories burned—and we know where the surplus calories are being stored!
- **Lifestyle:** As many of us now have fewer family-raising responsibilities and are entering our peak earnings years, we tend to eat out and travel more. Eating out tends to be a calorie-rich experience.

So, as you can see, while hormonal changes are somewhat responsible for weight gain during menopause, the aging process itself also has a substantial impact. The two are inextricably linked.

The one common element in all the factors I've mentioned is calorie intake and expenditure. The two must be brought into balance—and that is what the G.I. Diet is all about. I will show you how to reduce your calorie intake painlessly and without going hungry or feeling deprived. The traffic-light coding means you never have to count calories or points, or weigh and measure your food. The G.I. Diet is a nutritious, balanced diet that will keep you healthy and reduce your risk of major diseases, including most cancers (including breast cancer) heart disease, stroke, diabetes and dementia. The evidence that food is the most important controllable risk factor in our health is overwhelming. While exercise is important for overall good health, it is a poor tool when it comes to losing weight. As you will read later, losing weight is 90 percent diet and 10 percent exercise. However, when you reach your target weight, exercise is essential to help you maintain that weight and improve your health.

Why Do You Want to Lose Weight?

Everyone has their own reasons for wanting to lose weight. Let's look at the most common reasons and see if they match yours.

1. **Body image:** You want to look better. Weight loss boosts self-esteem and confidence for women in particular. It's amazing the difference the loss of just a few pounds can make, not only in how you look in your clothes but also in how you feel about yourself.

   My wife, Ruth, complains that the worst thing about a woman hitting fifty was becoming invisible. People appear not to notice you the way they used to. For some women, the end of the reproductive years can lead to a feeling of being less of a sexual being, which further compounds this sense of not being attractive or noticed. While there's nothing you can do about menopause itself, you can do a great deal about improving your appearance—particularly your weight.

2. **Health**: As mentioned earlier, a lighter you means a healthier you, and good health, which we tend to take for granted in our younger years, now

takes a new priority. Usually the first indications that we are not immortal are the growing health issues facing aging parents and relatives.

Most major health risks are now clearly associated with what we eat. This association of major diseases such as heart, stroke, diabetes and hypertension (high blood pressure) with being overweight is well established. More recently, major cancers, especially breast cancer in postmenopausal women, and Alzheimer's have been linked to being overweight. Living longer, healthier lives becomes a great incentive to losing weight.

In a recent research report from the University of Pittsburgh's School of Medicine, it was noted that women with a high percentage of body fat are more likely to suffer from the effects of menopause. In the sample of 1776 menopausal women, researchers found that as body fat increased so did the likelihood that a woman would have hot flashes and night sweats. Dr. Thurston, who headed the study, concluded that weight loss—especially loss of fat—may help women going through menopause reduce hot flashes and night sweats. How's that for motivation?

3. **Energy**: Being overweight means you have more to carry around, which translates into flagging energy levels; sore back, hips and knees; and decreased mobility. The problem is that we don't realize what weight actually weighs. Take a shopping bag and fill it up with say 20 pounds of food

As a person who studied biomedical sciences, when I read your book it all made perfect sense! … Your diet works like a miracle cure it's so simple to follow and I have now found a taste for porridge, I don't miss the carbohydrate laden junk food and have convinced lots of other people to join me on the diet … My clothes are falling off me, I nearly lost a skirt whilst on playground duty last week at school (had to catch it quick!). My husband hated following diets but loves yours because he is never hungry, gets to eat cranberry and cinnamon muffins and muesli bars (he thinks these taste like Christmas cake!) and most of all he can see the effects—his jeans are falling down too! … Thank you so much for your advice and inspiration, your diet is a true revelation. Helen

cans/books (use bathroom scales) and carry it up and down two flights of stairs. You'll be glad to put the bag down. I have no idea how some people carry around 50 or more extra pounds all the time. I doubt if many of them could actually lift that weight!

Below, I would like you to write your personal top three reasons for wanting to lose weight. Take a moment to be clear about your reasons and be absolutely honest—this is for your eyes only. Later on, being able to come back to this page and read what you have written will go a long way toward keeping you motivated.

My Top Three Reasons for Losing Weight

1._____

_____

_____

2._____

_____

_____

3._____

_____

_____

Making Permanent Change

As all of you know only too well, some 95 percent of diets fail and they fail for one simple reason: people just can't stay on them. Research has shown there are three principal reasons for this inability to stay with a diet:

1. You feel hungry or deprived.
2. It is too complex or time consuming, and you don't want to spend the rest of your life counting calories or points, or weighing and measuring foods.
3. You feel unhealthy and lack energy.

Well, on the G.I. Diet you will not go hungry or feel deprived. You will never have to count another calorie or point again—just follow the traffic lights. You will feel healthy and energetic eating the nutritious green-light way. This is not so much a diet as a new and permanent way of eating. No more yo-yo dieting. This is the way to lose weight permanently.

If there is only one thought I can leave with you in this first week, it is that if you wish to lose weight permanently, then you have to permanently change the way you eat.

It sounds simplistic but that is exactly why most diets and dieters fail time and time again. The assumption that you can go on a diet for a limited period of time and lose the weight you want to lose and then simply go back to your old way of eating will guarantee failure. Chances are that you will regain all the weight you have lost and perhaps even more.

Ultimately, the critical ingredient is you. I can provide you with the knowledge, tools and counsel to help make this an easy, simple and relatively painless transition to a new way of eating. But you have to make the commitment for it to work. Whether it's giving up smoking, getting fit or losing weight, nothing can be achieved until you decide you want to make it happen.

Top 5 Tips

Here are my top five tips for helping you achieve your weight-loss goals:

1. Eat three meals/three snacks per day

Always eat three meals and three snacks per day. Breakfast is particularly important. The idea is to keep your tummy busy all day digesting green-light foods.

2. Remember the 90 percent rule

The G.I. Diet is not a straitjacket. Most people are successful if they stay with the

Diet 90 percent of the time. That additional 10 percent can be used for special treats: that unavoidable drink, or lunch out with the friends who love all the "wrong" foods.

3. Don't rush your meals

Eat slowly. Do not rush your meals as it can take half an hour for the brain to realize the stomach is full—a principal reason we overeat. Always put your fork down between mouthfuls.

4. Exercise

Initially, exercise is not that important as the change in diet will account for at least 90 percent of your weight loss. However, as you get closer to your target weight, exercise will become more important.

5. Portions

Except for the dozen or so food items that have designated serving sizes, as listed on page 27), we leave green-light serving sizes primarily up to you. However, moderation is the key. Remember, the only person you are kidding is yourself.

E-Clinic Diaries

Each week I share some of the important questions or comments that the participants in the original menopause e-clinic made in their weekly diaries that you might find helpful on the journey to your target weight. The first couple of weeks are always the most challenging as your body adapts to this new healthy way of eating. Changes in shopping, meals and eating patterns, along with your body's "hey, what's going on here" response, can all be a little unsettling at first. This will soon pass as you rapidly adapt to the green-light way of eating that will shortly become second nature.

> Q: I am noted for my hospitality and my good cooking. I have a lot
> of friends who come for dinner and I go out for dinner a lot. I am

embarrassed about changing my eating habits once again and don't quite know how to tell my social circle what I am up to. Joyce

A: This is a familiar problem and our best advice is to be completely upfront about what you're doing and ask your friends for their support. It's not as if you have a hidden problem with your current weight and I'm sure your real friends will be supportive of you adopting a completely new lifestyle. Remember this is not so much a diet as a new and permanent way of eating. In the G.I. Diet books you will find many delicious recipes that you can share with your friends whether they need to lose weight or not. (Many people write in that their friends, husband and children couldn't believe the food served is "green light"!)

*Q: ... I have fears of failure and also of my "comfort source" (food) being taken away. That does things to my head, and so I am hungry for the first week or so. **Is it okay to eat fruit or a few nuts, or one of the green-light foods in between meals or snack times at first?** I feel like I need to be able to, just to prove to myself that I can follow this program, that I am **NOT** going to starve, and there are so many options out there. Marlene*

A: This is not an uncommon reaction. All I can say at this stage is that less than 1 percent of the letters I receive from readers who have been following the program talk about failure ... So, providing that you stay with the program, you have little to worry about failure. For people who have a BMI of 33 or more, I recommend that they increase their number of snacks from three to four per day. That means you are eating a meal or a snack seven times per day. I constantly hear from people surprised about the fact they always seem to be eating, yet losing weight.

Q: I have experienced some headaches and I am not sure if they are related to caffeine/sugar withdrawal? Carol

A: The headaches are almost certainly due to caffeine withdrawal but that will pass. If it continues to bother you, just limit your caffeine intake to 1 cup of coffee a day. And make sure it's a good one!

Q: *I have read that soy intake is very good for menopause symptoms. I have tried increasing my soy and find my night sweats and hot flashes almost disappear. I am using supplements and for breakfast I have a soy protein shake made for women ... Can I continue to take this? I absolutely detest tofu! Lynn*

A: As you are probably aware, soy is a rich source of isoflavones, an estrogen-like substance that acts in a similar way to human estrogen, though in a milder form. There is some evidence that eating moderate amounts of soy can help decrease menopause symptoms because of its ability to mimic estrogen replacement. There are, however, a couple of caveats. First, by taking large doses you may run the risk of duplicating the same health risks as with traditional HRT, namely heart disease, stroke and breast and ovarian cancer. Second, there is evidence that large doses of soy can affect the absorption of essential nutrients in the digestive process, particularly zinc and calcium. Calcium is particularly important to menopausal women because of the increased risk of osteo-porosis. Nevertheless, soy is recognized as an excellent source of low-fat protein and is a highly recommended green-light food. Due to the health risks for menopausal women, I recommend moderation. Serve a few times a week rather than several times daily. And do check with your physician/health care provider if additional soy products are right for you.

Now, congratulate yourself for getting through the first week on the program, and record your measurements on the next page. Also, take the time to write about your experiences and feelings this week. Diaries provide an opportunity to reflect on your progress, which helps reveal issues you might have to work on, ways of thinking that might be holding you back and strategies that could work well for you.

Week 1 Weight: _____

Week 1 Waist: _____

Week 1 Hips:_____

Week 1 Diary

_____

_____

_____

_____

_____

_____

_____

_____

_____

_____

_____

_____

_____

_____

Week 1 Optional Meal Plan

Note: You are *not* required to use these weekly meal plans and shopping lists.
Feel free to pick and choose and make up your own green-light meals.

	BREAKFAST	SNACK	LUNCH	SNACK	DINNER	SNACK
MON	Homey Oatmeal (p. 236) with chopped apple	Cranberry Cinnamon Bran Muffin (p. 301)	Open face chicken sandwich with with lettuce, tomato and onion, and Basic G.I. Salad (p. 255)	Laughing Cow Light cheese with crispbread	Lemon Linguine with Smoked Salmon (p. 266) Broccoli and salad	Mixed berries tossed in lime juice with sour cream
TUES	Mini Breakfast Puffs (p. 240)	Fruit yogurt	G.I. Pasta Salad (p. 259)	Hummus with carrot and celery sticks	Cheesy Lentil and Bean Bake (p. 267), basmati rice and salad	Orange and almonds
WED	Homemade Muesli (p. 237) with skim milk and fruit yogurt	Cranberry Cinnamon Bran Muffin (p. 301)	1/2 whole wheat pita with canned light tuna, lettuce, tomato and cucumber, and Basic G.I. Salad (p. 255)	Babybel Gouda Lite cheese with crispbread	Chicken Curry (p. 289) and Raita Salad (p. 253)	Cran-Apple Oatmeal Bars (p. 314) and glass of skim milk
THURS	Homey Oatmeal (p. 236) with blueberries	Small apple and glass of skim milk	Quick and Easy Chicken Noodle Soup (p. 248) and Basic G.I. Salad (p. 255)	Crunchy Chickpeas (p. 300)	Braised Pacific Halibut (p. 278), new or small potatoes and salad	1/2 nutrition bar
FRI	All-Bran Buds with skim milk, peach slices and sliced almonds	Fruit yogurt	Mixed Bean Salad (p. 261)	Laughing Cow Light cheese with crispbread	Marinated Flank Steak (p. 295), new potatoes, green beans and salad	Mixed berries tossed in lime juice with sour cream
SAT	Smoked Salmon Scrambled Eggs (p. 244)	1/2 nutrition bar	Greek Salad (p. 223)	Hummus with carrot and celery sticks	Orange Chicken with Almonds (p. 287), green beans and basmati rice	Creamy Raspberry Mousse (p. 307)
SUN	Oatmeal Buttermilk Pancakes with strawberries (p. 239)	Orange and almonds	Caesar Salad (p. 256) with canned tuna	Babybel Gouda Lite cheese with crispbread	Vegetarian Moussaka (p. 278), and basmati rice	Piece of Plum Crumble (p. 310)

Week 1 Grocery List for Meal Plan

PRODUCE
Almonds (whole and sliced)
Apples
Asparagus
Baby spinach

Blueberries (fresh or frozen)
Broccoli
Carrots
Celery
Cranberries (dried)
Cucumbers (English and field)
Eggplant
Fresh herbs (dill, flat-leaf parsley, thyme)
Garlic
Ginger root
Green beans
Green onions
Kale
Lemons
Lettuce (iceberg, leaf and romaine)
Limes
Onions (yellow and red)
Oranges
Peaches (fresh or canned in juice or water)
Peppers (green, red or yellow)
Potatoes (new, small)
Prune plums (e.g., damson or Italian)
Raisins
Raspberries
Strawberries
Sunflower seeds, shelled and unsalted
Tomatoes (plum)

DELI
Feta cheese (light)
Hummus (light)
Kalamata olives

BAKERY
100% stone-ground whole wheat bread
Crispbread (e.g., Wasa Fibre)
Whole wheat pita bread

FISH COUNTER
Pacific halibut
Smoked salmon

MEAT COUNTER
Chicken breasts (boneless, skinless)
Flank steak

**BEANS (LEGUMES) AND
CANNED VEGETABLES**
Black beans
Chickpeas
Diced tomatoes
Lentils (green)
Mixed beans
Tomato paste

PASTA AND SAUCES
Light tomato sauce (no added sugar)
Rotini or penne (whole wheat)
Small pasta (e.g., ditali or tubetti)

SOUP AND CANNED SEAFOOD AND MEAT
Anchovy fillets
Chicken stock (low-fat, low-sodium)
Tuna (light, in water)

GRAINS AND SIDE DISHES
Basmati rice
Flaxseeds (ground)

INTERNATIONAL FOODS
Soy sauce (low-sodium)
Tahini

COOKING OIL, VINEGAR, SALAD DRESSINGS AND PICKLES
Dijon mustard
Grainy mustard
Mayonnaise (fat-free)
Oil (canola and extra-virgin olive)
Red wine vinegar
Rice vinegar
Vegetable cooking oil spray (canola or olive oil)
Worcestershire sauce

SNACKS
Applesauce (unsweetened)
Nutrition bars (e.g., ZonePerfect, Balance Bar)

BAKING
Amaretto
Baking powder
Baking soda
Cornstarch
Oat bran
Spices (allspice, ground cardamom, Cajun seasoning, ground cinnamon, ground cumin, curry powder, ground ginger, dried oregano, black pepper, red pepper flakes, salt, dried thyme)
Splenda

Vanilla
Wheat bran
Wheat germ
Whole wheat flour

BREAKFAST FOODS
All-Bran Buds or 100% Bran cereal
Oatmeal (large-flake oats)

BEVERAGES
White wine

DAIRY CASE
Babybel Gouda Lite cheese
Buttermilk
Cheddar cheese (low-fat)
Cottage cheese (1%)
Fruit yogurt (non-fat with sweetener)
Laughing Cow Light cheese (extra-low-fat)
Liquid eggs (e.g., Naturegg Break Free)
Milk (skim)
Soft margarine (non-hydrogenated, light)
Sour cream (low-fat)
Whole Omega-3 eggs

FROZEN FOODS
Peas (or fresh)

Week 2

Preparing Food
the Green-Light Way

At this point in the clinic, enthusiasm is usually at a high. However, it does take a week or two for your body to become accustomed to this new way of eating. Be aware that the numbers on the scale may not have changed much or at all yet. Keep the faith!

Remember that our target weight loss is an *average* **of one pound per week** (see page 49). If you have a BMI of 33 or over, you may lose an average of up to two pounds per week especially in the first couple of months. It took you many years to achieve your current weight so don't fret if this seems a slow start. The G.I. Diet is not a quick fix, so-called miracle diet. Instead it is a highly nutritious way of eating that will improve your health and enable you to lose weight—and keep it off. Keep in mind what I said in Week 1: if you wish to lose weight permanently you must permanently change the way you eat.

Turning Your Standbys into Green-Light Recipes

... I'm going to have to be in the kitchen more (and) forced to get out of my cooking rut. I can no longer have the quick fix. Because I've been overweight forever, I think I have a mental block about baking and putting much time into cooking ... " Sheri

It's easy to make many of your own standby recipes green-light by following the guidelines below. You don't have to necessarily use the recipes listed in this book.

Green-Light Ingredients

First, ensure that all the ingredients in the recipe are green-light. If there are any red- or yellow- light ingredients, either omit or replace them with a green-light alternative. Some red- and yellow-light food can be used in recipes if there is a very limited quantity, such as ½ cup of wine in a dish that will serve six people, or ¼ cup raisins in a salad for four. Full-flavoured cheeses can also occasionally be used sparingly. For example, a tablespoon or two of grated Parmesan cheese

I've waited a year before writing, just to be sure that I didn't put back all the weight that I'd lost. Two years ago, I weighed nearly 147 pounds, and I'm short—only 5 ft 1". I was beginning to "feel my age" (58) but didn't want to accept what some people feel is inevitable. I looked and felt frumpy, didn't have much energy and my knees were sore at the end of the day. So I did the most sensible thing I have done in years, and bought a copy of "The G.I. Diet." In under a year, not feeling as if I was on a diet at all, I lost all my middle age flab, and by the time I got to my 59th birthday, I was a slender, fit and—according to my husband—dishy grandmother ... Since losing the weight, I've been on three walking holidays, walking about 20 miles a day, and I have taken up cycling and swimming, now that I look so good in a swimsuit. I urge anyone with a weight problem to try this way of eating. It is delicious, you feel fabulous and I'm sticking with it for life. It IS a bit expensive, though. All those new clothes! Margaret

sprinkled over a casserole will add flavour without too many calories. As long as the red- and yellow-light ingredients are used in very limited quantities and not as a core ingredient, they will not have a significant impact on the overall G.I. or green-light rating of the recipe.

Fibre

The fibre content of the recipe is critical. Fibre, both soluble and insoluble, is key to the overall G.I. rating of a recipe. The more, the better. If your recipe is light on fibre, consider adding fibre boosters such as oats, bran, whole grains or beans.

Fat

The recipes should be low in fat with little to no saturated fat. If fat is called for, use vegetable oil. Canola and olive oil are your best choices, but use as little as possible, as all fats are calorie-dense.

Sugar

Never add sugar or sugar-based ingredients such as corn syrup or molasses. There are some excellent sugar substitutes on the market. My favourite is

Splenda, or sucralose, which was developed from a sugar base but does not have as many calories. It works well in cooking and baking. Measure it by volume (not weight) to exactly replace sugar. For example, 1 tablespoon sugar = 1 tablespoon Splenda. Note that Brown Splenda is 50 percent sugar and is therefore not recommended. Sugar Twin Brown is an acceptable alternative.

Protein

Be sure that the recipe contains sufficient protein, or that you are serving it alongside some protein to round out the meal. Protein helps slow the digestive process, which effectively lowers the G.I. of a recipe. It is also the one component that is often overlooked at mealtime, particularly in recipes for salads and snacks. Useful protein boosters are low-fat dairy products; lean meats, poultry and seafood; egg whites; beans; and soy-based foods, such as tofu and isolated soy or whey powders.

Big-Batch Cooking Saves Time

If you don't always have time to cook, make big batches when you do have time, say on the weekends, and freeze green-light meals for busy nights. Having healthy meals in your freezer means you can always pull them out rather than grab a takeout menu. With a little planning, you won't have to rely on fast food to get you through your busy schedule. Organizing your pantry, fridge and freezer so that they keep you going when the going gets tough will ensure the weight-loss results you want.

Equipment

The right equipment will help you gain maximum nutritional benefit as well as save you time. Every G.I. Diet kitchen should have the following:

Microwave Oven

Heating and cooking foods is really the first step in the digestive process. The longer you cook your food, the more "digestible" it becomes. Ever tried eating a raw potato?

It will take you a week to digest it! As a result, cooking raises the G.I. of foods as it does what your tummy would otherwise be doing. Remember, it's important to have your body doing the processing of food. Though we don't recommend always eating uncooked foods, we do suggest keeping cooking times to a minimum; or cooking only until, as the Italians say, "al dente" or "with some firmness to the bite."

One of the best ways of doing this is with the microwave oven. Fresh or frozen vegetables can be cooked in minutes and that helps keep the G.I. low and often preserves nutrients better than other methods, because cooking time is reduced and little water is used. The microwave is a godsend at breakfast as my favourite cereal, oatmeal, can be made in three to four minutes rather than 15 minutes or more on the stove. A fillet of fish can be cooked in five minutes.

For thawing meats, and warming snacks and leftovers, the microwave is your best green-light kitchen friend.

Non-stick Frying Pans

You should have two different sizes plus lids. They require little or no oil, and cleaning up is a cinch. We are big on stir-fries in our household, so these non-stick skillets get a lot of use.

Barbecues/Indoor Grills

Cooking meat and fish on either a barbecue or indoor grill is a good idea as it allows any extra fat to drain away and always seem to taste better too.

E-Clinic Diaries

This week e-clinic participants were absorbing the basic information just as you are now. As a result, questions and comments cover a broad area. To help you stay focused, I have selected only those that are particularly relevant in helping you reach your goals.

Q: Is there any flexibility in this diet? Kathy

A: Yes, but only you can determine which rules you can break and still lose weight. Many readers tell me they can't live without certain red-light foods such as regular coffee or peanut butter. If there's a product that is important to you, go ahead and have it—but strictly limit the quantity you consume. Have only 1 cup of coffee or one tablespoon of peanut butter. My publisher told me she was on the "Vegas" version of the G.I. Diet, meaning she had a glass of red wine every day in Phase 1. She still lost 30 pounds and is wearing the same dress size she wore back in college. Although you would lose weight a little faster if you followed all the guidelines of the G.I. Diet, it really is okay to commit to 90 percent of the program. But don't try to accelerate the program by missing meals or snacks. Three meals a day and three snacks are absolutely essential if you are not going to go hungry or feel deprived.

Frozen fruits and vegetables

Q: *(I find that) groceries are more expensive (because) I am buying more out-of-season produce and somewhat more expensive cuts of meat. I am also cooking more—no takeout. Lynn*

A: You can reduce your cost of out-of-season fruits and vegetables by buying the family-size supermarket bags of frozen fruits or vegetables. These are a good deal and in some ways even better than fresh. Frozen fruits and vegs have the same nutritional content as fresh because they are picked at just the right ripeness stage—and there is usually less waste as leaves and stems have been removed.

Q: *Yogurt: fat-free, sugar-free? Any brand-name suggestions? I can find fat-free. I can find sugar-free. I cannot find fat-free and sugar-free. Ann*

A: There are several brands of fat-free, no-sugar-added, products on the market. You may be a little confused by the sugar content on the label but that simply reflects the fact that all dairy products contain some naturally occurring sugars. What we are trying to ensure is that there is no added sugar. So look for no-fat fruit yogurt with sweetener (such as Splenda).

Q: *I use a lot of artificial sweetener ... I prefer Splenda over NutraSweet. I recently became aware of agave nectar and xylitol, both which claim on their packages to be low glycemic, though I note that agave nectar has a lot of calories. I am interested in the xylitol because our dentist told me that it is actually GOOD for one's teeth in sugar-free gum. I purchased a small bag of the granulated xylitol sweetener. What do you think about the agave nectar and xylitol? Marlene*

A: NutraSweet is the brand name for aspartame, which some people appear to be sensitive to, even though it is completely safe to use. You cannot use aspartame for baking as it breaks down when heated. Splenda (sucralose), conversely, does not appear to have any sensitivity side effects as it is not absorbed by the body. It can also be used in baking. It is our preferred sweetener.

Sugar alcohols, such as maltitol or xylitol, (sugar alcohol names all end in "... tol") contain about 60 percent of the calories that are in sugar. They do metabolize more slowly than sugar, which gives them a lower G.I. Though they are obviously better than sugar, they still carry an unnecessary calorie load, and are therefore not recommended.

Agave nectar may have a low G.I., but as it is principally fructose, it has the same number of calories as sugar. Fructose is the sugar found in fruit, which is why it has a lower G.I. than regular sugar. However, calories are calories so, again, it is not recommended.

Q: *When I renovated my kitchen a few years ago, I deliberately did not buy a microwave oven. To me, they represent an opportunity to eat junk food: microwave popcorn and corn chips and cheese. Too tempting to have that for supper when you live alone! I have never been able to cook oatmeal in it without making a mess. I don't really miss it, and more often than not, I appreciate taking the time to pre-pare food in stages and not rush. You know that whole Slow Food movement? I think if you are eating slowly, enjoying and appreciating your food, then it is a sign of respect to take care in the preparation of the food as well. I find it easy to plan ahead and take things out of the freezer ahead of time. In fact, I love to cook and the time it takes. It makes up for eating in restaurants so much. And that brings me to my suggestion, what about some slow-cooker recipes for the G.I. diet? I have used mine for soups and all kinds of things. Louise*

A: It's good to read a counterpoint to the microwave recommendation. Most people complain they don't have enough time for cooking so the microwave becomes an indispensable tool for them. However, if you do have the time, then your comments about slow cooking are most appropriate.

By now you should be getting more comfortable with cooking and eating the green-light way. Next week we will be focusing on the single most important factor in successful weight loss: behaviour change.

Week 2 Weight: _____

Week 2 Waist: _____

Week 2 Hips: _____

Week 2 Diary

_____

_____

_____

_____

_____

Week 2 Optional Meal Plan

	BREAKFAST	SNACK	LUNCH	SNACK	DINNER	SNACK
MON	Homey Oatmeal (p. 236) with chopped apple	Carrot Muffin (p. 302)	Open-face lean deli ham sandwich with lettuce, tomato, red pepper and grainy mustard, and Basic G.I. Salad (p. 255)	Laughing Cow light cheese with crispbread	G.I. Fish Fillet (p. 280) asparagus, carrots and new potatoes	Mixed berries tossed in lime juice with sour cream
TUES	Mini Breakfast Puffs (p. 240)	Fruit yogurt	Vegetable Barley Soup au Pistou (p. 249) with Basic G.I. Salad (p. 255)	Hummus with carrot and celery	Bolognese Pasta Sauce (p. 297) with whole wheat pasta and Basic G.I. Salad (p. 255)	Orange and almonds
WED	Homemade Muesli (p. 237) with skim milk and fruit yogurt	Carrot Muffin (p. 302)	Cottage cheese with apple and grapes, and Basic G.I. Salad (p. 255)	Babybel Gouda Lite cheese with crispbread	Chicken Tarragon with Mushrooms (p. 288), broccoli and basmati rice	Pecan Brownie (p. 315) and glass of skim milk
THURS	Homey Oatmeal (p. 236) with blueberries	Small apple and glass of skim milk	Tuna Salad (p. 260)	Crunchy Chickpeas (p. 300)	Savoury Beans and Apple (p. 268), basmati rice and salad	1/2 nutrition bar
FRI	All-Bran Buds with skim milk, peach slices and sliced almonds	Fruit yogurt	1/2 whole wheat pita with deli turkey, lettuce, tomato and cucumber, and Basic G.I. Salad (p. 255)	Laughing Cow Light cheese with crispbread	Ginger-Wasabi Halibut (p. 281) Cold Noodle Salad with Cucumber and Sesame (p. 258), snow peas and carrots	Creamy Raspberry Mousse (p. 307)
SAT	Breakfast in a Glass (p. 242)	1/2 nutrition bar	Crab Salad in Tomato Shells (p. 263)	Hummus with carrot and celery sticks	Chicken Tikka (p. 283), snow peas, rice or bulgur and salad	Pecan Brownie (p. 315) and glass of skim milk
SUN	Cinnamon French Toast (p. 238), with back bacon	Orange and almonds	Minestrone (p. 246), and Basic G.I. Salad (p. 255)	Babybel Gouda Lite cheese with crispbread	Grilled Portobello Mushroom Pizzas (p. 270), and salad	Slice of Apple Raspberry Coffee Cake (p. 311)

Week 2 Grocery List for Meal Plan

PRODUCE
Almonds (whole and sliced)
Apples
Asparagus
Bananas
Broccoli
Carrots
Celery
Cucumbers (English and field)
Fresh herbs (basil, chives, cilantro, flat-leaf
   parsley, tarragon, thyme)
Garlic
Ginger root
Grapes
Green beans
Leeks
Lemons
Lettuce (leaf and romaine)
Limes
Mushrooms (white and Portobello)
Onions (yellow and red)
Oranges
Peaches (fresh or canned in juice or water)
Pecans
Peppers (green, red or yellow)
Potatoes (new, small)
Raisins
Raspberries
Snow peas
Strawberries
Sunflower seeds, shelled and unsalted
Tomatoes (large beefsteak and plum)
Zucchini

DELI
Feta cheese (light)
Hummus (light)
Lean deli ham
Lean deli turkey
Olives
Parmesan cheese, grated

BAKERY
100% stone-ground whole wheat bread
Crispbread (e.g., Wasa Fibre)
Whole wheat pita bread

FISH COUNTER
Frozen crab
Halibut fillets

MEAT COUNTER
Back bacon
Chicken breasts (boneless, skinless)
Ground beef (extra-lean)

BEANS (LEGUMES) AND CANNED VEGETABLES
Chickpeas
Crushed tomatoes
Kidney beans (red and white)
Tomato paste
Tomato sauce

PASTA AND SAUCES
Capellini or spaghettini (whole wheat)
Fettuccini or linguine (whole wheat)

SOUP AND CANNED SEAFOOD AND MEAT
Anchovy fillets
Chicken stock (low-fat, low-sodium)
Tuna (light, in water)
Vegetable stock (low-fat, low-sodium)

GRAINS AND SIDE DISHES
Barley
Basmati rice
Bulgar
Flaxseeds (whole and ground)

INTERNATIONAL FOODS
Mirin (or sweet sherry)
Rice vinegar
Soy sauce (low-sodium)
Sesame seeds (toasted)
Tahini
Wasabi powder

COOKING OIL, VINEGAR, SALAD DRESSINGS AND PICKLES
Buttermilk salad dressing (low-fat, low-sugar)
Capers
Dijon mustard
Dry mustard
Grainy mustard
Mayonnaise (fat-free)
Oil (canola and extra-virgin olive)
Red wine vinegar
Sherry vinegar
Worcestershire sauce

SNACKS
Nutrition bars (e.g., ZonePerfect, Balance Bar)

BAKING
Amaretto
Baking powder
Baking soda
Brown sugar substitute
Oat bran
Soy lecithin granules
Spices (cayenne pepper, chili powder, ground cumin, garam masala, ground ginger, ground cinnamon, ground nutmeg, dried

oregano, black pepper, salt, dried tarragon, dried thyme, turmeric)
Splenda
Unsweetened cocoa powder
Vanilla
Wheat bran
Wheat germ
Whey or soy protein isolate powder
Whole wheat flour

BREAKFAST FOODS
All-Bran Buds cereal
Oatmeal (large-flake oats)

BEVERAGES
Red wine
Tomato juice
Vermouth or white wine

DAIRY CASE
Babybel Gouda Lite cheese
Buttermilk
Cottage cheese (low-fat)
Fruit yogurt (non-fat with sweetener)
Laughing Cow Light cheese (extra-low-fat)
Liquid eggs (e.g., Naturegg, Break Free)
Milk (skim)
Mozzarella cheese (part-skim)
Soft margarine (non-hydrogenated, light)
Sour cream (low-fat)
Soy milk

FROZEN FOODS
Mixed berries
Raspberries

Week 3

Behaviour Change

By the time you reach menopause, your lifestyle patterns and personal habits are well established. Change, once so welcome in youth, is much more difficult to embrace. Over the years you have made choices that, for better or worse, have deeply entrenched your food habits. However, changing behaviours with regard to food is fundamental to your success with this program.

This week we will examine some behaviours that must be addressed. I can provide you with the tools to change what you eat but changing your food behaviours is something that only you can do. As the old saying goes, "you can lead a horse to water, but you cannot make it drink"!

Here are 10 important behaviours that must be addressed if you are to be successful in reaching your weight loss goals.

1. Skipping Breakfast

This is a very common bad habit: it is estimated that one-quarter of North Americans skip breakfast and the numbers are even worse for teenagers.

Breakfast is the most important meal of the day. By the time people rise in the morning, most haven't eaten for ten to twelve hours, and their blood sugar levels are low. As a result, skipping breakfast will most certainly cause you to snack throughout the day in an effort to boost your blood sugar or energy level. And chances are good that you will reach for high-calorie, high-fat foods such as doughnuts, muffins or cookies to give you that quick sugar fix your body feels it needs. But, as we are all well aware by now, the blood sugar high caused by these red-light foods will soon be followed by a sugar crash as your insulin kicks in, and you'll be looking for your next sugar fix.

2. Not Taking Time to Eat Properly

Saying "I don't have time to eat properly" creates a spawning ground for bad habits. People who don't take the time to eat properly tend to grab a coffee and Danish on their way to work, eat a store-bought muffin mid-morning to boost flagging energy levels, have a slice or two of pizza with a soft drink for lunch, snack on chocolate and cookies in the afternoon to help keep their eyes open, pick up some high-fat takeout food on the way home for dinner, and finally collapse in front of the TV for the evening with a beer and a bowl of chips.

It's easy to slip into this harmful cycle of fattening convenience food and short-term energy fixes, but you'll pay for the convenience with a growing girth, flagging energy and poor health. And really, the amount of incremental time required to prepare your own healthy meals and snacks is quite modest. Fifteen minutes in the morning is all it takes to eat a healthy breakfast—often the length of time it takes to line up for a coffee. If you can't manage to wake up fifteen minutes earlier to squeeze in a nutritious breakfast before rushing off to work, then bring along a box of green-light cereal, a carton of skim milk and piece of fruit. Another piece of fruit and a carton of skim milk take no time to prepare and make a filling, nutritious snack. And there are always places you can get a green-light sandwich so you don't have to resort to pizza. Eating healthily through the day will ensure that you have the energy when you arrive home to prepare a quick green-light dinner in the time it would have taken to drive to the takeout place and wait for your order.

3. Grazing

The world's best grazers are teenagers. They simply cannot avoid opening the fridge every time they pass it. Their rapid growth and (hopefully) high activity levels require a constant high-calorie intake. Unfortunately, grazing is a habit that many people continue into their adult lives with disastrous results for their waistlines and health. A few nuts here, a couple of cookies there, a tablespoon or two of peanut butter, and a few glasses of juice all look pretty harmless in themselves, but taken together they can easily total several hundred extra calories a day! And those can add up to over twenty pounds of additional weight in a year.

On the G.I. Diet, you should be eating three meals plus three to four snacks a day, which means you are eating approximately every two hours or so during your waking hours. This will reduce your temptation to graze. One reader wrote that she couldn't believe how she could be losing weight when she always seemed to be eating. She called it "green-light grazing"!

4. Unconscious Eating

How often have we all begun to nibble on a bowl of chips or nuts or a box of cookies while watching TV, reading a book or talking on the phone and then suddenly realized that we'd eaten the whole lot. Too often, I would guess.

Eating should never be the peripheral activity—it should always be the focus. Eat your meals at the table and set aside distractions such as the TV, computer, video game or telephone while you have your snacks. This will help you to always eat consciously and be aware of exactly how much you are eating.

5. Eating Too Quickly

The famous Dr. Johnson of the eighteenth century is said to have asserted that food should always be chewed thirty-two times before swallowing. Though this seems rather excessive, there is an important truth here. Many of us tend to eat far too quickly. It takes twenty to thirty minutes for the stomach to let the brain know it is full. If you eat too quickly, you'll continue to eat past the point at which you've had enough. The solution, then, is to eat slowly to allow the brain to catch up with your stomach.

That's probably another reason that Mediterranean countries have lower rates of obesity: they take far longer to eat their meals. There, mealtimes are for family and friends, for enjoying the pleasure of food—not simply a means to tackle hunger. To ensure you are not eating more than your appetite requires, slow down and really enjoy what you are eating. Put your fork down between mouthfuls. Savour the flavor and textures.

6. Not Drinking Enough

Did you know that by the time you feel thirsty you are already dehydrated? Your body's need for water is second only to its need for oxygen. Up to 70 percent of the body is water, and we should be drinking about eight glasses a day to replenish our supply. Yet many of us don't take the time to drink enough, and we go tired and hungry, which makes us reach for food when we really should be reaching for a glass of water. Our body isn't hungry, it's thirsty. So always carry water with you and make sure you are drinking your eight glasses. Being properly hydrated will go a long way toward helping you control your appetite and lose weight.

7. Rewarding for Exercise

Another common habit is rewarding yourself with food for doing some exercise. Rather than allowing the reward to be the exercise itself, many feel that the extra effort deserves some form of reward or treat, which more often than not takes the form of food or drink.

This raises a couple of issues. First, one of the great myths about weight loss is that it can be achieved through exercise. Though exercise is essential for long-term health and weight maintenance, it is actually a poor tool for losing weight. To give you an idea of how much exercise you would have to do to lose just one pound of fat, you would have to walk briskly for *forty-two* miles if you weighed 160 pounds or *fifty-three* miles if you weighed 130 pounds. That is a huge amount of effort and way beyond the capability or time availability of most people. Walking around the block or washing the car consumes only a handful of calories. So if you are using exercise as permission to cut a little slack in your diet, remember that cookie reward will add more calories than you expended on your activity.

By all means exercise to improve your health, but don't think it will contribute to your weight loss. I frequently tell people that losing weight is 90 percent diet and 10 percent exercise, particularly in the early stages.

8. Cleaning the Plate

Many of us were taught from the time we were small to finish what's on our plates before leaving the table. This becomes a deeply embedded habit that does not, unfortunately, help us in later life to lose or maintain weight. Not only do we finish our own, but we tend to also finish the leftovers on our children's plates or that last lonely slice in the pie dish after dinner. But this habit causes us to eat more than we need to satisfy our hunger and is therefore dreadful for weight control. Get into the habit of letting your stomach and brain decide when you are full, not the quantity of food on your plate. Leftovers can always be stored in the fridge, rather than around your waist or hips.

Prior to starting the G.I. Diet, I felt helpless to get rid of the bloated feeling I had. My husband would go through a large bottle of Tums a month with heartburn, and I was actually hospitalized with possible liver problems. I considered that I was doing a pretty good job at eating in a healthy manner ... I work in the health care field ... but all was for nought. Within a month of cleaning out the pantry and starting again we were both feeling better than in a long time. We have been at it now for 8 months, and to all those who laughed at my "diet," I am hearing nothing but admiration for the change. I have gone down from size 13 to 4, and my husband has lost 35 pounds so far. What do I tell those who ask? I tell them we have made a lifestyle change, and that we are enjoying the food, and the feeling of looking good and feeling well. We will not go back. Thanks Mr. Gallop for defining the guidelines of a good eating lifestyle. Pearl

9. Shopping on an Empty Stomach

Human nature can often be perverse, encouraging us to do the right thing but at the wrong time. When you are full and satisfied, food shopping is rarely top of mind. But when you are hungry, grocery shopping suddenly seems like a very good idea indeed. Unfortunately, it just isn't: you'll end up with a shopping cart that has been filled primarily by your stomach rather than your head. Those red-light foods will seem far more tempting than usual, and you will probably make some poor choices as a result.

So always shop after a meal, or at least take a green-light snack such as a muffin or a nutrition bar with you. You'll make far wiser choices this way.

10. Eating High-Sugar, High-Fat Treats

As we are all aware, food is a big part of holidays and celebrations—just think of Thanksgiving, a wedding, a bar mitzvah or Christmas and you'll probably picture the special foods that go along with them. Where would the candy industry be without Valentine's Day, Halloween or Easter? Food is inexorably linked with positive experiences, and that is one of reasons we often think of certain foods as "treats." Whether it's Granny doling out candies to a child who has been good, or a neighbour presenting you with a freshly baked pie as reward for raking up her leaves, we are accustomed to using food treats to reward the people in our lives as well as ourselves. Unfortunately, these so-called treats tend to be high in calories, sugar and fat and are certainly not your friends. They are a major contributor to the obesity crisis and to weight-related diseases such as diabetes and heart disease. We should start to view these foods as penalties rather than rewards.

Instead, choose treats that are lower in calories and fat. If candy is your thing, there is a plethora of low- and no-sugar brands available. Fresh fruit, low-fat, no-sugar-added yogurt and ice cream are even better treats. And there are many delicious green-light dessert and snack recipes in all my G.I. Diet books. Treats are a wonderful part of our lives—just make sure they are the right sort of treats.

Keep in mind that while it will take some effort and can be challenging at times to change old bad habits, it's well worth your while to persevere with beneficial new behaviours. Before you know it, they'll be second nature, new habits as firmly entrenched as old ones used to be. But these ones will help you slim down to a brand new you.

E-Clinic Diaries

To end this week on a positive note, here are some observations from e-clinic participants as they completed Week 3 of the program:

> I'm adjusting to eating green-light foods and find that it's not as difficult or restrictive as I thought. If I make a few substitutions here and there, I can still have the occasional treat. The key for me is "occasional" instead of indulging every day which has been my downfall. I'm excited with the program and look forward to seeing weekly weight reduction and health benefits. Jacinthe

> This week I was able to really get in to the swing of the meal plans and, as I'd read in your book, the lack of hunger actually occurs. As a result,

I'm feeling far more in control of my food choices rather than them being in control of me. Christine

I just wanted to let you know that since I've started your program, it's amazing how much you start realizing what's good and bad for you. I think and check before I eat something. I feel great, not only physically but mentally to know that I'm going through a phase in my life that will require a lot of healthy choices. This to me is not a diet—it's a plan with rewarding benefits every way you look at it. Grace

Last week, I ... learned a technique which has been overwhelmingly useful to me ... I learned to put my fork down between each bite, chew and then take another mouthful. No distractions like reading and watching TV either! So this way, I end up enjoying what I am eating, tasting it and stopping eating when I am full. Louise

Q: How can I change our family eating habits and the groceries in the house so that food appeals to my boys and husband who don't need to lose weight and still cook so that I can? Kathy

A: We received so much correspondence on whether the G.I. Diet can be applied to the whole family that I wrote a whole book on the subject entitled *The Family G.I. Diet.* The simple answer is that this is an ideal way for the whole family to eat because it is fundamentally a healthy and nutritious way of eating with its focus on fruits, vegetables, whole grains, low-fat dairy, lean protein and "good" fats. All you have to do is adjust the serving sizes depending on whether the individuals need to manage their weight. There is no need to be a short-order cook dealing with everybody's individual needs. One size fits all!

Q: [At work] they are talking about starting aerobics, cardio, weight training, ab workouts, etc., in a couple of weeks. They do it twice a week. Is it too early to start taking these classes? Linda

A: I do strongly advocate some resistance training to help maintain or build muscle mass. I would advocate this form of exercise at this stage rather than aerobic, if you have to choose. As I will be demonstrating later, losing weight is 90 percent diet and 10 percent exercise. However, any exercise is beneficial because it produces a healthier body and helps maintain weight loss (see Week 5).

Q: I am finding that cooking "green" really isn't that tough once you get used to it. The one thing I am still finding a challenge is sauces. It seems they all contain butter and/or sugar. I used to purchase ready-made sauces for quick meals when I had minimal time to cook dinner. Can you suggest any guidelines for purchasing sauces from the super-market? (i.e., better brand names, guidelines for calorie count, fat and sugar content.) It is a bit of a confusing exercise. Kathy

A: The best guideline I can give you for sauces is to compare labels. It's usually quite easy to identify those categories of brands that are posi-tioned as healthy alternatives, such as Campbell's Healthy Choice products and, among those, look for the ones that have the lower fat, sodium (salt) and calorie ratings. I think you'll find it quite an educa-tional experience!

Q: Totally blew it this week. However, after some real soul searching, I know, without a doubt, I am an emotional eater and I am finding ways to counteract that, like substitute candy for a creamy shake made from frozen strawberries, Splenda, and skim milk. That is okay, isn't it? (Happy I am finally thinking how to use the correct foods in a way that will satisfy some bad, nasty old habits.) Janice

A: While I'm delighted to see you are experimenting with alternative green-light choices for some of your traditional favourites, I have one caution: You should try and minimize the use of shakes as the blender is doing most of the food processing. Blending fruits in this way substantially raises the G.I. level. I'd rather you drink the milk and eat the strawberries with some Splenda on them.

Changing ingrained behaviours can be a challenge, particularly by the time you reach menopause. Check off the ones that you have already addressed and focus on those that you recognize need attending to. Don't try to change them all at once or you will likely become frustrated and give up.

Next week we'll discuss getting family and friends on your team.

Week 3 Weight: _____

Week 3 Waist: _____

Week 3 Hips: _____

Week 3 Diary

_____

_____

_____

_____

_____

_____

_____

_____

_____

Week 3 Optional Meal Plan

	BREAKFAST	SNACK	LUNCH	SNACK	DINNER	SNACK
MON	Homey Oatmeal (p. 236) with chopped apple	Apple Bran Muffin (p. 303)	Open-face chicken sandwich with lettuce, tomato and onion, and Basic G.I. Salad (p. 255)	Laughing Cow Light cheese with crispbread	Lemony Grilled Vegetable Pasta Salad (p. 253) with canned tuna or salmon	Mixed berries tossed in lime juice with sour cream
TUES	Mini Breakfast Puffs (p. 240)	Fruit yogurt	Tuscan White Bean Soup (p. 247) with Basic G.I. Salad (p. 255)	Hummus with carrot and celery sticks	Spicy Roasted Chicken with Tomatoes and Tarragon (p. 289), green beans and basmati rice	Orange and almonds
WED	Homemade Muesli (p. 237) with skim milk and fruit yogurt	Apple Bran Muffin (p. 303)	1/2 whole wheat pita with canned light tuna, lettuce, tomato and cucumber, and Basic G.I. Salad (p. 255)	Babybel Gouda Lite cheese with crispbread	Pork Medallions Dijon (p. 298), green beans, carrots and new potatoes	Creamy Lemon Square (p. 310) and glass of skim milk
THURS	Homey Oatmeal (p. 236) with blueberries	Small apple and glass of skim milk	Quick and Easy Chicken Noodle Soup (p. 248) and Basic G.I. Salad (p. 255)	Crunchy Chickpeas (p. 300)	Quinoa, Bean and Vegetable Chili (p. 270), and Basic G.I. salad (p. 255)	1/2 nutrition bar
FRI	All-Bran Buds with skim milk, peach slices and sliced almonds	Fruit yogurt	Waldorf Chicken and Rice Salad (p. 262)	Laughing Cow Light cheese with crispbread	Thai Red Curry Shrimp Pasta (p. 279)	Mixed berries tossed in lime juice with sour cream
SAT	Vegetarian Omelette (p. 243)	1/2 nutrition bar	Greek Salad (p. 257)	Hummus with carrot and celery sticks	Zesty Barbecued Chicken (p. 290), Tangy Red and Green Coleslaw (p. 254)	Creamy Lemon Square (p. 316) and glass of skim milk
SUN	Oatmeal Buttermilk Pancakes (p. 239) with strawberries	Orange and almonds	Tuna Salad (p. 260)	Babybel Gouda Lite cheese with crispbread	Blueberry Beef Burgers (p. 296) broccoli and cauliflower tossed in lemon	Piece of Berry Crumble (p. 309)

Week 3 Grocery List for Meal Plan

PRODUCE
Almonds (ground, sliced and whole)
Apples
Blueberries (fresh or frozen)
Broccoli
Brussels sprouts
Cabbage (green, red or yellow)
Carrots
Cauliflower
Celery
Cucumbers
Eggplant
Fresh herbs (chives, cilantro, mint, tarragon)
Hot pepper
Garlic
Green beans
Green onions
Kale
Leeks
Lemons
Lettuce (leaf and romaine)
Limes
Mushrooms (white and shiitake)
Onions (yellow and red)
Oranges
Peaches (fresh or canned in juice or water)
Pecans
Peppers (green, red or yellow)
Potatoes (new, small)
Raisins
Shallots
Strawberries
Sunflower seeds, shelled and unsalted
Tomatoes (cherry and plum)
Walnuts
Zucchini

DELI
Feta cheese (light)
Hummus (light)
Kalamata olives

BAKERY
100% stone-ground whole wheat bread
Crispbread (e.g., Wasa Fibre)

FISH COUNTER
Shrimp (large raw)

MEAT COUNTER
Chicken breasts (boneless, skinless)
Ground beef (extra-lean)
Lean ground chicken or turkey
Pork tenderloin

BEANS (LEGUMES) AND CANNED VEGETABLES
Black beans
Chickpeas
Kidney beans (red and white)
Diced tomatoes
Pinto beans
Stewed tomatoes
Tomato paste

PASTA AND SAUCES
Penne or rotini (whole wheat)
Macaroni or small shells (whole wheat)
Spagettini or linguine (whole wheat)
Small pasta (e.g., ditali or tubetti)
Light tomato sauce

SOUP AND CANNED SEAFOOD AND MEAT
Chicken stock (low-fat, low-sodium)
Tuna (light, in water)
Vegetable stock (low-fat, low-sodium)

GRAINS AND SIDE DISHES
Barley
Basmati rice
Celery Seeds
Flaxseed (ground)
Quinoa

INTERNATIONAL FOODS
Thai red curry paste

COOKING OIL, VINEGAR, SALAD DRESSINGS AND PICKLES
Balsamic vinegar
Buttermilk salad dressing (low-fat, low-sugar)
Capers
Cider vinegar
Dijon mustard
Oil (canola and extra-virgin olive)
Red wine vinegar
Worcestershire sauce

SNACKS
Nutrition bars (e.g., ZonePerfect, Balance Bar)

BAKING
Baking powder
Baking soda
Cornstarch
Oat bran
Spices (ground allspice, cayenne
   pepper, chili powder, ground cinnamon,
   ground cloves, ground cumin, dried
   oregano, Hungarian paprika, parsley, black
   pepper, salt)
Splenda
Vanilla
Wheat bran
Wheat germ
Whole wheat flour
Unsweetened cocoa powder

BREAKFAST FOODS
All-Bran Buds cereal
Oatmeal (large-flake oats)

BEVERAGES
Apple juice (unsweetened)
Dry white wine (or vermouth)

DAIRY CASE
Babybel Gouda Lite cheese
Buttermilk
Cheddar cheese (low-fat)
Fruit yogurt (non-fat with sweetener)
Laughing Cow Light cheese
Liquid eggs (e.g., Naturegg, Break Free)
Milk (skim)
Orange juice (unsweetened)
Soft margarine (non-hydrogenated, light)
Sour cream (low-fat)
Whole omega-3 eggs

FROZEN FOODS
Apple juice concentrate
Mixed berries
Peas (or fresh)

Week 4

Family and Friends

Having a supportive spouse/partner is vital in a successful weight-loss program. It helps you to have your own cheering section rather than someone who is running interference and undermining your best efforts. And if you are the one who does most of the cooking, having a supportive partner means you will not have to prepare separate meals—which means there are fewer red-light temptations to deal with.

Where a male partner is concerned, helping you helps him because men also suffer from middle-age spread. Look around to see how many beer bellies strike men over 50. They are equally at risk from heart disease, stroke, diabetes and cancer (prostate cancer is as prevalent for men as breast cancer is for women) as you are. Should your partner be female, and particularly if she is experiencing similar weight issues, it is important that you support each other. If you want to grow old together, then the sooner you adopt the green-light way of eating, the better.

Like women, men experience their own version of menopause known as andropause. Andropause results from a drop in testosterone levels. It's testosterone that gives men their male characteristics, both physical and attitudinal, in the same way estrogen gives the female form to women. However, during andropause men's testosterone levels do not fall off as precipitously as do women's estrogen levels during menopause, and generally andropause occurs a few years later than with menopause. (Okay, I know it's not fair, but I didn't write the script!) The reduction in testosterone leads to a slowing metabolism and, along with aging, men experience the same weight-gain issues.

Worse, men are naturally an "apple" shape, versus women's "pear" shape, which means men carry their excess weight around their waists. Andropause simply accelerates that belly fat accumulation. Unfortunately, carrying fat around your waist is highly detrimental to health. The "beer belly" acts very much like a tumour, feeding the body with a dangerous combination of free fatty acids and proteins, which promote out-of-control cell growth associated with malignant cancers; causes inflammation of the arteries, leading to heart disease and stroke; and increases insulin resistance, a precursor to diabetes. If your waist measurement is 37 inches or more (40 inches or more for men), your health is at serious risk.

If your spouse/partner appears hesitant about getting on side, here are three approaches that could be persuasive:

First: *Logic*. You are overweight and that is damaging your health. We can help each live longer and healthier lives.

Second: *Blackmail*. Your spouse, children and grandchildren will suffer when you die prematurely from a heart attack or cancer. How could you abandon us!

Third: *Stealth*. If all else fails, just change to green-light foods without saying anything. One reader wrote that she did this and the only thing her husband noticed was that his pants were falling down!

Even if your partner is not overweight, he or she will benefit from eating a healthy diet, as many diseases connected with obesity are also associated with diet. All the principal medical and nutritional authorities agree that a diet rich in fruits, vegetables, whole grains, unsaturated fats and lean protein is essential for good health and a longer life—an approach you already know as the G.I. Diet! If weight is not an issue, simply adjust serving sizes and introduce some yellow-

> I've been battling to lose weight for 35 years. Every time I tried it was misery—I was always very hungry and the choice of food was very limited. Within months I always seemed to weigh ... more than before the diet.
>
> One day I was standing in the checkout queue at the supermarket and noticed that on the front of their free magazine it said "eat chocolate and lose weight." Being a chocoholic, I picked it up and glanced at it. It referred to your book on the G.I. diet.
>
> Months later I was in a bookshop and saw your book on the shelf. I started to look through it and realized that far from being another fad, this was actually the same advice I was giving to newly diagnosed diabetics. (I was a nurse at the time.) My patients never seemed to take the advice on board, any more than I practiced what I preached.
>
> I thought I'd give it a try. I was never hungry and often found I had missed a snack. Food choice was extensive and I realized that this was not "a" diet but my diet for life. That was so important to my success. And, thanks entirely to you, I lost 56 pounds, reached my target size and have maintained it since. I cannot thank you enough, Rick. Sue

light foods. Getting your spouse/partner on side is clearly important and well worth the investment.

With regards to family, most menopausal and post-menopausal women are past the child-rearing years so are not faced with the dietary tantrums of the young, or teen social eating angst, which can make family green-light eating a hassle. Adult children are normally very supportive of their mother trying to improve her health and how she looks and feels.

Friends, and I include co-workers here as well, can be a curse or a blessing—often a combination of the two. In an e-clinic, Pat was upset by the unhelpful attitude of some of her friends. Here is the response that I wrote to her at the time:

There is no magic to dealing with friends who appear to want to lead you astray. You simply have to tell them that "no" means "no" and that you would appreciate your real friends helping you achieve your goals, rather than making it more difficult. You probably only have to say this once, and if you upset one or two people, then it is worth asking whether they are in fact your real friends ... in addition you should look to your friends' motivation. If your friends are overweight and see that you are being successful, then they may feel threatened. At least you would know where they are coming from and it may be their own insecurities that are the issue here.

While you have some control over who are your friends, coworkers are another thing. Few of us can control whom we have to work with, and office politics can play havoc with personal relationships. We've all dealt with office gifts of boxes of chocolates, birthday cakes, the "go on, be a devil" office celebratory lunches. Here is what Joan had to say about this:

I've spent many years working through an eating disorder ... I learned that my abusing food was not different than an alcoholic's abusing alcohol. Food just happened to be the substance that I chose to abuse, to use so I didn't have to feel my feelings. I was such a "good girl" who wouldn't be a drunk and drugs weren't really available in those days. I couldn't hang out with my old "eating buddies" anymore than a drunk getting sober can hang out with their old drinking buddies. I had to find new friends who wanted me to succeed at becoming healthy.

I determine who my friends are by remembering this example: someone I love has a serious drinking or drug problem that is destroying his or her life. He/she goes into treatment or Alcoholics Anonymous, and is attempting to stay sober. As a friend, do I give her/him a bottle of liquor for their birthday or offer them a nice, cold beer on a hot day, telling them that "just one drink" won't hurt them. Do I tell them that having a drink just this once won't hurt them? No, as a friend I want what is best for them, telling them I was so proud of them and letting them know that I am here to help them remain sober.

People are dying from diseases caused by obesity but food doesn't get the same rap as alcohol or drugs. I cannot change the world's views on eating, but I can change my own. If need be I am open about my history of my eating disorder to let the person know that food is a serious issue with me. If after they know me and my history, they still push foods on me, I've had to get them out of my life. I can't take the gamble that sometime they'll push food when I'm in a bad place and I might just say "Ok, just for this time."

Out of envy or insecurity, many people cannot stand others being successful—and delight in undermining their progress. Sometimes this is called the "tall poppy" syndrome where everyone has to be cut down to the same level.

There are no easy answers here except to be upfront about what you are doing, changing the way you eat and why. Ask for their support and, who knows, you may become, as one reader told me, the diet guru of the office, where coworkers, impressed with your success, come to be coached.

However, I'll give the final word on this to Karen, a member of an e-clinic who wrote:

I've also learned that I share my home and office with "diet assassins." I think they think if they can get me to cheat, it absolves their bad eating habits. Last night I found myself making chocolate chip cookies because my husband and co-workers requested them because "[mine] are the best ever." As I was dropping the dough on to the cookie sheet I had an epiphany. I told my husband he could bake as many as he wanted and I wrapped up the rest of the raw dough and brought it into my co-workers with baking instructions. YOU GO GIRL!

E-Clinic Diaries

As we enter Week 4, some of you may start to worry about your rate of weight loss just as the clinic participants did:

> *Q: I was disappointed to GAIN 0.2 lb ... Is this normal to gain a little? I DID lose 3.8 the first week, but since I am so overweight, I thought maybe I would lose at least a pound per week. I DO feel better, and I did get out an old pair of jeans and was able to wear them. (They used to be too tight). I just want to make sure that I am not eating too much. I COULD go back to measuring everything. [AM] I ... seriously behind where I should be at this time? Marlene*

A: Remember that you are playing the averages, and the average is 1 pound per week or sometimes a little more, if your BMI is high. I must keep stressing that you are making a fundamental lifestyle change. As one reader wrote to me "I realize now that it might take me a year or even two years to reach my target weight but it doesn't matter because I know I will eventually get there. What is more important is that I've made a basic lifestyle change which I know is helping me lead a longer and healthier life." I couldn't have put it better myself.

This week has been very emotional for me. I am not sure if I am in another phase of menopause or if perhaps it has something to do with the G.I. Diet but I am just not comfortable in my clothes as I used to be and every time I look in the mirror I could just cry. I feel like I am getting bigger around the mid section rather than smaller. Even though I go 4 to 5 times a week to the gym, and have lost pounds (which I am grateful for) my inches are still the same. I used to be firm around the mid section but now it seems to have changed shape and looks like I have gained weight and it is all around the mid section. Rita

I empathize with Rita and the horror of seeing weight around the middle that wasn't there before the onset of menopause. That is one of the areas I first noticed too, along with a new layer of what felt like "flab" basically all over. It wasn't a lot to start but enough that one day I realized I just wasn't as firm all over as I had been previously ... Anyhow, after months of full blown menopause, I noticed the "flab" and contacted a doctor who highly recommends natural progesterone cream for menopausal women. I was thinking it was the cream that may somehow have caused the flab. Yeah, wishful thinking. The doctor, in a very diplomatic way, let me know my body was changing, I needed to watch what I ate to restrain from gaining more weight, and needed some form of exercise on a regular basis. If I had listened to him seven years ago I doubt I would be in the shape I am now. Janice

The weight is coming off slowly, but then again, I'm not feeling hungry or deprived. Every other time I've "dieted," I felt like either A) that I had eaten my quotient of calories for the day and couldn't eat anything else no matter how hungry I was, or B) that because I was restricting carbs, I couldn't even eat a piece of fruit or bread without going off the diet. Now, I eat when I'm hungry, but really, my appetite is much smaller than it was a month ago. I never thought I'd enjoy eating whole grain bread and muffins, but I really do. I used to overeat at every meal. The way I would tell when to stop eating was when I started to feel sick. I know that sounds horrible and it is. I haven't overeaten at all in the last month, and I feel so much better. Laura

Having your partner, family and friends as cheerleaders—or better still participants—in your green-light journey will help you immeasurably. It's never too soon to start bringing them onside.

Next week we will look at what is arguably the main reason that our obesity rate in Canada is so high: portion sizes, or as some nutritionists have termed it, portion creep. I think you will be surprised to see how far portion sizes have ballooned over the past few years.

Week 4 Weight: _____

Week 4 Waist: _____

Week 4 Hips: _____

Week 4 Diary

_____

_____

_____

_____

_____

_____

_____

_____

_____

_____

_____

_____

_____

_____

Week 4 Optional Meal Plan

	BREAKFAST	SNACK	LUNCH	SNACK	DINNER	SNACK
MON	Homey Oatmeal (p. 236) with chopped apple	Whole Wheat Fruit Scone (p. 304)	Open-face lean deli ham sandwich with lettuce, tomato, red pepper and grainy mustard, and Basic G.I. Salad (p. 255)	Laughing Cow Light cheese with crispbread	Fettucine Primavera (p. 273) and Caesar Salad (p. 256)	Mixed berries tossed in lime juice with sour cream
TUES	Mini Breakfast Puffs (p. 240)	Fruit yogurt	Waldorf Chicken and Rice Salad (p. 262)	Hummus with carrot and celery sticks	Tomato and Cheese Catfish (p. 277) serve with Fettuccini Primavera	Orange and almonds
WED	Homemade Muesli (p. 237) with skim milk and fruit yogurt	Whole Wheat Fruit Scone (p. 304)	Cottage cheese with apple and grapes, and Basic G.I. Salad (p. 255)	Babybel Gouda Lite cheese with crispbread	Chicken Schnitzel (p. 285), green beans, carrots and new potatoes	Slice of Strawberry Tea Bread (p. 305) and glass of skim milk
THURS	Homey Oatmeal (p. 236) with blueberries	Small apple and glass of skim milk	Minestrone Soup (p. 246) and Basic G.I. Salad (p. 255)	Crunchy Chickpeas (p. 300)	Meatloaf (p. 294) green beans, carrots and new potatoes	1/2 nutrition bar
FRI	All-Bran Buds with skim milk, peach slices and sliced almonds	Fruit yogurt	1/2 whole wheat pita with deli turkey, lettuce, tomato and cucumber, and Basic G.I. Salad (p. 255)	Laughing Cow Light cheese with crispbread	Indian Vegetable Curry (p. 272) and Basic G.I. Salad (p. 255)	Fancy Fruit Salad (p. 308)
SAT	Smoked Salmon Scrambled Eggs (p. 244)	1/2 nutrition bar	Vegetable Barley Soup au Pistou (p. 249) with Basic G.I. Salad (p. 255)	Hummus with carrot and celery sticks	Roasted Pork Tenderloin with Balsamic Glaze and Gingered Peach Salsa (p. 293) new potatoes, asparagus and Basic G.I. Salad (p. 255)	Slice of Strawberry Tea Bread (p. 305) and glass of skim milk
SUN	Cinnamon French Toast (p. 238) with back bacon	Orange and almonds	Grilled Shrimp and Pear Salad (p. 264)	Babybel Gouda Lite cheese with crispbread	Chicken Stir-Fry with Broccoli (p. 284) and Basic G.I. Salad (p. 255)	Slice of One-Bowl Chocolate Cake (p. 313) with berries

Week 4 Grocery List for Meal Plan

PRODUCE
Almonds (whole and sliced)
Apples
Asparagus
Baby spinach
Bean sprouts
Blackberries
Blueberries (fresh or frozen)
Broccoli
Carrots
Cashews
Celery
Chili pepper
Cucumbers
Dried apricots
Fresh herbs (basil, chives, cilantro, oregano,
  flat-leaf parsley, mint, thyme)
Garlic
Ginger root
Grapes
Green beans
Green onions
Hot pepper
Kiwis
Leeks
Lemons
Lettuce (leaf and Romaine)
Limes
Mushrooms
Onions (red, yellow and Vidalia)
Oranges
Peaches (fresh or canned in juice or water)
Pears
Peppers (green, red and yellow)
Potatoes (new, small)
Strawberries
Sunflower seeds, shelled and unsalted
Tomatoes (large beefsteak and plum)

Walnuts
Zucchini

DELI
Hummus (light)
Lean deli ham
Lean deli turkey
Parmesan cheese, grated

BAKERY
100% stone-ground whole wheat bread
Crispbread (e.g., Wasa Fibre)
Whole wheat breadcrumbs
Whole wheat hamburger buns
Whole wheat pita bread

FISH COUNTER
Catfish fillets
Frozen crab
Shrimp (large raw)
Smoked salmon

MEAT COUNTER
Back bacon
Chicken breasts (boneless, skinless)
Ground beef (extra-lean)
Pork tenderloin

**BEANS (LEGUMES) AND
CANNED VEGETABLES**
Chickpeas
Kidney beans (red)
Plum tomatoes
Tomato paste

PASTA AND SAUCES
Small pasta (e.g., ditali or tubetti)

SOUP AND CANNED SEAFOOD AND MEAT
Anchovy fillets
Chicken stock (low-fat, low-sodium)
Vegetable stock (low-fat, low-sodium)

GRAINS AND SIDE DISHES
Barley
Basmati rice

INTERNATIONAL FOODS
Hoisin sauce
Mild curry paste
Oyster sauce
Rice vinegar
Soy sauce
Tahini

COOKING OIL, VINEGAR, SALAD DRESSINGS AND PICKLES
Balsamic vinegar
Buttermilk salad dressing (low-fat, low-sugar)
Dijon mustard
Grainy mustard
Oil (canola, extra-virgin olive, and sesame)
Red wine vinegar
Worcestershire sauce

SNACKS
Applesauce (unsweetened)
Nutrition bars (e.g., ZonePerfect, Balance Bar)

BAKING
Baking powder
Baking soda
Honey
Oat bran
Spices (cayenne, chili powder, ground
  cinnamon, cumin seeds, ground
  nutmeg, dried oregano, black pepper, red
  pepper flakes, salt)

Splenda
Vanilla
Wheat bran
Wheat germ
Whole wheat flour

BREAKFAST FOODS
All-Bran Buds cereal
Oatmeal (large-flake oats)

BEVERAGES
Tomato juice

DAIRY CASE
Cottage cheese (low-fat)
Babybel Gouda Lite cheese
Buttermilk
Cheddar cheese (low-fat)
Fruit yogurt (non-fat with sweetener)
Laughing Cow Light cheese
Liquid eggs (e.g., Naturegg, Break Free)
Milk (skim)
Sour cream (low-fat)
Whole omega-3 eggs

FROZEN FOODS
Mixed berries

We are now just over one-third of the way through the 13-week program. At this point, most people will be feeling comfortable with the basic principles of eating the green-light way. Making the right food choices is not as difficult as you thought! However, it's still all too easy to trip up over the question of **how much** you should eat and jeopardize your weight-loss results.

One of the principal reasons that we have an obesity crisis is the size of servings and portions. A serving size is what is recommended whereas a portion size is what you choose to eat. We have undergone a radical change in our perception of portion sizes over the past 20 years or so, principally because of the super-sizing of fast-food and family restaurant meals during this time. These have now become our serving-size norms in what is described as "portion distortion." Let me give you some examples with a list prepared by the U.S. National Heart, Lung and Blood Institute:

SNACKS	TWENTY YEARS AGO		TODAY	
	Size	Calories	Size	Calories
Bagel	3 inches	140	6 inches	350
French fries	2.4 ounces	210	7 ounces	610
Muffin	1.5 ounces	210	5 ounces	500
Cookie	1 1/2 inches	55	4 inches	275
MEALS	**Calories**			**Calories**
Spaghetti and meatballs	500			1025
Turkey sandwich	320			820
Chicken Caesar salad	390			700
Chicken stir-fry	435			865

As you can see, the size and corresponding calories have doubled or even trebled over this relatively short time period. These new sizes have become today's serving norms and that translates into how you see portions on your plate. No wonder there's "portion distortion" and ballooning waistlines. Does this mean that we were all starving in the disco era—or are we simply eating more now because it's there?

A study done of college students on their consumption of their favourite food, macaroni and cheese, shows that the more that was put in front of them, the more they ate (if the food was there, they ate it). Yet they reported that they felt no fuller on the larger portions than they felt with the smaller ones! Moral: if it's not on your plate, you won't miss it.

To further reinforce the message, when researchers were trying to discover why the French are far less obese than Americans, they compared similar eateries in Paris and Philadelphia. They found the average serving size was 25 percent greater in Philadelphia. In supermarkets a similar pattern emerged with fourteen of seventeen items larger in the U.S. stores (e.g. candy bars, 41 percent larger; soft drink 52 percent larger; hot dogs 63 percent larger; and yogurt 82 percent larger.

Though most of us have been aware of the super-sizing of foods in recent years, what we don't realize is that this portion distortion has slipped into home-prepared meals too. To make it easier to reduce our green-light portions, especially as no one likes to weigh and measure foods, here are some ways of eyeballing your portion sizes using familiar objects:

½ cup breakfast cereals	1/2 baseball
½ tsp margarine	top half of thumb
4 oz. meat	palm of your hand
4 oz. fish	small hotdog bun
¾ cup pasta (cooked)	size of your fist
⅔ cup rice (cooked)	one tennis ball

Note: These serving sizes are for the regular Phase 1 in the G.I. Diet. In the Preliminary Phase, for those with a BMI of 33 plus, you may increase these serving sizes by up to 50 percent. If you can manage on less, that's just fine.

Although we don't recommend particular serving sizes for most green-light foods, we do stress moderation and common sense. For example, typical servings should be

Fruit (e.g., an apple) equals a tennis ball.
Vegetable (e.g., broccoli) equals a lightbulb.
Dairy product (e.g. cottage cheese) equals half a baseball.

I have always eaten healthy food, but learning that some of my favorites—beets, squash, turnip—were not green light made me revamp what I was eating. I am amazed at the weight loss in 8 months—down 85 pounds—and I am feeling fantastic. You can imagine my excitement at finally being able to wear regular sized clothes … I have no desire to stray off the path of green light foods because I am completely satisfied with the program. Just the smell of greasy foods makes me cringe! … thank you for making me feel so much better about myself! Donna

Here are some helpful tips for watching those serving sizes:

- Don't eat in front of the TV as you will be unaware of how much food you've eaten.
- Eat slowly as it takes 20 to 30 minutes for the message to get from your tummy to your brain. Put down your fork/spoon between mouthfuls.
- Divide your plate into three:
  - One quarter for meat/fish/chicken/tofu
  - One quarter for rice/potatoes/pasta
  - One half for vegetables (a minimum of two).
- Don't snack from a bag (e.g., count out a serving of nuts and put into a bowl).
- Ask for small servings when eating out, or split an entree with your companion.
- Use a smaller luncheon-sized plate rather than a dinner plate.

Soon you will look back aghast at the amount you used to eat. I look around restaurants today when dining out and never cease to be amazed at what people can put away in a sitting!

E-Clinic Diaries

Week 5 found many of the e-clinic participants getting into the swing of reducing their serving sizes and finding some interesting benefits of the G.I. Diet:

I picked up a 1 kg bag of brown sugar yesterday and hefted it in my hand. I realized that I had just lost that amount of weight off my body this week ... I kept reminding myself of that as I dealt with urges to snack last night. But then I remembered I COULD have a snack and so I had a healthy one. That is the marvellous thing about this new relationship I have with food—a reminder that a snack is a good thing, eating slowly is a good thing and losing weight is the best darn thing of all! Louise

I have been using the smaller plate at dinner time and it is surprising how much I had eaten before on a regular sized plate. I don't overpile the smaller plate and am quite satisfied with the serving. Did you notice I said "serving"? I don't get usually get second servings. First I ask myself if I am really hungry. If I'm not, the plate goes to the dishwasher, the kitchen gets straightened, and I find something to get busy with. One problem I am still having, though, and I'm really mentally working on it, is wanting something to nibble late in the evening. Haven't found the answer to that one yet but am still working on it. Janice

Q: I think I am just eating way too much portion-wise. I see the stories in the books about the weight just flying off, and though I know that is unrealistic, I am discouraged that I am losing so slowly. I AM in the "BIG" people category, so do allow myself larger portions (per your okay), but would that completely STALL OUT weight loss? I know I am eating so much healthier, and plan to continue for life, but I really want to lose the unhealthy weight too ... I know that I occasionally would measure some half and half into my coffee, about 30 calories worth, but have now gone back to just skim milk. Maybe I have sabotaged myself somehow. Any ideas? ... I was in tears this morning when I stepped on the scale. Marlene

A: Don't be too hard on yourself. You appear to have made significant progress on the number of inches you have lost ... and you have also lost an average of 1 pound per week since the program started. While that weight loss is on the lower side for somebody with your BMI, it is also not that unusual. It may take you a year to lose 50 pounds or 18 months to lose 75 pounds. I'm sure you would be delighted to lose that much weight, and if you continue to maintain your current progress, this is exactly what will happen.

I have said previously that if I do any physical work, it brings on the flashes. I have been doing heavy duty cleaning, and when I stopped to rest, it hit me that I hadn't had a hot flash. Linda

Next week is a hot topic when we will be delving into the emotional reasons that many of you overeat. My wife, Dr. Ruth Gallop, is an expert in behaviour and she will be leading the discussion on "Food for Comfort."

Week 5 Weight: _____

Week 5 Waist: _____

Week 5 Hips: _____

Week 5 Diary

_____

_____

_____

_____

_____

_____

Week 5 Optional Meal Plan

Note: You are *not* required to use these weekly meal plans and shopping lists. Feel free to pick and choose and make up your own green-light meals.

	BREAKFAST	SNACK	LUNCH	SNACK	DINNER	SNACK
MON	Homey Oatmeal (p. 236) with chopped apple	Cranberry Cinnamon Bran Muffin (p. 301)	Open face chicken sandwich with with lettuce, tomato and onion, and Basic G.I. Salad (p. 255)	Laughing Cow Light cheese with crispbread	Lemon Linguine with Smoked Salmon (p. 266), Broccoli and salad	Mixed berries tossed in lime juice with sour cream
TUES	Mini Breakfast Puffs (p. 240)	Fruit yogurt	G.I. Pasta Salad (p. 259)	Hummus with carrot and celery sticks	Cheesy Lentil and Bean Bake (p. 267), basmati rice and salad	Orange and almonds
WED	Homemade Muesli (p. 237) with skim milk and fruit yogurt	Cranberry Cinnamon Bran Muffin (p. 301)	½ whole wheat pita with canned light tuna, lettuce, tomato and cucumber, and Basic G.I. Salad (p. 255)	Babybel Gouda Lite cheese with crispbread	Chicken Curry (p. 285) and and Raita Salad (p. 252)	Cran-Apple Oatmeal Bars (p. 314) and glass of skim milk
THURS	Homey Oatmeal (p. 236) with blueberries	Small apple and glass of skim milk	Quick and Easy Chicken Noodle Soup (p. 248) and Basic G.I. Salad (p. 255)	Crunchy Chickpeas (p. 300)	Braised Pacific Halibut (p. 278), new or small potatoes and salad.	½ nutrition bar
FRI	All-Bran Buds with skim milk, peach slices and sliced almonds	Fruit yogurt	Mixed Bean Salad (p. 261)	Laughing Cow Light cheese with crispbread	Marinated Flank Steak (p. 295), new potatoes, green beans and salad	Mixed berries tossed in lime juice with sour cream
SAT	Smoked Salmon Scrambled Eggs (p. 244)	½ nutrition bar	Greek Salad (p. 256)	Hummus with carrot and celery sticks	Orange Chicken with Almonds (p. 287), green beans and basmati rice	Creamy Raspberry Mousse (p. 307)
SUN	Oatmeal Buttermilk Pancakes with strawberries (p. 239)	Orange and almonds	Caesar Salad (p. 256) with canned tuna	Babybel Gouda Lite cheese with crispbread	Vegetarian Moussaka (p. 274), and basmati rice	Piece of Plum Crumble (p. 310)

Week 5 Grocery List for Meal Plan

PRODUCE
Almonds (whole and sliced)
Apples
Asparagus
Baby spinach
Peppers (green, red or yellow)
Blueberries (fresh or frozen)
Broccoli
Carrots
Celery
Cranberries (dried)
Cucumbers (English and field)
Eggplant
Fresh herbs (dill, flat-leaf parsley, thyme)
Garlic
Gingerroot
Green beans
Green onions
Kale
Lemons
Lettuce (iceberg, leaf and romaine)
Limes
Onions (yellow and red)
Oranges
Peaches (fresh or canned in juice or water)
Peppers (green, red or yellow)
Potatoes (new, small)
Prune plums (e.g., damson or Italian)
Raisins
Raspberries
Strawberries
Sunflower seeds, shelled and unsalted
Tomatoes (plum)

DELI
Feta cheese (light)
Hummus (light)
Kalamata olives

BAKERY
100% stone-ground whole wheat bread
Crispbread (e.g., Wasa Fibre)
Whole wheat pita bread

FISH COUNTER
Pacific halibut
Smoked salmon

MEAT COUNTER
Chicken breasts (boneless, skinless)
Flank steak

BEANS (LEGUMES) AND CANNED VEGETABLES
Black beans
Chickpeas
Diced tomatoes
Lentils (green)
Mixed beans
Tomato paste

PASTA AND SAUCES
Light tomato sauce (no added sugar)
Rotini or penne (whole wheat)
Small pasta (e.g., ditali or tubetti)

SOUP AND CANNED SEAFOOD AND MEAT
Anchovy fillets
Chicken stock (low-fat, low-sodium)
Tuna (light, in water)

GRAINS AND SIDE DISHES
Basmati rice
Flaxseeds (ground)

INTERNATIONAL FOODS
Soy sauce (low-sodium)
Tahini

COOKING OIL, VINEGAR, SALAD DRESSINGS AND PICKLES
Dijon mustard
Grainy mustard
Mayonnaise (fat-free)
Oil (canola and extra-virgin olive)
Red wine vinegar
Rice vinegar
Vegetable cooking oil spray (canola or olive oil)
Worcestershire sauce

SNACKS
Applesauce (unsweetened)
Nutrition bars (e.g., ZonePerfect, Balance Bar)

BAKING
Amaretto
Baking powder
Baking soda
Cornstarch
Oat bran
Spices (allspice, ground cardamom, Cajun seasoning, ground cinnamon, ground cumin, curry powder, ground ginger, dried oregano, black pepper, red pepper flakes, salt, dried thyme)
Splenda

Vanilla
Wheat bran
Wheat germ
Whole wheat flour

BREAKFAST FOODS
All-Bran Buds or 100% Bran cereal
Oatmeal (large-flake oats)

BEVERAGES
White wine

DAIRY CASE
Babybel Gouda Lite cheese
Buttermilk
Cheddar cheese (low-fat)
Cottage cheese (1%)
Fruit yogurt (non-fat with sweetener)
Laughing Cow Light cheese (extra-low-fat)
Liquid eggs (e.g., Naturegg Break Free)
Milk (skim)
Soft margarine (non-hydrogenated, light)
Sour cream (low-fat)
Whole Omega-3 eggs

FROZEN FOODS
Peas (or fresh)

This week we will address the issue of emotional eating, frequently described as using "food for comfort." I have asked my wife, Dr. Ruth Gallop, Professor Emeritus at the University of Toronto, to write this section, as one of her specialties is childhood trauma and how that plays out in adult life. This has given her considerable insight into the whole question of the role of food in helping people deal with their emotional issues. We realize that this is a very large topic but hope to provide you with some guidance. Here are some of her thoughts:

We all eat for comfort. When we are sick, many of us have favourite foods—often foods from our childhood that we associate with being looked after. There are foods we eat rarely and foods we could eat every day—often foods that make us feel good, satiated or even happy.

When we have reasonably balanced lives, food plays an important but not dominant role in our day-to-day lives. When our lives are out of balance and we don't feel good about certain aspects of our lives, then food can take over. When we don't feel good about ourselves and experience low self-esteem, food can be a powerful and damaging force. This is particularly true for women. Women live in a society fixated on how we should look. Putting aside all the healthy reasons for being at a "normal" weight, our society just doesn't approve of big people. And, more importantly, big people often don't approve of themselves.

Frequently, eating to feel better is preceded by negative feeling. For some people these feelings may include sadness, loneliness or even boredom. For others the feelings can be more in the range of anger, irritability or high stress. These feelings can lead to a vicious eating cycle. It goes something like this:

> I feel: depressed; angry; bored; sad; bad about myself (low self-esteem) → so I eat to feel better → I experience a brief blood sugar high and feel better → I experience a blood sugar crash and feel terrible → I feel bad about myself for eating, for failing → so I eat to feel better ... and around I go.

In many situations the original reasons for feeling bad about oneself or getting angry, overwhelmed or disappointed may have origins in our childhood; overeating, negative body image and low self-esteem are the current consequence.

Usually we do not make any conscious link between past events and current behaviour. For example, as a child parental approval/love may have been connected with food via treats or eating all that was put in front of us. Or we may have been punished (love withdrawn) if we didn't eat our vegetables! Eating becomes connected to trying to recapture that good feeling of being loved. Although we are unaware of these motives or psychological reasons for the behaviour, we have done it for so long it becomes part of our food and eating habits.

Congratulations on an excellent diet program. I am a GP and have practiced in a rural community for 30 years. I have developed a special interest in managing my diabetics better. Along with using a CDA flowsheet on all of their charts, I discuss diet and exercise. Living in a rural community means that I have access to only one dietitian and a monthly diabetic clinic run by one of our dedicated nurse managers at our local hospital so, guess what? The GP gets to do much of the teaching.

Your books and your web-site have found a very important place in my teaching. I have many patients who have already been successful beyond their wildest expectations. It was really exciting to see a morbidly obese woman who had really almost given up on any hopes of health (her GTT was in the diabetic range also) walk into my office tenderly clutching your book The G.I. Diet and proudly announcing that she had already lost 12 pounds in 2 weeks.

My wife and I also latched onto your program and WOW!!!!! what a difference. With regular walking, some weight lifting and your marvellous recipes I have lost 33 pounds and am well on my way to my ideal weight. We have had a wonderful time preparing the meals and an even more wonderful time eating them. Even the two teens in our home enjoy the food. We rarely get to enjoy leftovers as the kids find them first. One of the things we learned is that it is much easier when both husband and wife prepare the meals together. I have incorporated this suggestion into my teaching and use it as a method of encouraging healthier relationships as well as healthier bodies. Thanks so much, Rick for what you have accomplished. Bill

Rick's mother cannot bear to see food that is on the table unfinished regardless of whether or not a person is still hungry. At ninety-eight years of age she still says, "I do like to see a clean plate" when all the food on the table has disappeared. I have learned to deal with this learned behaviour—a behavior that earned Rick love and approval from his mother—by never putting excess food on the table at mealtimes or making up the dinner plates before I serve them. I don't put out bowls of food for individual selection; otherwise, Rick will unconsciously graze on a lot of extra food!

Menopause, of course, plays havoc with our body image. We lose our reproductive ability, and fine lines and wrinkles have started to appear. And of course we also may be trying to deal with sugar cravings, irritability, night sweats and mood swings.

On the other hand, the children are moving toward independence, our jobs and careers are for the most part reasonably stable, and we finally have some time to do things for ourselves. But, as the sandwich generation, we now run the risk of being caregivers to elderly parents; all the more reason to relearn how to look after ourselves. Fortunately, thanks to the Boomer generation, marketers are paying attention to women our age. We can still look good even if it takes a little more makeup, hair colour and time!

If you are ready to change your eating habits, the first thing to do is to become *aware* of them. For example, every time you walk in the front door is the first stop the fridge or cookie cupboard? When you have had a bad day do you deal with it by eating something sweet or creamy? When you feel bored and have nothing structured to do, do you eat? Are you unable to watch TV without food in your hand so that you end up eating more than you realize unconsciously? I have one piece of dark chocolate most evenings if I am watching TV. The other night I realized I was in the middle of eating a second piece with no memory of reaching down and picking it up!

Take a day or two to jot down your patterns and work out when automatic behaviours take over and when it is most difficult for you to avoid eating in excess. It is important to recognize high-risk situations. Bad habits include:

- Grazing—a teenage habit that many have not grown out of
- Eating when stressed, angry, irritable, tired or frustrated
- Eating when sad, bored or lonely
- Eating too quickly—remember, it takes 20 to 30 minutes for the stomach to tell the brain it is full
- Eating unconsciously—especially in front of the TV or at the movies
- Eating portions that are far too large. Thanks to fast food and restaurants, many portion sizes have doubled and we have brought this portion distortion into our homes
- Keeping red-light snacks in your desk drawer to eat when you are stressed at work
- Always eating during any social activity, whether it's a sports events, a social visit or even just walking with a friend.

If food comforts you when you are stressed, or when you set unrealistic expectations for yourself, such as getting the household and family errands done, cooking all the meals, or looking after aged parents, then recognize these patterns so you can consider alternative ways to cope, such as sharing tasks with others.

Once you are aware of how comfort eating plays a role in your life, you can begin to change your eating behaviour. You have already taken the first step by making sure that all the food in your house and workplace, as well as all food going into your mouth, is green-light. Reward yourself for this accomplishment. Do something nice for yourself—a little treat like a new lipstick, makeup or perfume—just make sure it isn't red-light food!

Start by trying to modify one behaviour at a time. If you usually walk in the front door and eat a snack, make sure it is one of your snack times and you have a green-light snack at the ready.

During menopause it is particularly important to have snacks that taste sweet in case sugar cravings occur. Fruit muffins (use raspberries, blueberries, strawberries or peaches) make an excellent sweet snack as do fresh berries sweetened with Splenda and perhaps served with a dollop of Splenda-sweetened no-fat sour cream. Even sugar-free candies are better than a red-light chocolate bar. Sugar cravings and irritability will lessen as long as you stick with green-light foods, and eat three meals and three snacks a day.

Make a list of pleasurable activities you could be doing instead of eating. For example, if you sit in front of TV and eat, what else could you be doing? Many women like to do something while watching TV; I read books or magazines. Some women like to knit, work on scrapbooking or even do the ironing! Are there pleasurable things you could do instead of watching TV, such as go for a walk? Substituting pleasurable activities helps to break the vicious cycle I have described above.

It is very important to realize that as you lose weight, you will feel better not only physically but also psychologically—being successful will improve your self-esteem. Feeling better about how you look is the best reinforcement for holding back on red-light foods, and breaking those bad eating habits. You will notice your body changing and soon others will too. As you start to experience success in weight reduction—and we are talking here about permanent weight reduction—you start to consider yourself successful. Successful people hold their bodies differently and interact with people differently. As one reader wrote: "I no longer hide behind a tree every time a camera comes out." You will find that a more-confident you may feel safe enough to come out into the world. Let people compliment you.

Let me stress again the need to find substitute activities. This an important tool for breaking bad eating habits. Make a substitute-activities list and use it until you feel sure that your new behaviours and eating patterns are your new habits. Don't beat up on yourself if you slip—happens to all of us—just get back on the wagon. Having the guts and determination to do this program takes courage. So pat yourself on the back and get on with the journey.

I have been stressing immediate substitute activities but it may also be help-ful to think about long-term goals. Have you always had a secret dream or goal—always wanted to take dance lessons, be a tango star or belly dancer, or learn to ski? If you've avoided those dreams because of your self-esteem or body image, maybe now is the time to say this could be possible. Keep that long-term goal in mind when you reach for that red-light food; will that snack help you get on the dance floor?

A cardiologist friend of ours, who is struggling with some bad food habits and poor food choices, wears a plastic bracelet on his left wrist. When he makes a wrong choice he switches the bracelet to his right wrist. This reminds him every time he reaches for something to eat that he has already made one poor choice that day already. He says it's worked for him, so if you want a visual aid to help remind you to break bad eating habits, then you might want to try this innovative idea. If you try this, Rick would be interested in getting your feedback to share with others.

Finally, I encourage you to plan a reward for each week of success on the program—go to a show, buy some flowers, have a long scented bath. Don't buy the new wardrobe yet—that is for later. Remember, be good to yourself.

Ruth Gallop

E-Clinic Diaries

Ruth's comments elicited a great deal of self-recognition among the e-clinic participants. See if you can hear yourself in their comments:

> I was one of those people, the first thing I did when I got in the front door was check out the fridge for a snack whether I needed it or not. Then one day someone gave me an idea to try the following: I bought myself a timer at the dollar store and every time I thought I needed to reach for food, I set the timer for 20 minutes and then walked away from the room. After 20 minutes if I was still thinking of eating then and only then would I have something to eat. Guess what, 98% of the time, I forgot all about that timer and the fact that I wanted food. Rita

> Nailed Me! I dread the thought of getting on the scales, even though our house is ALL green-light food. You and your wife nailed me with the emotional eating. I eat if I am unhappy, sad, stressed, and etc. (I have been giving myself rewards for weight lost ... I go out to the movies on the weeks I lose weight). I am outgoing and I think I am self-confident

and I do like myself. But the emotional eating is me. It is true that I will eat when I am not hungry. The only thing I have going for me is now the only food I eat is green-light food. I would like to learn how to control this habit I have had. Carol Ann

I could relate to much of what Ruth said. I grew up in a house where my parents were totally fixated on appearance and being thin. It was a very dysfunctional environment in a number of ways. I was also genetically coded to be very thick in the trunk. "Closet eating" became a norm and a habit that I've dealt with all my life. Recognizing when I'm stressed and not falling into compulsive eating patterns (grazing all evening is my style) continues to be challenging, as I mentioned last week. I am getting much better overall, but I do have lapses ... weekly ones, it seems. I weigh in on Saturday mornings and seem to have developed this feeling that if I'm going to put the 10% rule in effect, I'll do it Sat. night when I still have the week ahead of me ... Rewarding myself with food is an age old habit for me, one I MUST break! I obviously really need to work on the substitute list that Ruth mentioned. It always seems to me that other rewards pale in comparison to food or that alternatives are more expensive. Poor excuses! I also need to put thought into THE long-term goal that packs a significant punch for me. Getting into various "thinner" clothes, currently stored in our basement, is a great incentive but not THE goal I need. I'll keep working on that one. Sheri

My mother was of the belief you clean your plate and in doing so you got dessert. Dessert was used as a reward in our house. Isn't it pathetic that it took me until adulthood to realize how wrong that is ... Janice

And here is a remarkable diary entry that encapsulates the very important message that you must look after your own well-being. Rightly or wrongly, women have been the traditional gatekeepers for both health and nutrition in the family. As a result of being the chief caregiver, women often let their own health and well-being slide.

I made a positive decision to take care of myself. We were going to my sister's surprise 60th birthday party. When I called and said that I couldn't make it, I knew I was doing the right thing. The party went on without me; my sister understood why I wasn't there, everyone there seemed to have a great time even if I wasn't there. Doing these once-a-week journals helped me realize how much effort I expend doing things I think other people think I "should" do. I realized that so much of my "busy" stuff had to do with my guilt feelings of getting remarried, moving away from my family, and living such a peaceful, happy life on our farm with my new husband. I felt like the "bad mom" and "bad grandma." In the past weeks, I've made a couple runs (6–1/2 hours one way)—one to baby-sit for a week, and one to be with my son who is having medical problems. Another of my sons was down here for a few days and I made certain I was the perfect mom, making him all kinds of special dishes (but they were green-light)—even going turkey hunting with him. Three times my husband's kids stopped unexpectedly and I hurried to make supper for six people when I had only taken out food for two. Of course, I reassured them that their stopping by without calling was no problem. I just needed them to know I was the "perfect" mom, step-mom or grandma. I learned in Overeaters Anonymous that if you don't take care of yourself first, you're no good to anyone else. I have to work on this and check to see if I'm doing something because I want to do it or if I'm doing it to assure that everyone will like me. I can't be everything to everyone ... If I wasn't staying conscious of my goal to become healthier, I would have hidden those feelings of discomfort with a pound of chocolate (literally) and buried the feelings inside. Without having food as my tranquilizer, I expect other "feelings" will emerge and call for action on my part. Joan

Something we all do, which is always a challenge, is eating out. Next week we'll show you how to dine out the green-light way even in a fast-food restaurant!

Week 6 Weight:_____

Week 6 Waist:_____

Week 6 Hips:_____

Week 6 Diary

_____

_____

_____

_____

_____

_____

_____

_____

_____

_____

_____

_____

_____

_____

_____

_____

Week 6 Optional Meal Plan

	BREAKFAST	SNACK	LUNCH	SNACK	DINNER	SNACK
MON	Homey Oatmeal (p. 236) with chopped apple	Carrot Muffin (p. 302)	Open-face lean deli ham sandwich with lettuce, tomato, red pepper and grainy mustard, and Basic G.I. Salad (p. 255)	Laughing Cow light cheese with crispbread	G.I. Fish Fillet (p. 280), asparagus, carrots and new potatoes	Mixed berries tossed in lime juice with sour cream
TUES	Mini Breakfast Puffs (p. 240)	Fruit yogurt	Vegetable Barley Soup au Pistou (p. 249) with Basic G.I. Salad (p. 255)	Hummus with carrot and celery	Bolognese Pasta Sauce (p. 297) with whole wheat pasta and Basic G.I. Salad (p. 255)	Orange and almonds
WED	Homemade Muesli (p. 237) with skim milk and fruit yogurt	Carrot Muffin (p. 302)	Cottage cheese with apple and grapes, and Basic G.I. Salad (p. 255)	Babybel Gouda Lite cheese with crispbread	Chicken Tarragon with Mushrooms (p. 288), broccoli and basmati rice	Pecan Brownie (p. 315) and glass of skim milk
THURS	Homey Oatmeal (p. 236) with blueberries	Small apple and glass of skim milk	Tuna Salad (p. 260) Basic G.I. Salad	Crunchy Chickpeas (p. 300)	Savoury Beans and Apple (p. 268), basmati rice and salad	1/2 nutrition bar
FRI	All-Bran Buds with skim milk, peach slices and sliced almonds	Fruit yogurt	1/2 whole wheat pita with deli turkey, lettuce, tomato and cucumber, and Basic G.I. Salad (p. 255)	Laughing Cow Light cheese with crispbread	Ginger Wasabi Halibut (p. 281) Cold Noodle Salad with Cucumber and Sesame (p. 258), snow peas and carrots	Creamy Raspberry Mousse (p. 307)
SAT	Breakfast in a Glass (p. 242)	1/2 nutrition bar	Crab Salad in Tomato Shells (p. 263)	Hummus with carrot and celery sticks	Chicken Tikka, (p. 283) snow peas, rice or bulgur and salad	Pecan Brownie (p. 315) and glass of skim milk
SUN	Cinnamon French Toast (p. 238), with back bacon	Orange and almonds	Minestrone (p. 246) and Basic G.I. Salad (p. 255)	Babybel Gouda Lite cheese with crispbread	Grilled Portobello Mushroom Pizzas (p. 269), and salad	Slice of Apple Raspberry Coffee Cake (p. 311)

Week 6 Grocery List for Meal Plan

PRODUCE
Almonds (whole and sliced)
Apples
Asparagus
Bananas
Broccoli
Carrots
Celery
Cucumbers (English and field)
Fresh herbs (basil, chives, cilantro, flat-leaf
  parsley, tarragon, thyme)
Garlic
Ginger root
Grapes
Green beans
Leeks
Lemons
Lettuce (leaf and romaine)
Limes
Mushrooms (white and Portobello)
Onions (yellow and red)
Oranges
Peaches (fresh or canned in juice or water)
Pecans
Peppers (green, red or yellow)
Potatoes (new, small)
Raisins
Raspberries
Snow peas
Strawberries
Sunflower seeds, shelled and unsalted
Tomatoes (large beefsteak and plum)
Zucchini

DELI
Feta cheese (light)
Hummus (light)
Lean deli ham
Lean deli turkey
Olives
Parmesan cheese, grated

BAKERY
100% stone-ground whole wheat bread
Crispbread (e.g., Wasa Fibre)
Whole wheat pita bread

FISH COUNTER
Frozen crab
Halibut fillets

MEAT COUNTER
Back bacon
Chicken breasts (boneless, skinless)
Ground beef (extra-lean)

BEANS (LEGUMES) AND CANNED VEGETABLES
Chickpeas
Crushed tomatoes
Kidney beans (red and white)
Tomato paste
Tomato sauce

PASTA AND SAUCES
Capellini or spaghettini (whole wheat)
Fettuccini or linguine (whole wheat)

SOUP AND CANNED SEAFOOD AND MEAT
Anchovy fillets
Chicken stock (low-fat, low-sodium)
Tuna (light, in water)
Vegetable stock (low-fat, low-sodium)

GRAINS AND SIDE DISHES
Barley
Basmati rice
Bulgar
Flaxseeds (whole and ground)

INTERNATIONAL FOODS
Mirin (or sweet sherry)
Rice vinegar
Soy sauce (low-sodium)
Sesame seeds (toasted)
Tahini
Wasabi powder

COOKING OIL, VINEGAR, SALAD DRESSINGS AND PICKLES
Buttermilk salad dressing (low-fat, low-sugar)
Capers
Dijon mustard
Dry mustard
Grainy mustard
Mayonnaise (fat-free)
Oil (canola and extra-virgin olive)
Red wine vinegar
Sherry vinegar
Worcestershire sauce

SNACKS
Nutrition bars (e.g., ZonePerfect, Balance Bar)

BAKING
Amaretto
Baking powder
Baking soda
Brown sugar substitute
Oat bran
Soy lecithin granules
Spices (cayenne pepper, chili powder,
   ground cinnamon, cumin, garam masala,
ground ginger, ground nutmeg, dried
   oregano, black pepper, salt, dried tarragon,
   dried thyme, turmeric)
Splenda
Unsweetened cocoa powder
Vanilla
Wheat bran
Wheat germ
Whey or soy protein isolate powder
Whole wheat flour

BREAKFAST FOODS
All-Bran Buds cereal
Oatmeal (large-flake oats)

BEVERAGES
Red wine
Tomato juice
Vermouth or white wine

DAIRY CASE
Babybel Gouda Lite cheese
Buttermilk
Cottage cheese (low-fat)
Fruit yogurt (non-fat with sweetener)
Laughing Cow Light cheese (extra-low-fat)
Liquid eggs (e.g., Naturegg, Break Free)
Milk (skim)
Mozzarella cheese (part-skim)
Soft margarine (non-hydrogenated, light)
Sour cream (low-fat)
Soy milk

FROZEN FOODS
Mixed berries
Raspberries

Eating away from home presents several challenges. The first obstacle you'll face is that the restaurant or fast-food menu naturally limits your choice of food as well as how it is prepared. This is why it's critical to decide ahead of time where you want to dine. To help, I have listed your best green-light choices for most restaurants, family restaurants and fast-food categories.

The second challenge is social. More often than not, dining out is a social occasion with family and friends or co-workers at lunch. You don't want to be a party pooper by making everyone feel uncomfortable with your dietary concerns. More often than not there is the risk of fellow diners egging you to "live a little" which usually means poor food choices, extra drinks and decadent desserts! While there is no easy solution, honesty is the best policy. Be upfront that you have a weight problem that's affecting your health and you would like your family and friends to help you reach your weight goals. No need to ram your diet down the throats of others but be clear in asking for their support.

Fast Food

Most of the leading fast-food restaurants have introduced menu items that are lower in fat and calories. However, the amount of sodium (salt) that is often added to offset any perceived flavour loss is a concern. Remember, salt retains liquid, which is the last thing you need when you're trying to lose weight, yet alone trying to keep your blood pressure down. If you are not sure about salt levels, ask your server for a nutritional information sheet, which most family and fast food restaurant chains carry.

A couple of ground rules:
1. Always eat burgers and sandwiches opened-faced, throwing away the top slice of bread or bun.
2. Use at most, one-third of the salad dressing normally provided in a sachet as it contains far more than you would ever need, and only adds unnecessary calories and salt to your meal. Choose the light or vinaigrette dressings over creamy ones.

Here is a more detailed rundown of your best choices at some of the larger fast-food chains:

Subway

This chain has been a pacesetter in the fast-food industry in reducing fat and calories in its meals. Subway's 6-inch/6g fat subs on whole wheat or honey oat bread are your best choices. Just be careful not to load on those high-fat/-calorie extras such as cheese, bacon and high-sugar sauces. Mr. Sub and other similar sandwich chains are following this lead.

McDonald's

McDonald's grilled chicken salads are a good bet with a low-fat dressings. You can even go for a Fruit 'n' Yogurt Parfait dessert (hold the granola).

Burger King

Again, grilled chicken salads, or a chicken sandwich with garden salad, are your best options. You also may consider a Veggie Burger (without mayo) and a garden salad.

Wendy's

Grilled chicken sandwich or salads are acceptable along with low-fat dressings. You might consider a large chili with side salad.

Pizza Hut

Normally I recommend avoiding pizza restaurants so I am delighted to see that Pizza Hut has made a real effort to improve its offerings. Your best bet is Thin 'N' Crispy Pizzas and Fit 'n Delicious Pizzas (2 slices maximum) with garden salads and light dressings.

Taco Bell

Their line of Fresco tacos and burritos are acceptable green-light choices but are very high in sodium. Steer clear of the rest of the menu except the side salads.

KFC

Until just recently, KFC was a place to avoid. Stick to salads and chicken if you must eat here, and get the chicken without skin, grilled not fried.

Restaurants

As it's impossible to list restaurants by name, I've provided a quick rundown of different types of restaurants instead.

All-You-Can-Eat Buffets

This can be your worst or best option depending on your level of self-control. Best to do a quick reconnaissance of the whole buffet before you start to fill your plate. This way you can pick out your best green-light choices ahead of time.

Italian

Start with a good bean and vegetable soup such as minestrone. For the main course your best option is grilled, roasted or braised fish, chicken or veal. You may order pasta as a side dish if you wish, though you would be better off with an extra serving of vegetables.

Greek

Grilled or baked seafood is an excellent choice as well as the classic chicken souvlaki. Just watch your serving sizes. Instead of the potatoes, which are frequently served along with rice, order double vegetables. You must ask for both your salad dressing and feta to be served on the side so you can control your servings.

Chinese

This type of food can present some real challenges. Much of the food is deep-fried with sweet sauces. Sodium levels are usually astronomic and the rice is glutinous and red-light (short-grain rice has a much higher G.I. than long-grain rice such as basmati). Though you can make do with steamed or stir-fried vegetables, it's probably not worth the effort. This kind of restaurant would be my last resort when eating out.

Indian/South Asian

This is one of your best restaurant choices because of the cuisine's focus on vegetables, legumes and long-grain rice. Servings of meat, poultry or fish tend to be modest. However, make sure that food is not fried, particularly not in "ghee" or clarified butter, which is a highly saturated fat. Also be cautious with the side dishes such as mangoes/papayas, raisins and coconut slices as they have a higher G.I. and can pack a lot of calories if you aren't careful.

Mexican/Latin American

Tex-Mex dishes can be heavy on cheese, refried beans and sour cream, which are all red-light. Your best bet is to look for grilled seafood, chicken or meat, as well as dishes made with beans (not refried). Vegetable-based soups such as gazpacho are an excellent choice.

Thai

Thai restaurants tend to be heavy on red-light sauces, often using full-fat coconut milk. Here it's best to stick with a starter such as lemongrass soup, green mango salad, or mussels in a lemongrass broth. Follow this with a Thai beef salad or stir-fry with chicken and vegetables. Skip the peanut sauce.

Japanese

This is a good green-light choice once you get beyond the sushi and tempura. Sushi is red-light because of the glutinous rice it is made with. Order the sashimi instead. Watch the quantity of soy sauce, which should be thought of as liquid salt! The beef and vegetable stir-frys and grilled fish are excellent choices. You might try Nabemono, a healthy fondue with broth rather than oil as the cooking medium.

If you are dining in a group you might not have any say as to the choice of restaurant. In that case, a little planning and some careful choices can help you over the hurdles:

I am a family physician in Louisiana, and I bought the G.I. Diet book for myself several months ago. I found it to be the healthiest wellness plan that I had ever read. It makes good scientific sense, it's "do-able," and it is an excellent long-term lifestyle change. I've now been recommending both of your books to my patients and the results are unbelievable. Several of my morbidly obese diabetic patients are losing 8–12 pounds per month and are having excellent glycemic control and their cholesterol is markedly improved as well. The local bookstore can't keep up with the demand, because I'm probably recommending it as much as 10 times a day to people. I can't applaud you enough for coming up with such a great plan. I thank you on behalf of myself and my patients. Judith

Top Ten Dining Tips

1. Just before you go out, have a small bowl of high-fibre, green-light cold cereal (such as All Bran) with skim milk and sweetener. I often add a couple of spoonfuls of fruit yogurt (fat-free with sweetener). This will take the edge off your appetite and get some fibre into your digestive system, which will help reduce the G.I. of your upcoming meal.

2. Once seated in the restaurant, drink a glass of water. It will help you feel fuller.

3. Remember to eat slowly to allow your brain the time it needs to realize you are full. Put your fork down between mouthfuls and savour your meal.

4. Once the basket of rolls or bread—which you will ignore—has been passed around the table, ask the server to remove it. The longer it sits, the more tempted you will be to dig in.

5. Order a soup or salad first and tell the server you would like this as soon as possible. This will keep you from sitting there hungry while others are filling up on bread. For soups, go for vegetable or bean-based, the chunkier the better. Avoid any that are cream-based, such as vichyssoise. For salads, keep the dressing on the side. Then you can use a fraction of what the restaurant would normally pour over your greens.

Avoid Caesar salads, which come predressed and often pack as many calories as a burger.

6. Since you probably won't get boiled new potatoes and can't be sure of what kind of rice is being served, ask for a double serving of vegetables instead. I have yet to find a restaurant that won't oblige.

7. Stick with low-fat cuts of meat or poultry. If necessary, you can remove the skin. Duck is usually too high in fat. Fish and shellfish are excellent choices but shouldn't be breaded, battered or fried. Tempura is more fat and flour than filling. Remember that servings tend to be generous in restaurants, so eat only 4 to 6 ounces (the size of a pack of cards) and leave the rest.

8. As with salads, ask for any sauces to be served on the side.

9. For dessert, fresh fruit and berries—without the ice cream—are your best choice. Most other desserts are a dietary disaster. My advice to you is to avoid dessert. If a birthday cake is being passed around, share your piece with someone. A couple of forkfuls with your coffee should get you off the hook with minimal dietary damage!

10. Order only decaffeinated coffee. Skim-milk decaf cappuccino is our family's favorite choice.

SWEET AND SALTY CRAVINGS

As discussed earlier, menopause plays havoc with your hormones, and as a result, your blood-sugar levels. Low blood sugar often generates the desire for something sweet. So if you are hankering for something sweet, check for fruit in the menu particularly in the appetizers or desserts. You can always sprinkle on some sweetener from the packages available for coffee and tea. This will heighten the natural sweetness of the fruit and ease those cravings. It's a good idea to carry some sweetener packages with you at all times.

Conversely, some women crave savory food. When you are feeling this way, select the spicier choices on the menu. Just be careful it is not salt that is giving the food that extra kick as it will exacerbate any hot flashes. If in doubt, ask your waiter to check with the chef.

E-Clinic Diaries

After the reality check of Week 6, many of the clinic participants begin to sense that making that all-important permanent change is happening after all:

I'm really pleased with how easy this [diet] is to incorporate into my "lifestyle." I had an instance where "green-light" options were totally not available. In past situations when I have attempted to lose weight, I would have viewed this as a huge failure and a reason to "blow it." With this plan, I simply assessed the food choices, tried to go for the lower calorie/healthiest available and stuck to smaller portions. I didn't have to feel deprived or defeated because I couldn't have what everyone else was eating and enjoying. I went right back to green-light choices the next day as if nothing happened and I still lost a pound and another inch in my waist this week. Cindy

The diet suits me and I am sticking to it very well. I went out to lunch twice this week and ordered salads with protein and light dressing. I am looking forward to my daughter's wedding at the end of August. I have not bought my dress yet because I am determined to lose more weight in the next few weeks. Carol

I continue to feel that the rewards of "being good" and sticking to greenlighters outweigh the pleasures of eating other foods, especially since I really don't feel deprived or hungry. Good thing I kept some of my smaller clothes, as now they are coming out of the closet. Great feeling! Friday's huge challenge was a tasting of the foods our caterer will be preparing for our wedding in June. I felt I owed it to my guests to make sure they'd be getting the best and the tasting was a real treat, but I had only enough to sample the red foods and the caterer must have been surprised when I left most of it behind. My weight didn't change the following day. This shows me that the most important thing is regularly eating properly and the odd exception shouldn't get you de-railed. Again, this only helps me understand that this is indeed a long-range plan, not a temporary diet. Susan

Q: I am going for a few days to a conference and my only dilemma is what to have for breakfasts. Lunch and dinner are no problem as there will always be salads or vegetables and protein. So what should I be eating for breakfasts when I am sure there will be no oatmeal available? Carol

A: When Ruth and I are travelling, we take along packets of instant oatmeal. We bring them to breakfast, empty one in a cereal bowl and simply add hot water. As sugar is unfortunately a major factor in the commercially prepared packages, I suggest you purchase a box of instant oatmeal and prepackage in small baggies individual portion sizes and take those with you instead. You can then add yogurt and fresh fruit, which are usually available at most conference breakfasts. If they are not, I suggest you ask the conference organizer for them. Explain that you need these for health reasons. A former e-clinic member told me she had done this many times and it had worked each time.

We always go to our favorite buffet restaurant, the Shady Maple, where they serve the best "fat food" in the world for my "FREE" birthday dinner. We have been going there for years but not this year ... I do not want to even be tempted yet with all those fat foods which I am proud to say are no longer my friends. This would be too much like having red light foods at my fingertips ... I am not sure I can resist the temptation at this stage of my "healthy eating the green light way." I don't want to deal with the temptation (the desserts are to die for)! I just know I would not do well and I could blow away my 7 weeks of good healthy eating in just 1 hour time there. It is not worth the "FREE" meal. We plan on just staying home and eating healthy. So thank you Shady Maple for the "FREE" birthday dinner offer but "no thank you" this year! Ann

Neighbours asked us out to dinner with them last night and they picked a Thai restaurant. First mistake was not looking at your dining out book before I went. I went with the idea that I could pick something for myself that was reasonably green-light. WRONG!! I had never eaten Thai food before, so my neighbour, who doesn't know I am on the G.I. diet (second mistake) was suggesting food, and being a little uncomfortable with what to order, went along with her suggestion. Dinner was good, enjoyed everything and tried to watch my portions ... when I did return home and check the book, everything we ordered was RED light. Felt awful, but learned a valuable lesson, plan before heading out to a restaurant ... now right back on track. Helen

Next week we will be dealing with arguably two of the biggest frustrations in losing weight: reaching a weight-loss plateau and falling off the wagon.

Week 7 Weight: _____

Week 7 Waist: _____

Week 7 Hips: _____

Week 7 Diary

_____

_____

_____

_____

_____

Week 7 Optional Meal Plan

	BREAKFAST	SNACK	LUNCH	SNACK	DINNER	SNACK
MON	Homey Oatmeal (p. 236) with chopped apple	Apple Bran Muffin (p. 303)	Open-face chicken sandwich with lettuce, tomato and onion, and Basic G.I. Salad (p. 255)	Laughing Cow Light cheese with crispbread	Lemony Grilled Vegetable Pasta Salad (p. 253) with canned tuna or salmon	Mixed berries tossed in lime juice with sour cream
TUES	Mini Breakfast Puffs (p. 240)	Fruit yogurt	Tuscan White Bean Soup (p. 247) with Basic G.I. Salad (p. 255)	Hummus with carrot and celery sticks	Spicy Roasted Chicken with Tomatoes and Tarragon (p. 289), green beans and basmati rice	Orange and almonds
WED	Homemade Muesli (p. 237) with skim milk and fruit yogurt	Apple Bran Muffin (p. 303)	½ whole wheat pita with canned light tuna, lettuce, tomato and cucumber, and Basic G.I. Salad (p. 255)	Babybel Gouda Lite cheese with crispbread	Pork Medallions Dijon (p. 298), green beans, carrots and new potatoes	Creamy Lemon Square (p. 316) and glass of skim milk
THURS	Homey Oatmeal (p. 236) with blueberries	Small apple and glass of skim milk	Quick and Easy Chicken Noodle Soup (p. 248) and Basic G.I. Salad (p. 255)	Crunchy Chickpeas (p. 300)	Quinoa, Bean and Vegetable Chili (p. 270) and, Basic G.I. Salad (p. 255)	½ nutrition bar
FRI	All-Bran Buds with skim milk, peach slices and sliced almonds	Fruit yogurt	Waldorf Chicken and Rice Salad (p. 262)	Laughing Cow Light cheese with crispbread	Thai Red Curry Shrimp Pasta (p. 279)	Mixed berries tossed in lime juice with sour cream
SAT	Vegetarian Omelette (p. 243)	½ nutrition bar	Greek Salad (p. 257)	Hummus with carrot and celery sticks	Zesty Barbecued Chicken (p. 290)	Creamy Lemon Square (p. 316) and glass of skim milk
SUN	Oatmeal Buttermilk Pancakes (p. 239) with strawberries	Orange and almonds	Tuna Salad (p. 260)	Babybel Gouda Lite cheese with crispbread	Blueberry Beef Burgers (p. 296) broccoli and cauliflower tossed in lemon	Piece of Berry Crumble (p. 309)

Week 7 Grocery List for Meal Plan

PRODUCE
Almonds (ground, sliced and whole)
Apples
Blueberries (fresh or frozen)
Broccoli
Brussels sprouts
Cabbage (green, red or yellow)
Carrots
Cauliflower
Celery
Cucumbers
Eggplant
Fresh herbs (chives, cilantro, mint, tarragon)
Hot pepper
Garlic
Green beans
Green onions
Kale
Leeks
Lemons
Lettuce (leaf and romaine)
Limes
Mushrooms (white and shiitake)
Onions (yellow and red)
Oranges
Peaches (fresh or canned in juice or water)
Pecans
Peppers (green, red or yellow)
Potatoes (new, small)
Raisins
Shallots
Strawberries
Sunflower seeds, shelled and unsalted
Tomatoes (cherry and plum)
Walnuts
Zucchini

DELI
Feta cheese (light)
Hummus (light)
Kalamata olives

BAKERY
100% stone-ground whole wheat bread
Crispbread (e.g., Wasa Fibre)

FISH COUNTER
Shrimp (large raw)

MEAT COUNTER
Chicken breasts (boneless, skinless)
Ground beef (extra-lean)
Lean ground chicken or turkey
Pork tenderloin

BEANS (LEGUMES) AND CANNED VEGETABLES
Black beans
Chickpeas
Kidney beans (red and white)
Diced tomatoes
Pinto beans
Stewed tomatoes
Tomato paste

PASTA AND SAUCES
Penne or rotini (whole wheat)
Macaroni or small shells (whole wheat)
Spagettini or linguine (whole wheat)
Small pasta (e.g., ditali or tubetti)
Light tomato sauce

SOUP AND CANNED SEAFOOD AND MEAT
Chicken stock (low-fat, low-sodium)
Tuna (light, in water)
Vegetable stock (low-fat, low-sodium)

GRAINS AND SIDE DISHES
Barley
Basmati rice
Flaxseed (ground)
Quinoa

INTERNATIONAL FOODS
Thai red curry paste

COOKING OIL, VINEGAR, SALAD DRESSINGS AND PICKLES
Balsamic vinegar
Buttermilk salad dressing (low-fat, low-sugar)
Capers
Cider vinegar
Dijon mustard
Oil (canola and extra-virgin olive)
Red wine vinegar
Worcestershire sauce

SNACKS
Nutrition bars (e.g., ZonePerfect, Balance Bar)

BAKING
Baking powder
Baking soda
Cornstarch
Oat bran
Spices (ground allspice, cayenne
   pepper, chili powder, ground cinnamon,
   ground cloves, ground cumin, dried
   oregano, Hungarian paprika, black
   pepper, salt)
Splenda
Vanilla
Wheat bran
Wheat germ

Whole wheat flour
Unsweetened cocoa powder

BREAKFAST FOODS
All-Bran Buds cereal
Oatmeal (large-flake oats)

BEVERAGES
Apple juice (unsweetened)
Dry white wine (or vermouth)

DAIRY CASE
Babybel Gouda Lite cheese
Buttermilk
Cheddar cheese (low-fat)
Fruit yogurt (non-fat with sweetener)
Laughing Cow Light cheese
Liquid eggs (e.g., Naturegg, Break Free)
Milk (skim)
Orange juice (unsweetened)
Soft margarine (non-hydrogenated, light)
Sour cream (low-fat)
Whole omega-3 eggs

FROZEN FOODS
Apple juice concentrate
Mixed berries
Peas (or fresh)

Week 8

Staying the Course

By the end of the first two months of the program, two issues preoccupied many of the e-clinic participants, as evidenced in their diaries: reaching a weight-loss plateau and falling off the wagon. These are perhaps the most frustrating challenges that people on any diet experience. Let me give you a sense of why these challenges present themselves and suggest some strategies for coping with them.

Reaching a Plateau

After diligently eating the green-light way and losing weight steadily for successive weeks, it is difficult to accept that a break in the pattern, unfair as it may be, is inevitable. Weight loss never occurs in a straight line, but always in a series of steps or plateaus.

There are a couple of principal causes. First, hormonal shifts triggered by menopause cause the body to retain fluid (for example, if you usually wear rings they might feel tight on your fingers). This is nearly always a temporary state. As your hormones shift back to their previous levels, so will your fluids. This symptom is also typical of PMS symptoms that you may have experienced during menstrual cycles.

The second most common cause is "portion creep" for a weight-loss plateau can occur when you have let your guard down and allowed your portion or serving size to increase. This is easy to do as you have watched the pounds steadily drop off; not surprisingly, complacency can set in. A useful tool in keeping you on track is dividing your place into three sections (see page 26): half the plate should consist of at least two vegetables; one-quarter should consist of a protein (meat, fish or tofu); and the remaining quarter can consist of rice, potatoes or pasta. Remember to use small lunch-sized plates instead of oversized dinner plates.

Since hormonal shifts and complacency can cause your weight to fluctuate significantly from day to day, I suggest you restrict your weigh-in to once a week. Then you can avoid the disappointment of the short-term aberrations and focus on your long-term success. One reader wrote to me and said that she had become very frustrated with the daily variations in weight and decided to weigh herself once a month. She said there was not a single month in the past 18 months when she had not lost some weight and her frustration level had dropped significantly.

When playing the averages, patience is a virtue! Just keep on the green-light track and the weight will continue to come off. Some clinic participants also wondered why they sometimes seem to be losing inches but not pounds, and sometimes pounds but not inches. Remember, everyone is different, and weight loss doesn't ever happen in a straight line; eventually both the inches and pounds will come off—guaranteed!

So don't let an irregularity on the scale get you down, although nothing is quite as frustrating as hitting a weight-loss plateau. But if you hang in there and don't use food to console yourself, you will reach your weight-loss target.

Falling Off the Wagon

Like a weight-loss plateau, falling off the wagon is bound to happen sooner or later. And while I don't encourage it, it's acceptable as long as it's the exception and not the rule. The diet isn't meant to be a straitjacket, after all. If you do your best to eat the green-light way 90 percent of the time, you will still lose weight. The odd lapse, at worst, will delay you by a week or two from reaching your target weight. So don't be too hard on yourself; just get right back on the plan with the next meal. Some people make the mistake of feeling so bad about having a slip-up that they just give up. But you should anticipate that you will fall off the wagon from time to time. The best way to handle it is to learn why it happened and decide how you will handle the situation the next time. By now you have the knowledge and tools to do just that.

Although most people find that their cravings diminish after a few weeks on the G.I. Diet, because of the levelling effects green-light eating has on blood sugar levels, there will be times when a craving will surface. Here's how to handle the situation:

1. Try to distract yourself with an activity. Call a friend, fold a basket of laundry, take out the garbage or just go for a walk. Sometimes a craving will pass.

2. If you are still have the craving, pinpoint the flavour that you want and find a green-light food that has it. For example, if you want something sweet and creamy, try low-fat yogurt or ice cream with no added sugar. If you want something salty, have a couple of olives or a dill pickle, or some hummus with veggies. If it's chocolate you crave, try half a chocolate-flavoured nutrition bar or a mug of instant light hot chocolate. There are many green-light versions of the foods we normally reach for when a craving strikes.

3. Sometimes nothing but a piece of chocolate or a spoonful of peanut butter will do. If this is case, have a *small* portion and really enjoy it. Eat it slowly and savour the experience. Chalk it up to that 10 percent leeway you're allowed on the G.I Diet. Just make sure you're staying green-light 90 percent of the time.

Remember, the 10 percent "wriggle room" I mentioned earlier gives you permission to enjoy that extra serving or occasional drink. It is meant to help you stay with the program so use it wisely.

> My husband and I started on your G.I. diet the first of the year. We both have lost weight without being hungry. I have lost 31 pounds and Jim has lost 12. (I haven't told him how much I have lost because I don't want him to be discouraged). I must admit that he gets extra portions sometimes. Anyway, we are both thrilled that we have found a program that we can live with. I am 57 and a diabetic with severe osteoarthritis. I can't really do much exercise, just my PT; but I still am losing weight! My entire family is obese as far back as the caveman. It has been a lifelong battle for me. I finally have hope that I can lose and maintain a "normal" weight. Thank you so much for your enjoyable, readable, doable book. Kathy

E-Clinic Diaries

If you really want to make a permanent change in the way you eat and look, keep planning ahead—especially if you've hit a plateau or find yourself repeatedly falling off the wagon. Think about where you might have slipped back, consciously or unconsciously, into your old food habits. Here is what some of our e-clinic members had to say about their frustrations and successes when weight loss stalled:

> I think I am slipping back into some "old habits." Like just a "taste" of that cream pie won't make a difference. Obviously too many "tastes" do make a difference. Lynn

> I think I'm getting sloppy in timing my meals and snacks. We live on a farm and I've been working outside much of the time ... and get so involved that I forget to come in for meals and snacks. Of course, then I'm really hungry and want something quickly. Maybe I'm going to have to set a timer for myself to remember to keep my stomach happy. Joan

> I was on a retreat on Saturday and the food was to be provided, but ... I thought I had better be careful and bring my food just in case. At first I figured that I didn't have to bring anything because I would just eat the fruit and vegs and drink bottled water; was I glad that I brought my own food. The lunch was sandwiches, sweet pickles and olives; a little bit of fruit which I didn't feel I should take too much as there was so little of it and so many others to have some. Absolutely no vegs. And no bottled water, just fruit drinks and coffee and tea. I had brought tabouli and strawberries with yogurt and some cheese and crispbread for snack. Thank goodness I did that because I wasn't tempted to eat sandwiches and dessert ... I now realize if I want to get rid of these pounds that I definitely have to plan ahead. Carol

This week was very bad for me. I'm house/pet sitting my brother's house. Unfortunately, all they have [to eat] I consider 'junk' food. I tried my very best to stay on target but coming home from a stressful day/week at work, on top of that—it was that time of the month. I had no energy to go shopping/prepare a healthy meal. I just let myself go. I realize there is no excuse for my behaviour and by not losing anything this week it is very depressing for me right now, especially after seeing results in the past weeks and feeling good about myself. No excuse!!! Grace

It seems that I reached the stage where I thought I had "the cure." Was happy accepting slow weight loss—"all the experts say that's the best kind." But, what was really happening was that I was getting complacent. I acted as if I had the green-light way of living down pat. I realized there is the 90% rule, but I was using the 90% rule a few times a day: it's OK to have a sandwich "this time" with two slices of bread (how could 5 grams of fiber per slice hurt?) and we'll just use real mayonnaise this time since we're out of non-fat sour cream. If this had been one day, I could accept my actions better, but it wasn't. It was frequent during the week. Each time I called it "the exception" but it was pretty much the rule. This morning I cannot take off my rings that are usually very loose. The old me is angry at myself for being a fool but the other part of me has decided that since what is done is done, I'd better look at it as a lesson. I could lie to myself all week about the "changes" I was making to my green-light diet, but my body didn't believe the lies. It counted every indiscretion. Since before this week, I thought I was on the way to a cure, I didn't do the water bottles you suggested and other members tried. This morning I did. My one-gallon bleach bottle filled with water is marked "Weight Lost." The large kitty litter container (weighing 22 pounds) is marked "Extra weight on Joan." I'm temporarily disappointed in myself but I know my history. I remember when I first wrote to you I said that I was a great sprinter—but a lousy long-distance person. Joan

I paid attention to my portion sizes this week and have been to the gym every day doing an hour of exercise classes and as of this morning I am still at my current weight. This is what usually happens to me, I lose a little weight and then I reach a plateau ... For the most part, I watch what I eat and I will stay at that weight until the next diet plan catches my eye ... It is a real battle just to maintain my weight, which believe me when I say, I really do try because I refuse to be like most of my family, obese. Oh and if that wasn't bad enough, I now have entered the world of MENOPAUSE. Even though it may sound like I have given up, I am very much determined to succeed with this G.I. Diet plan. I am still focused and I must say I have noticed I lost inches in other places. Rita

Underlying all we have discussed about plateauing and falling off the wagon is the importance of staying motivated. Without motivation, you are unlikely to stay the course. Next week we will look at ways to help keep your commitment and enthusiasm from flagging—especially at those difficult times we all inevitably experience.

Week 8 Weight: _____

Week 8 Waist: _____

Week 8 Hips: _____

Week 8 Diary

_____

_____

_____

Week 8 Optional Meal Plan

	BREAKFAST	SNACK	LUNCH	SNACK	DINNER	SNACK
MON	Homey Oatmeal (p. 236) with chopped apple	Whole Wheat Fruit Scone (p. 304)	Open-face lean deli ham sandwich with lettuce, tomato, red pepper and grainy mustard, and Basic G.I. Salad (p. 255)	Laughing Cow Light cheese with crispbread	Fettucine Primavera (p. 273) and Caesar Salad (p. 256)	Mixed berries tossed in lime juice with sour cream
TUES	Mini Breakfast Puffs (p. 240)	Fruit yogurt	Waldorf Chicken and Rice Salad (p. 262)	Hummus with carrot and celery sticks	Tomato and Cheese Catfish (p.277), serve with leftover Fettuccini Primavera	Orange and almonds
WED	Homemade Muesli (p. 237) with skim milk and fruit yogurt	Whole Wheat Fruit Scone (p. 304)	Cottage cheese with apple and grapes, and Basic G.I. Salad (p. 255)	Babybel Gouda Lite cheese with crispbread	Chicken Schnitzel (p. 286), green beans, carrots and new potatoes	Slice of Strawberry Tea Bread (p. 305) and glass of skim milk
THURS	Homey Oatmeal (p. 236) with blueberries	Small apple and glass of skim milk	Minestrone Soup (p. 246) and Basic G.I. Salad (p. 255)	Crunchy Chickpeas (p. 300)	Meatloaf (p. 294), green beans, carrots and new potatoes	1/2 nutrition bar
FRI	All-Bran Buds with skim milk, peach slices and sliced almonds	Fruit yogurt	1/2 whole wheat pita with deli turkey, lettuce, tomato and cucumber, and Basic G.I. Salad (p. 255)	Laughing Cow Light cheese with crispbread	Indian Vegetable Curry (p. 272) and Basic G.I. Salad	Fancy Fruit Salad (p. 308)
SAT	Smoked Salmon Scrambled Eggs (p. 244)	1/2 nutrition bar	Vegetable Barley Soup au Pistou (p. 249) with Basic G.I. Salad (p. 255)	Hummus with carrot and celery sticks	Roasted Pork Tenderloin with Balsamic Glaze and Gingered Peach Salsa (p. 293) new potatoes, asparagus and Basic G.I. Salad (p. 255)	Slice of Strawberry Tea Bread (p. 305) and glass of skim milk
SUN	Cinnamon French Toast (p. 238) with back bacon	Orange and almonds	Grilled Shrimp and Pear Salad (p. 264)	Babybel Gouda Lite cheese with crispbread	Chicken Stir-Fry with Broccoli (p. 284) and Basic G.I. Salad (p. 255)	Slice of One-Bowl Chocolate Cake (p. 313) with berries

Week 8 Grocery List for Meal Plan

PRODUCE
Almonds (whole and sliced)
Apples
Asparagus
Baby spinach
Bean sprouts
Blackberries
Blueberries (fresh or frozen)
Broccoli
Carrots
Cashews
Celery
Chili pepper
Cucumbers
Dried apricots
Fresh herbs (basil, chives, cilantro, oregano,
   flat-leaf parsley, mint, thyme)
Garlic
Ginger root
Grapes
Green beans
Green onions
Hot pepper
Kiwis
Leeks
Lemons
Lettuce (leaf and Romaine)
Limes
Mushrooms
Onions (red, yellow and Vidalia)
Oranges
Peaches (fresh or canned in juice or water)
Pears
Peppers (green, red and yellow)
Potatoes (new, small)
Strawberries
Sunflower seeds, shelled and unsalted
Tomatoes (large beefsteak and plum)
Walnuts
Zucchini

DELI
Hummus (light)
Lean deli ham
Lean deli turkey
Parmesan cheese, grated

BAKERY
100% stone-ground whole wheat bread
Crispbread (e.g., Wasa Fibre)
Whole wheat breadcrumbs
Whole wheat hamburger buns
Whole wheat pita bread

FISH COUNTER
Catfish fillets
Frozen crab
Shrimp (large raw)
Smoked salmon

MEAT COUNTER
Back bacon
Chicken breasts (boneless, skinless)
Ground beef (extra-lean)
Pork tenderloin

BEANS (LEGUMES) AND CANNED VEGETABLES
Chickpeas
Kidney beans (red)
Plum tomatoes
Tomato paste

PASTA AND SAUCES
Small pasta (e.g., ditali or tubetti)

SOUP AND CANNED SEAFOOD AND MEAT
Anchovy fillets
Chicken stock (low-fat, low-sodium)
Vegetable stock (low-fat, low-sodium)

GRAINS AND SIDE DISHES
Barley
Basmati rice

INTERNATIONAL FOODS
Hoisin sauce
Mild curry paste
Oyster sauce
Rice vinegar
Soy sauce
Tahini

COOKING OIL, VINEGAR, SALAD DRESSINGS AND PICKLES
Balsamic vinegar
Buttermilk salad dressing (low-fat, low-sugar)
Dijon mustard
Grainy mustard
Oil (canola, extra-virgin olive, and sesame)
Red wine vinegar
Worcestershire sauce

SNACKS
Applesauce (unsweetened)
Nutrition bars (e.g., ZonePerfect, Balance Bar)

BAKING
Baking powder
Baking soda
Honey
Oat bran
Spices (cayenne, chili powder, ground cinnamon,
   cumin seeds, ground nutmeg, dried oregano,
   black pepper, red pepper flakes, salt)
Splenda

Vanilla
Wheat bran
Wheat germ
Whole wheat flour

BREAKFAST FOODS
All-Bran Buds cereal
Oatmeal (large-flake oats)

BEVERAGES
Tomato juice

DAIRY CASE
Cottage cheese (low-fat)
Babybel Gouda Lite cheese
Buttermilk
Cheddar cheese (low-fat)
Fruit yogurt (non-fat with sweetener)
Laughing Cow Light cheese
Liquid eggs (e.g., Naturegg, Break Free)
Milk (skim)
Sour cream (low-fat)
Whole omega-3 eggs

FROZEN FOODS
Mixed berries

Week 9

Keeping Motivated

We are now two-thirds of the way through the first stage of the program.

This is a good time to reflect on your progress to date and what still needs to be done to keep your motivation high. Some people may have taken to the G.I. Diet like the proverbial duck to water, while others have struggled to make the transition from their red-light habits to the green-light way of eating. Many of you have work and home and unrelated health pressures that have complicated matters.

However, the one common thread that has run through all the correspondence I received from the e-clinic participants was a determination to get this weight devil off their backs. It's how to maintain this motivation that I want to discuss in this week, especially during those times when you feel you are not making enough progress or your stress levels become overwhelming.

You wouldn't be human if you didn't feel your resolve starting to waver occasionally. When it does, there are a number of things you can do to encourage yourself to keep going.

1. Remember your initial reasons.

Reread your reasons for wanting to lose weight in Week 1 (see page 62). Remember why it was so important to you to slim down when you started this journey, and why you need to persevere.

2. Use physical reminders of your goal.

Keep a picture of an outfit you're going to buy when you reach your goal, or a photograph of a thinner you where you will see it every day. One reader, who is blind, kept a picture in her mind's eye. She told me "I am using my beautiful red leather coat as the motivator for me. Last winter when I went to put it on, it was about two inches too small. I was not able to close the zipper. Now when I put the coat on, I am able to zip up the coat. Tight yes, but I know that I have made progress. What an incredible feeling. What motivation for me ... I am determined to wear the coat this winter."

3. Keep in mind how far you've come.

Compare yourself now to where you were before you started the diet. How much weight have you lost? How much better do your clothes fit you? How has your energy level and health improved? What can you do now that you couldn't do before? Going back to your old eating habits won't seem so tempting when you think how it will undermine all the good things that weight loss has brought you so far.

4. Try the shopping bag motivator.

Often people don't realize how much weight actually weighs. Sounds crazy, but when people tell me they've only lost 20 pounds, I ask them to fill a couple of shopping bags with 20 pounds of books and carry them up and down the stairs a few times. Everyone is always glad to put the bags down and report they had no idea how heavy 20 pounds really is.

So the next time you're feeling uninspired, fill a shopping bag or two with the amount of books or cans of food that equals how much weight you've lost over the last eight weeks of the program and carry them up and down a flight of stairs three times. You'll be amazed at what you've lost, and you'll be relieved to put the bag down. You couldn't have put that weight down weeks ago when it was still around your waist, hips and thighs.

One lady used potatoes for weight and when the bag reached 40 pounds she couldn't even lift it, let alone walk around with it. She had absolutely no idea this is what she had been carrying around for years. No wonder," she wrote "I lacked energy and my back and knees were always sore!"

Several e-clinic members found this incentive very motivating and also suggested filling empty bottles with water equivalent to the weight they had lost overall each week. This struck me as a very simple and flexible idea. Their experiences are recorded in the diary section on the next page.

> I can't express to you how much your book has helped me. [When] I bought your book ... I weighed 188 lbs at 5 ft and as of today (15 months later) I have lost 75 lbs. I now weigh 113 lbs. I have told everyone who will listen to buy your book[;] even my family doctor is giving her other patients who need to lose weight the name of the book and the author of this marvelous book ... My doctor is amazed as at my age 72 it is usually hard to lose weight but I am living testimony that it can be done on this wonderful diet. Elaine

5. Get support.

Buddy up with friends, a spouse or family members who are trying to lose weight. They will give you a sense of camaraderie and encouragement as you strive for your goal, and you can turn to them for support when you need it.

6. The $10 cure.

This is a motivator that people often stumble upon by accident. The siren song of a red-light lunch draws them into a fast-food chain, where they order a burger with the works, a large french fries and a shake. Mid-afternoon, they feel lousy and can barely keep their eyes open. They've found out the hard way where straying from the green-light gets you.

I call this the $10 cure because it's the food version of what immigrants (like me!) used to call the $1,000 cure. Whenever a new arrival, after a long cold winter in Canada, used to pine for the "old country," the cure was to get on a plane and go home for a week. All the reasons that originally persuaded the person to emigrate would come crashing back, and the thought of flying back to Canada would begin to look pretty good again.

With food, the cure costs less—say $10 (maybe $15 with inflation!). But this is a motivator of last resort only; I certainly don't want to encourage people to abuse their bodies and feel awful! However, if you've been unceasingly pining for red-light foods, go out for lunch with some friends and order a high G.I. meal—perhaps a couple of slices of double cheese pizza, a soft drink and a brownie. Your mouth may enjoy it, but I guarantee that a couple of hours later you'll be regretting the deviation.

E-Clinic Diaries

Motivation comes in many forms, whether it's one of the coping strategies I've outlined above, a reduction in menopausal symptoms or simply the knowledge that while it didn't happen this week, if you keep at it, the weight loss will come. Take a moment to think about what motivates you while you are on this journey. Here are some thoughts from our clinic participants on the subject:

I like doing lists and I usually work from a list for just about everything. I made myself a list of snack ideas and posted it to the fridge. I made a list of rewards for myself for losing weight and have also made a list of pleasurable activities to do other than eating. I have purchased three items from my rewards list and have used the pleasurable activities list to deter myself from eating when I didn't need to. Joyce

I just realized—I DO NOT SUFFER FROM HOT FLASHES, NIGHT SWEATS OR INSOMNIA ANYMORE!!!! I do still go to the restroom in the night, but don't lay there and watch the clock the rest of the night, I GO BACK TO SLEEP!!!!! I stopped taking the hormone replacement pills after I read that more studies are not encouraging with long term side effects. [Add]the fact that I had gained 10.5 pounds[;] I just did not want to take them, so stopped. So the only thing I am doing differently is EATING the LOW G.I. way of eating. WOW. Marlene

The weight is slower coming off now, but I am still happy it's coming off. It took time to put it on, so I know it will take time to get it off. I will not ever go back to the way I was eating before … I was a chip-a-holic and a choc-o-holic … I use to eat a large bag a day and a few chocolate bars. Now when I'm stressed at work (instead of having my junk at my desk), I get up go to the fridge, grab a yogurt and think of the weight that has come off and is still coming off. Debbie

It is still a huge struggle for me to get on the scales once a week because I avoided weighing myself at all costs for so long. But when I saw I had lost another pound since last weigh in and with all the compliments I am getting from friends lately, I am trying to believe that the news will continue to be good because my efforts have been steady and I am forgiving myself the odd trespass. Louise

I did the bottles of water (the amount I have lost) just to see if this would really matter. Well with 5 back surgeries I could not carry them up and down stairs. But I did carry them around the room with me ... Well I sure did not know what weight weighs. So I took another set of bottles and filled them with water for my goal weight to lose. Talk about a shock ... I left the bottles I have lost to the right of my scales and the ones I am going to lose to the left of my scales. I will transfer the water to the right side of the scales as I progress. The visual is very effective for me. Carol Ann

Probably the most rewarding thing has been to be able to feel the difference in my clothes and take out the ones which hadn't fit for awhile. Being a "professional" at yoyo dieting, I have every size in my closet(s) from 8–16 and I have now worked my way down to a 12. Nothing tastes as good as thin feels. Sharon

I was struck by your idea ... of filling a bag with the amount of weight I had lost. I got up from the computer and put a bag of books together. Then, I carried it around the house all day, off and on, to remind myself of my accomplishment. It is just as motivating as trying on smaller clothes! In fact, I may put that weight into a backpack and take it with me in the car when I leave for out of town work later today. Louise

Staying motivated is crucial to successful weight loss. It keeps you focused and on the green-light path and it will get you through the pitfalls you'll encounter. Next week we'll be looking at how to eat when you are celebrating with family or friends, a time when diets often get thrown out the window. These strategies will help keep you on track as you slim down to your ideal weight.

Week 9 Weight:_____

Week 9 Waist:_____

Week 9 Hips:_____

Week 9 Diary

_____

_____

_____

_____

_____

_____

_____

_____

_____

_____

_____

_____

_____

_____

_____

_____

Week 9 Optional Meal Plan

	BREAKFAST	SNACK	LUNCH	SNACK	DINNER	SNACK
MON	Homey Oatmeal (p. 236) with chopped apple	Cranberry Cinnamon Bran Muffin (p. 301)	Open face chicken sandwich with with lettuce, tomato and onion, and Basic G.I. Salad (p. 255)	Laughing Cow Light cheese with crispbread	Lemon Linguine with Smoked Salmon (p. 266), broccoli and salad	Mixed berries tossed in lime juice with sour cream
TUES	Mini Breakfast Puffs (p. 240)	Fruit yogurt	G.I. Pasta Salad (p. 259)	Hummus with carrot and celery sticks	Cheesy Lentil and Bean Bake (p. 267), basmati rice and salad	Orange and almonds
WED	Homemade Muesli (p. 237) with skim milk and fruit yogurt	Cranberry Cinnamon Bran Muffin (p. 301)	½ whole wheat pita with canned light tuna, lettuce, tomato and cucumber, and Basic G.I. Salad (p. 255)	Babybel Gouda Lite cheese with crispbread	Chicken Curry (p. 285) and Raita Salad (p. 252)	Cran-Apple Oatmeal Bars (p. 314) and glass of skim milk
THURS	Homey Oatmeal (p. 236) with blueberries	Small apple and glass of skim milk	Quick and Easy Chicken Noodle Soup (p. 248) and Basic G.I. Salad (p. 255)	Crunchy Chickpeas (p. 300)	Braised Pacific Halibut (p. 278), new or small potatoes and salad	½ nutrition bar
FRI	All-Bran Buds with skim milk, peach slices and sliced almonds	Fruit yogurt	Mixed Bean Salad (p. 261)	Laughing Cow Light cheese with crispbread	Marinated Flank Steak (p. 295), new potatoes, green beans and salad	Mixed berries tossed in lime juice with sour cream
SAT	Smoked Salmon Scrambled Eggs (p. 244)	½ nutrition bar	Greek Salad (p. 257)	Hummus with carrot and celery sticks	Orange Chicken with Almonds (p. 287), green beans and basmati rice	Creamy Raspberry Mousse (p. 307)
SUN	Oatmeal Buttermilk Pancakes with strawberries (p. 239)	Orange and almonds	Caesar Salad (p. 256) with canned tuna	Babybel Gouda Lite cheese with crispbread	Vegetarian Moussaka (p. 274), and basmati rice	Piece of Plum Crumble (p. 310)

Week 9 Grocery List for Meal Plan

PRODUCE
Almonds (whole and sliced)
Apples
Asparagus
Baby spinach
Blueberries (fresh or frozen)
Broccoli
Carrots
Celery
Cranberries (dried)
Cucumbers (English and field)
Eggplant
Fresh herbs (dill, flat-leaf parsley, thyme)
Garlic
Gingerroot
Green beans
Green onions
Kale
Lemons
Lettuce (iceberg, leaf and romaine)
Limes
Onions (yellow and red)
Oranges
Peaches (fresh or canned in juice or water)
Peppers (green, red or yellow)
Potatoes (new, small)
Prune plums (e.g., damson or Italian)
Raisins
Raspberries
Strawberries
Sunflower seeds, shelled and unsalted
Tomatoes (plum)

DELI
Feta cheese (light)
Hummus (light)
Kalamata olives

BAKERY
100% stone-ground whole wheat bread
Crispbread (e.g., Wasa Fibre)
Whole wheat pita bread

FISH COUNTER
Pacific halibut
Smoked salmon

MEAT COUNTER
Chicken breasts (boneless, skinless)
Flank steak

**BEANS (LEGUMES) AND
CANNED VEGETABLES**
Black beans
Chickpeas
Diced tomatoes
Lentils (green)
Mixed beans
Tomato paste

PASTA AND SAUCES
Light tomato sauce (no added sugar)
Rotini or penne (whole wheat)
Small pasta (e.g., ditali or tubetti)

SOUP AND CANNED SEAFOOD AND MEAT
Anchovy fillets
Chicken stock (low-fat, low-sodium)
Tuna (light, in water)

GRAINS AND SIDE DISHES
Basmati rice
Flaxseeds (ground)

INTERNATIONAL FOODS
Soy sauce (low-sodium)
Tahini

COOKING OIL, VINEGAR, SALAD DRESSINGS AND PICKLES
Dijon mustard
Grainy mustard
Mayonnaise (fat-free)
Oil (canola and extra-virgin olive)
Red wine vinegar
Rice vinegar
Vegetable cooking oil spray (canola or olive oil)
Worcestershire sauce

SNACKS
Applesauce (unsweetened)
Nutrition bars (e.g., ZonePerfect, Balance Bar)

BAKING
Amaretto
Baking powder
Baking soda
Cornstarch
Oat bran
Spices (allspice, ground cardamom, Cajun seasoning, ground cinnamon, ground cumin, curry powder, ground ginger, dried oregano, black pepper, red pepper flakes, salt, dried thyme)
Splenda

Vanilla
Wheat bran
Wheat germ
Whole wheat flour

BREAKFAST FOODS
All-Bran Buds or 100% Bran cereal
Oatmeal (large-flake oats)

BEVERAGES
White wine

DAIRY CASE
Babybel Gouda Lite cheese
Buttermilk
Cheddar cheese (low-fat)
Cottage cheese (1%)
Fruit yogurt (non-fat with sweetener)
Laughing Cow Light cheese (extra-low-fat)
Liquid eggs (e.g., Naturegg Break Free)
Milk (skim)
Soft margarine (non-hydrogenated, light)
Sour cream (low-fat)
Whole Omega-3 eggs

FROZEN FOODS
Peas (or fresh)

Week 10

Celebrations:
Holidays and Entertaining

Food and celebrations are inextricably intertwined. Since earliest recorded times, food and drink have been central when people get together for social or celebratory reasons. Whether it's events driven by the calendar—such as Thanksgiving, Christmas, New Year—or family affairs such as anniversaries, birthdays, weddings—all have one thing in common, food and drink—usually lots of it and often the red-light sort! However, it really is not that hard to not only survive, but also enjoy and eat well at these gatherings. So if such occasions are not imminent, the same considerations will apply to having friends over for a summer barbecue.

If you are worried that people will be watching what you eat, always keep some green-light food on your plate, and nibble very slowly. Don't assume the skinny people are having loads of fun—they are probably as worried as or more worried about the food than you! Remember, as you lose weight, people may comment—usually positively. Thank them for the compliment. If they ask, "Have you lost weight?" Just answer, "Yes I have. Thanks for noticing" and move on. No detailed explanations!

Entertaining at Home

When you are entertaining friends or family at a cocktail party or buffet you can control the kind of food that is served. Nibbles and snacks can all be green-light. For example, serve hummus or salsa with raw vegetables and smoked salmon on cucumber. Meats can be lean deli meats with assorted mustards. Make rice salads such as the Waldorf Chicken and Rice Salad on page 262. Put out fruit platters with flavoured yogurt dips. Serve decaf coffee with our homemade Whole Wheat Fruit Scones (see page 304) and fresh berries.

If you are cooking a meal for your family other than the traditional holiday ones mentioned above, try some of the recipes mentioned in Part 4, or check out the *G.I. Cookbook* for more entertaining suggestions.

> Your diet has been a godsend to me! I weighed 196 pounds. My doctor told me I needed to go on high blood pressure medicine. I convinced her to let me try to lower my blood pressure naturally. She gave me two months. Two weeks later I read an article in Woman's World about your diet. I bought food from the sample of the diet in the article. In three days I lost 3 pounds! I knew I had to buy the book. It is now one year later and I weigh 137 pounds, my blood pressure is perfect without medicine and I have lost approximately 40 inches. As an added bonus, people see how good I look and feel and they try it too. At least 20 people have bought your book and tried the G.I. Diet. Most couldn't be happier about the results. I feel so much better; I will never go back to my old bad eating habits. Jeri

The Celebratory Family Dinner

You may be preparing the dinner or attending someone else's. Some of the traditional foods are yellow- or even red-light, but with adjustments you can enjoy many of them.

As an example, we have taken the classic turkey-based dinner normally associated with Thanksgiving and Christmas, but with many components that can be featured any time of the year. This will please even the fussiest relative.

The Classic Turkey Dinner

Soup: If you have soup before the turkey, prepare a stock- or broth-based soup. Use fresh herbs and vegetables to flavour the soup, avoiding cream or butter additions.

The turkey: This is easy. You can prepare a traditional bird and eat the white breast meat—skin off, of course. Make a stuffing using wild or basmati rice, apples or mushrooms, celery, onions and seasoning, leaving out the bread crumbs. Pork loin or even a short leg of lamb, with the fat well trimmed, are other acceptable alternatives.

Cranberry sauce: This can be made from scratch using sucralose (Splenda) to sweeten the cranberries. Add some orange pieces and slivered almonds for a delicious crunch.

Salad: Always serve a large salad with homemade green-light dressing. Try serving this before the main course to help fill you up. Fancy it up with toasted pecans, a sprinkling of dried cranberries or a scattering of crumbled blue cheese. Ruth makes a simple salad using romaine lettuce, sliced strawberries and a raspberry or balsamic vinaigrette. It's very easy and quite pretty.

Sweet potatoes: If sweet potatoes are an essential part of the feast then go ahead, but instead of using brown sugar, orange juice, or maple syrup, try mashing them with some powdered ginger, light non-hydrogenated margarine, pepper and hot water if needed. Or you can try roasted butternut squash with a balsamic vinegar glaze.

Vegetables: For vegetable side dishes make a colourful dish of steamed vegetables that are lightly sautéed in olive oil and seasoning. This can be a very festive holiday dish if you use red and green peppers and snow peas as the main vegetables.

Dessert: No need to feel cheated when it comes to dessert. Dessert can be a crustless apple pie with a crumble topping served with fat-free yogurt cheese sweetened with Splenda or a fat-free flavored yogurt with sweetener. Or use a no-sugar-added ice cream (Breyers or Nestlé's Legend are good choices and taste great too). For an elegant dessert, make a Pavlova with lemon-flavored yogurt cheese and fresh berries.

No one will leave the table feeling hungry! Just remember to fill half of your plate with vegetables, one-quarter with protein and one-quarter with potatoes or rice. Keep portion sizes in line with G.I. Diet requirements and enjoy.

Cocktail and Drinks Parties

It is quite easy to enjoy cocktail parties on the G.I. Diet. Keep a glass in your hand. It can be soda water with a twist of lime; or, if you want alcohol, try one long drink such as a white wine spritzer; or have one glass of red and then switch to soda water. If you don't have something in your hand, someone will pass you a drink you haven't chosen, or your hands will find bowls of food to graze on. Make sure you consume the alcohol with some food to slow the rate at which your body will metabolize it. Try to avoid beer and fancy cocktails, which are caloric nightmares. Look for nibbles that are green-light if possible. Do not station yourself beside the bowls of nuts—they may be green-light but restricting yourself to a small handful may be difficult.

Buffets

Buffets can be heaven or hell: heaven in that you usually have a wide choice of foods, which enables you to make better choices; hell because of all the fancy, calorie-laden temptations laid out before you. How many times have you kept loading your plate as you progress down the line, finding yet another delicious temptation that you just have to try? By the end of the line, you're wishing you had a larger plate and you hadn't included, or at least had taken a smaller serving, of some of your earlier choices.

Start with just a salad. This helps fill you up a little and takes the edge off your appetite. Then take a plate—look for a luncheon and not an enormous dinner plate—and focus on vegetables and lean protein.

For dessert, look for fruit platters only. Give all other desserts a miss unless you are absolutely certain they are green-light. Finish up with a decaf coffee or tea.

E-Clinic Diaries

As the e-clinic did not run during the traditional holiday season, we did not receive any diary feedback on these celebrations. We did however hear about Passover and the experiences of a new bride. Enjoy!

> Well, I was down to 151.8 just a couple of days ago but then family came into town for Passover and I was caught up with a dinner out and food preparations. Even though I stuck with green[-light] foods almost exclusively, no wine, and made a flourless chocolate almond cake without even licking one finger, I think the focus on food had me

eating larger quantities. It's amazing how quickly the weight comes back when it takes so long to get it off. Holiday times are really difficult in that you really don't want to call attention to yourself eating somewhat differently, and the temptations abound. The best way I found is to cook green[-light] for everyone, with just a couple of other choices for folks that you stay away from. The cake was wonderful (I was told) and I wrapped what was left and gave it to my guests to take home. Susan

Well, it's been quite a week. As you know, my wedding was Sunday, but the dinners and celebrations began earlier. I decided I'd suspend the diet for a few days and see where I went with that. Some interesting observations:

(1) My main "suspension" was the wine, to toast our marriage (a number of times) and relax during all the excitement. It wasn't too hard to stay fairly green[-light] in restaurants by ordering salads with dressing served separately and no sides other than veggies. My niece made me a "bachelorette" on Saturday and I asked for the food to be sushi and I had my sashimi.

(2) During the wedding itself, I was too engaged with people and too excited to eat, and ended up having far less than I would have eaten as a guest.

(3) The wedding cake was my other downfall. It was so fantastic and there was a lot left which we served at the brunch as well. When everyone finally took off, I packaged the remaining pieces for my neighbours just to get it out of the house. Both joyful and sorry to see it go.

(4) Tuesday, Bob's clinic made us a celebratory lunch and bought us another cake. It was a small group and they were very proud of the trouble they had gone to for us. I couldn't tell them I didn't want the cake and so I had a small piece. The whole afternoon I felt incredibly fatigued and lethargic. I knew it was from the cake and hated that feeling. It was a good chance to observe my body and say "no way is this worth it" in the future.

(5) Since the wedding I definitely feel my motivation somewhat weakened. There are still great leftovers of high fat cheese, bagels, etc. from the brunch, I'm not seeing that wedding dress as a carrot anymore, and I've gained a pound or two. On the other hand, the week was spectacular and I'm not going to get too down on myself for a pound when I know what I have to do to continue the terrific direction I was going in. (6) Cannot tell you how many people told me I looked like I had lost weight!

[2 days later] Thanks, Rick. I'm happy to say I'm back down to 149.4 lbs, so I guess the wedding weight wasn't permanent. Let's hope the marriage is. Susan

Q: I was out one evening and was served a piece of pineapple upside down cake with a cup of tea. Rather than refuse it I ate it and noticed within a few minutes that I got quite hot and had to take off my sweater and roll up the sleeves of my blouse. Would this have been the sugar or the tea or a combination of both? Joyce

A: Getting overheated—other than from hot flashes—was almost certainly due to the sugar in the cake. There is not sufficient caffeine in tea to make that much difference. Your body has become accustomed to green-light foods, which deliver the sugar slowly and steadily into your bloodstream. A sudden spike in blood sugar as a result of eating a high G.I. food, such as the cake, causes your body to react strongly to this now-unaccustomed stimulus. Your own built-in warning or warming system!

This week we have been discussing celebrations and food, and next week we will be discussing the ultimate celebration, life. And nothing makes more of a contribution to your life than your health. The research evidence grows daily regarding the negative impact on our health from being overweight or obese. Other than quitting smoking, getting your weight under control will do more to add not just years, but active years, to your life than anything else.

Week 10 Weight: _____

Week 10 Waist: _____

Week 10 Hips: _____

Week 10 Diary

_____

_____

_____

_____

_____

_____

_____

_____

_____

_____

Week 10 Optional Meal Plan

	BREAKFAST	SNACK	LUNCH	SNACK	DINNER	SNACK
MON	Homey Oatmeal (p. 236) with chopped apple	Carrot Muffin (p. 302)	Open-face lean deli ham sandwich with lettuce, tomato, red pepper and grainy mustard, and Basic G.I. Salad (p. 255)	Laughing Cow light cheese with crispbread	G.I. Fish Fillet (p. 280) asparagus, carrots and new potatoes	Mixed berries tossed in lime juice with sour cream
TUES	Mini Breakfast Puffs (p. 240)	Fruit yogurt	Vegetable Barley Soup au Pistou (p. 249) with Basic G.I. Salad (p. 255)	Hummus with carrot and celery	Bolognese Pasta Sauce (p. 297) with whole wheat pasta and Basic G.I. Salad (p. 255)	Orange and almonds
WED	Homemade Muesli (p. 237) with skim milk and fruit yogurt	Carrot Muffin (p. 302)	Cottage cheese with apple and grapes, and Basic G.I. Salad (p. 255)	Babybel Gouda Lite cheese with crispbread	Chicken Tarragon with Mushrooms (p. 288), broccoli and basmati rice	Pecan Brownie (p. 315) and glass of skim milk
THURS	Homey Oatmeal (p. 236) with blueberries	Small apple and glass of skim milk	Tuna Salad (p. 260)	Crunchy Chickpeas (p. 300)	Savoury Beans and Apple (p. 268), basmati rice and salad	1/2 nutrition bar
FRI	All-Bran Buds with skim milk, peach slices and sliced almonds	Fruit yogurt	1/2 whole wheat pita with deli turkey, lettuce, tomato and cucumber, and Basic G.I. Salad (p. 255)	Laughing Cow Light cheese with crispbread	Ginger-Wasabi Halibut (p. 281) Cold Noodle Salad with Cucumber and Sesame (p. 258), snow peas and carrots	Creamy Raspberry Mousse (p. 307)
SAT	Breakfast in a Glass (p. 242)	1/2 nutrition bar	Crab Salad in Tomato Shells (p. 263)	Hummus with carrot and celery sticks	Chicken Tikka (p. 283), snow peas, rice or bulgur and salad	Pecan Brownie (p. 315) and glass of skim milk
SUN	Cinnamon French Toast (p. 238), with back bacon	Orange and almonds	Minestrone (p. 246), and Basic G.I. Salad (p. 255)	Babybel Gouda Lite cheese with crispbread	Grilled Portobello Mushroom Pizzas (p. 269), and salad	Slice of Apple Raspberry Coffee Cake (p. 311)

Week 10 Grocery List for Meal Plan

PRODUCE
Almonds (whole and sliced)
Apples
Asparagus
Bananas
Broccoli
Carrots
Celery
Cucumbers (English and field)
Fresh herbs (basil, chives, cilantro, flat-leaf
  parsley, tarragon, thyme)
Garlic
Ginger root
Grapes
Green beans
Leeks
Lemons
Lettuce (leaf and romaine)
Limes
Mushrooms (white and Portobello)
Onions (yellow and red)
Oranges
Peaches (fresh or canned in juice or water)
Pecans
Peppers (green, red or yellow)
Potatoes (new, small)
Raisins
Raspberries
Snow peas
Strawberries
Sunflower seeds, shelled and unsalted
Tomatoes (large beefsteak and plum)
Zucchini

DELI
Feta cheese (light)
Hummus (light)
Lean deli ham
Lean deli turkey
Olives
Parmesan cheese, grated

BAKERY
100% stone-ground whole wheat bread
Crispbread (e.g., Wasa Fibre)
Whole wheat pita bread

FISH COUNTER
Frozen crab
Halibut fillets

MEAT COUNTER
Back bacon
Chicken breasts (boneless, skinless)
Ground beef (extra-lean)

BEANS (LEGUMES) AND CANNED VEGETABLES
Chickpeas
Crushed tomatoes
Kidney beans (red and white)
Tomato paste
Tomato sauce

PASTA AND SAUCES
Capellini or spaghettini (whole wheat)
Fettuccini or linguine (whole wheat)

SOUP AND CANNED SEAFOOD AND MEAT
Anchovy fillets
Chicken stock (low-fat, low-sodium)
Tuna (light, in water)
Vegetable stock (low-fat, low-sodium)

GRAINS AND SIDE DISHES
Barley
Basmati rice
Bulgar
Flaxseeds (whole and ground)

INTERNATIONAL FOODS
Mirin (or sweet sherry)
Rice vinegar
Soy sauce (low-sodium)
Sesame seeds (toasted)
Tahini
Wasabi powder

COOKING OIL, VINEGAR, SALAD DRESSINGS AND PICKLES
Buttermilk salad dressing (low-fat, low-sugar)
Capers
Dijon mustard
Dry mustard
Grainy mustard
Mayonnaise (fat-free)
Oil (canola and extra-virgin olive)
Red wine vinegar
Sherry vinegar
Worcestershire sauce

SNACKS
Nutrition bars (e.g., ZonePerfect, Balance Bar)

BAKING
Amaretto
Baking powder
Baking soda
Brown sugar substitute
Oat bran
Soy lecithin granules
Spices (cayenne pepper, chili powder, ground cinnamon, ground cumin, garam masala, ground ginger, ground nutmeg, dried oregano, black pepper, salt, dried tarragon, dried thyme, turmeric)
Splenda
Unsweetened cocoa powder
Vanilla
Wheat bran
Wheat germ
Whey or soy protein isolate powder
Whole wheat flour

BREAKFAST FOODS
All-Bran Buds cereal
Oatmeal (large-flake oats)

BEVERAGES
Red wine
Tomato juice
Vermouth or white wine

DAIRY CASE
Babybel Gouda Lite cheese
Buttermilk
Cottage cheese (low-fat)
Fruit yogurt (non-fat with sweetener)
Laughing Cow Light cheese (extra-low-fat)
Liquid eggs (e.g., Naturegg, Break Free)
Milk (skim)
Mozzarella cheese (part-skim)
Soft margarine (non-hydrogenated, light)
Sour cream (low-fat)
Soy milk

FROZEN FOODS
Mixed berries
Raspberries

Week 11

What Menopause
Means for Your Health

Unfortunately, menopause heralds the beginning of that stage in our lives when we become increasingly prone to life's major diseases. Heart disease, stroke, hypertension, cancer, diabetes and Alzheimer's are all diseases primarily associated with aging. This is demonstrated by health care expenditures in North America that are four to five times higher for those over 65 years of age. The following Canadian chart indicates this change in spending as we age.

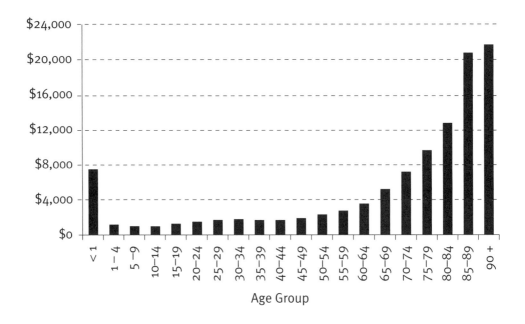

Age Group

Sources: National Health Expenditure Database, CIHI; Population, Statistics Canada, 2005.

The kind of food you choose to eat—and the resulting impact upon your weight—is undoubtedly the single most significant controllable factor in determining whether you are at risk of these killer diseases ("controllable" means those things you can influence, as opposed to factors such as your genes, which you cannot). "You are what you eat" has never been more true.

Menopause is a wake-up call to the realization that if you want to live a longer, active life, you need to eat foods that support your health—not damage it—and help you maintain a healthy weight. Do it both for yourself as well as for your family and friends.

Are You an Apple or Pear?

As you are now aware, there is a strong correlation between obesity and health. What you may not know is that obesity, as traditionally measured by your BMI, is not necessarily the best guide to assessing your health risk. It's where the fat is stored that is the real issue.

The results of a major worldwide survey involving 27,000 people were released recently and showed that people who carried their extra weight around their waists were at far greater risk of serious diseases than those who carried their weight on their hips. Such people are described as "apple shaped," whereas people who carry fat on their hips are called "pear shaped." So it's the apple shaped among us who need to be particularly concerned about their health. This is not to dismiss the relationship between being overweight and therefore at greater risk of disease; but it's a major refinement. From this study came the table below, showing the risk of life-threatening diseases versus weight and waist measurement. (I have included men's measurements because many of you have partners who could also be at risk.)

This information is particularly important for women in their menopausal years when the reduction in estrogen levels results in losing the traditional pear-shaped figure. As we discussed at the outset of the program, your body begins to adopt the traditional male apple shape, which as you can see below, is a major predictor of your health risk.

WEIGHT	BMI	WAIST	WAIST
		Women less than 35" Men less than 40"	Women 35" plus Men 40" plus
Normal	18.0–24.9	No risk increase	No risk increase
Overweight	25.0–29.9	Increased risk	High risk
Obese	30.0–39.9	High risk	Very high risk

So those of you who have a BMI of 30 or more; a waist measurement of 35 inches or more for women puts you in the Very High Risk category for developing diabetes, heart disease, stroke, hypertension (high blood pressure) and certain types of cancer—breast, uterus and colon.

A further refinement is your waist-to-hip ratio. This is measured by dividing your hip measurement into your waist measurement. A healthy ratio for women is 0.85 or below, and 0.95 or below for men. So as a woman, for instance, if your hips measure 48 inches and your waist 44 inches, you waist to hip ratio is 0.92 which puts you firmly at risk. Conversely, if your hips were 48 inches but your waist was reduced to 40 inches, your ratio would be an acceptable 0.83.

This "beer belly" is not just surplus weight, which would be bad enough, but it acts more like a huge tumour in that it boosts hormone levels, which stimulates cell growth, and causes inflammation, leading to clogged arteries. This is not a passive depository of fat; rather, it is a hostile member that is actively undermining your health.

Diabetes

Other than heart disease, stroke, hypertension and cancer, the other principal disease outcome of being overweight is diabetes. Fortunately, the G.I. Diet is extremely effective in managing the causes and symptoms of diabetes by regulating your blood sugar. I have had thousands of diabetics write that they had been able to reduce, or in some cases—with their doctor's supervision and approval—go off their medication entirely. By reducing your weight and better managing your blood sugar levels with your green-light foods, you have every opportunity to reduce your risk of this dreadful disease.

Heart Attack and Stroke

U.S. researchers followed 88,000 healthy women for 24 years to see how their food choices impacted their risk of heart attack and stroke. Those who ate a diet that emphasized fruits, vegetables, whole grains, low-fat milk and plant-based protein rather than meat were 24 percent less likely to have a heart attack and 18 percent less likely to have a stroke than women with more typical U.S. diets.

> I would prefer calling this a lifestyle more than a weight loss diet, though a change in diet is crucial for this lifestyle to be successful. People around me all tell me how much better I look but, even more so, how much healthier, happier, more active and pro-active I actually am. Battling conditions such as PTSD, fibromyalgia, adult acne with severe flare ups ... have become more manageable ... Considering that many women feel that diets don't address the menopausal and post menopausal segment of the population ... I believe that this one does. That this diet does not require [you] to measure everything, go hungry and eat wacky or papery food such as rice cakes ... I am by no means slim at this point but in no way am I discouraged by the amount left to lose or by the time it will take me to lose this ... I don't feel deprived—I feel free. Claire-Anne

Considering some 40 percent of women over the age of 50 will eventually develop some form of heart disease and stroke, these statistics are very significant. For many years, heart attacks were considered to be a man's domain, which still is more often than not the case for men under the age of 50, but after that it becomes a common concern for both men and women.

You will have noted that the diet mentioned above, with its emphasis on fruits, vegetables, whole grains and low-fat milk, pretty well sums up the G.I. Diet. The question of plants—such as soy—rather than meat as the major source of protein is worth noting. Most meats tend to be high in saturated (bad) fats, while protein from plant sources, such as soy, is not. The reality is that most of us are meat eaters, so it is extremely important to ensure you are eating low-fat lean meats such as chicken and fish—in other words, green-light meats—if you are to experience the maximum health benefits.

Cancer

In one of the largest studies to date, British scientists pooled information from 141 studies on 20 different cancers. They found conclusive evidence that obesity was replacing smoking as the number one risk factor for cancer. They demonstrated a depressing series of linkages between being overweight and:

- Thyroid, kidney, esophageal and colon cancers; multiple myeloma; leukemia; and non-Hodgkin lymphoma in both sexes
- Rectal cancer and malignant melanoma in men
- Gallbladder, pancreas, endometrial and postmenopausal breast cancers in women.

Knee and Hip Replacement

Finally, there is the issue of joint degeneration caused by excessive weight. Just recently the Canadian Institute of Health published a survey of knee and hip replacements performed in Canada in 2004/5. The results showed that not only had the number of operations nearly doubled over the past 10 years, but also that overweight and obese patients accounted for a startling 87 percent of knee replacements and 74 percent of hips. Some 54 percent of the knee replacement patients were obese though this group accounts for only 23 percent of the population. Interestingly 60 percent of patients were women whose smaller bone structure makes them more vulnerable to extra weight stress. The United States has recorded similar figures with a 48 percent increase in hip and 63 percent increase in knee operations between 1997 and 2004.

So if you want to reduce your risk of experiencing these leading killer diseases—heart disease, stroke, diabetes, hypertension and cancer—and keep your joints intact—then stay with the program. I can't think of a better motivator.

Sleep and Menopause

A common experience amongst menopausal women is a lack of sleep usually caused by hot flashes. Sleep apnea, when breathing becomes shallow or irregular and is often accompanied by snoring, is frequently seen as a male problem. Unfortunately, menopausal and post-menopausal women also become susceptible to sleep apnea. As a result, overweight women in particular find it hard to get a good night's sleep because they're coping with both hot flashes and sleep apnea.

The reason I raise this frustrating issue is that sleep deprivation causes weight gain. So a good night's sleep is important in our weight-loss journey. If hot flashes and/or sleep apnea are seriously interfering with your sleep patterns, then I strongly suggest you see your doctor and ask for advice. While there are many contributors to hot flashes and sleeplessness, it is clear that excessive weight is certainly one that you can do something about.

E-Clinic Diaries

Over the past weeks we received a great deal of positive comment about improvements in members' health, particularly menopause symptoms and diabetes. Here are three typical diary entries:

> This week on the road, I had my biggest help from two colleagues who are also on weight loss programs—one because she was borderline diabetic and the other because I introduced her to the G.I. Diet—so we were doing great snacks and smart lunches together. I have also been running and eating smaller portions as you suggested ... and the results have been amazing to me this week—I am pretty thrilled with the way things are going. Louise

> I also notice a big difference in my hot flashes. Usually I get up two to three times a night due to my night sweats but this past week has been excellent for me. At the beginning of the week I woke up only once a night, but the last two nights I went to bed and slept like a baby (I couldn't believe it!). I still get the hot flashes during the day which I seem to be able to handle more so than those night sweats. There is nothing worse than not being able to have a good night's sleep especially since I was the person who as soon as my head hit the pillow I was out like a light. Rita

> My visit to the doctor this week was exceptional. All my tests came back perfect (cholesterol, blood pressure, sugar). She was really excited about my weight loss and if I continued on she would start decreasing my medicines. She is the one that got me on to your book and she couldn't believe I was doing this clinic with you. I think she was more excited about that. She is definitely one of your fans. Linda

Though exercise is not everyone's favourite topic and has limited value in helping you lose weight, we will show in next week's letter how important it is to your long-term health and weight maintainance.

Week 11 Weight: _____

Week 11 Waist: _____

Week 11 Hips: _____

Week 11 Diary

_____

_____

_____

_____

_____

_____

_____

_____

_____

_____

Week 11 Optional Meal Plan

	BREAKFAST	SNACK	LUNCH	SNACK	DINNER	SNACK
MON	Homey Oatmeal (p. 236) with chopped apple	Apple Bran Muffin (p. 303)	Open-face chicken sandwich with lettuce, tomato and onion, and Basic G.I. Salad (p. 255)	Laughing Cow Light cheese with crispbread	Lemony Grilled Vegetable Pasta Salad (p. 253) with canned tuna or salmon	Mixed berries tossed in lime juice with sour cream
TUES	Mini Breakfast Puffs (p. 240)	Fruit yogurt	Tuscan White Bean Soup (p. 247) with Basic G.I. Salad (p. 255)	Hummus with carrot and celery sticks	Spicy Roasted Chicken with Tomatoes and Tarragon (p. 289), green beans and basmati rice	Orange and almonds
WED	Homemade Muesli (p. 237) with skim milk and fruit yogurt	Apple Bran Muffin (p. 303)	1/2 whole wheat pita with canned light tuna, lettuce, tomato and cucumber, and Basic G.I. Salad (p. 255)	Babybel Gouda Lite cheese with crispbread	Pork Medallions Dijon (p. 298), green beans, carrots and new potatoes	Creamy Lemon Square (p. 316) and glass of skim milk
THURS	Homey Oatmeal (p. 236) with blueberries	Small apple and glass of skim milk	Quick and Easy Chicken Noodle Soup (p. 248) and Basic G.I. Salad (p. 255)	Crunchy Chickpeas (p. 300)	Quinoa, Bean and Vegetable Chili (p. 270), and Basic G.I. Salad (p. 255)	1/2 nutrition bar
FRI	All-Bran Buds with skim milk, peach slices and sliced almonds	Fruit yogurt	Waldorf Chicken and Rice Salad (p. 262)	Laughing Cow Light cheese with crispbread	Thai Red Curry Shrimp Pasta (p. 279)	Mixed berries tossed in lime juice with sour cream
SAT	Vegetarian Omelette (p. 243)	1/2 nutrition bar	Greek Salad (p. 257)	Hummus with carrot and celery sticks	Zesty Barbecued Chicken (p. 290),	Creamy Lemon Square (p. 316) and glass of skim milk
SUN	Oatmeal Buttermilk Pancakes (p. 239) with strawberries	Orange and almonds	Tuna Salad (p. 260)	Babybel Gouda Lite cheese with crispbread	Blueberry Beef Burgers (p. 296) broccoli and cauliflower tossed in lemon	Piece of Berry Crumble (p. 309)

Week 11 Grocery List for Meal Plan

PRODUCE
Almonds (ground, sliced and whole)
Apples
Blueberries (fresh or frozen)
Broccoli
Brussels sprouts
Cabbage (green and red)
Carrots
Cauliflower
Celery
Cucumbers
Eggplant
Fresh herbs (chives, cilantro, mint, tarragon)
Hot pepper
Garlic
Green beans
Green onions
Kale
Leeks
Lemons
Lettuce (leaf and romaine)
Limes
Mushrooms (white and shiitake)
Onions (yellow and red)
Oranges
Peaches (fresh or canned in juice or water)
Pecans
Peppers (green, red or yellow)
Potatoes (new, small)
Raisins
Shallots
Strawberries
Sunflower seeds, shelled and unsalted
Tomatoes (cherry and plum)
Walnuts
Zucchini

DELI
Feta cheese (light)
Hummus (light)
Kalamata olives

BAKERY
100% stone-ground whole wheat bread
Crispbread (e.g., Wasa Fibre)

FISH COUNTER
Shrimp (large raw)

MEAT COUNTER
Chicken breasts (boneless, skinless)
Ground beef (extra-lean)
Lean ground chicken or turkey
Pork tenderloin

BEANS (LEGUMES) AND CANNED VEGETABLES
Black beans
Chickpeas
Kidney beans (red and white)
Diced tomatoes
Pinto beans
Stewed tomatoes
Tomato paste

PASTA AND SAUCES
Penne or rotini (whole wheat)
Macaroni or small shells (whole wheat)
Spagettini or linguine (whole wheat)
Small pasta (e.g., ditali or tubetti)
Light tomato sauce

SOUP AND CANNED SEAFOOD AND MEAT
Chicken stock (low-fat, low-sodium)
Tuna (light, in water)
Vegetable stock (low-fat, low-sodium)

GRAINS AND SIDE DISHES
Barley
Basmati rice
Flaxseed (ground)
Quinoa

INTERNATIONAL FOODS
Thai red curry paste

COOKING OIL, VINEGAR, SALAD DRESSINGS AND PICKLES
Balsamic vinegar
Buttermilk salad dressing (low-fat, low-sugar)
Capers
Cider vinegar
Dijon mustard
Oil (canola and extra-virgin olive)
Red wine vinegar
Worcestershire sauce

SNACKS
Nutrition bars (e.g., ZonePerfect, Balance Bar)

BAKING
Baking powder
Baking soda
Cornstarch
Oat bran
Spices (ground allspice, cayenne
   pepper, chili powder, ground cinnamon,
   ground cloves, ground cumin, dried
   oregano, Hungarian paprika, black
   pepper, salt)
Splenda
Vanilla

Wheat bran
Wheat germ
Whole wheat flour
Unsweetened cocoa powder

BREAKFAST FOODS
All-Bran Buds cereal
Oatmeal (large-flake oats)

BEVERAGES
Apple juice (unsweetened)
Dry white wine (or vermouth)

DAIRY CASE
Babybel Gouda Lite cheese
Buttermilk
Cheddar cheese (low-fat)
Fruit yogurt (non-fat with sweetener)
Laughing Cow Light cheese
Liquid eggs (e.g., Naturegg, Break Free)
Milk (skim)
Orange juice (unsweetened)
Soft margarine (non-hydrogenated, light)
Sour cream (low-fat)
Whole omega-3 eggs

FROZEN FOODS
Apple juice concentrate
Mixed berries
Peas (or fresh)

Week 12

Getting Active

At the beginning of this program, I suggested that weight loss was 90 percent diet and 10 percent exercise, even though exercise is essential for weight maintenance and a healthy lifestyle.

To recap, there are two principal reasons that exercise is not as efficient as diet when you are trying to lose weight. First, it requires a huge amount of effort to burn off those pounds. For example, simply to lose just one pound of fat, a 160 lb person would have to walk briskly for 42 miles/67 km or bike 79 miles/127 km! This is something that not many of you are likely to do, even if you physically could.

A recent issue of *Nutrition Action* magazine reported how much exercise effort is required for a 150 lb person to burn off the calories in some popular foods:

One doughnut = 20 minutes on a stair machine
One muffin = 50 minutes jogging
One slice cheesecake = 2 hours and 40 minutes of brisk walking
One slice of cheese pizza = 1 hour playing tennis
One café mocha = 40 minutes continuous lap swimming

Food for thought, if you'll pardon the pun!

I'm sure many of you have tried a treadmill or exercise bike at some time and have been amazed at how much effort it takes to burn off even 200 calories. And as you can see, you can blow that and more with just a latte on the way home from the gym.

As one pound of fat contains 3,600 calories, you can see why taking the dog for a walk around the block or washing the car has little or no impact on losing weight. Obviously any exercise is better than none, as it all helps to burn extra calories. Just don't expect it to have any significant impact during the weight-loss phase.

The second reason I recommended diet rather than exercise during the weight-loss period was the difficulty obese people—those with a BMI of 30 and over—experience when moving. Quite frankly, I am astonished that many of the Big People I have met can actually support their weight. The stress on joints and back carrying an additional 80–100 pounds or more is absolutely enormous.

My husband and I had been talking about how we did not like the way we looked and felt and this diet looked like something we could do. We bought the book, started following the guidelines of the "diet" and by the end of November of that same year my husband had [gone] from a 36 waist to a 32 (at age 67) and I had gone from wearing nearly a 14 to a size 4/6 ... We look at food value in a new prospective. G.I. is just the way we eat. If anyone out there gave it a try they would find that after the first few weeks it is no longer a diet, it is just a sensible way to eat ... You will feel better as well as look better. Jana

Most people couldn't even lift that weight, yet alone carry it around all the time. This puts a serious limitation on what overweight people can do to exercise, even if they wanted to.

However, as we are now twelve weeks into the program and many of you have lost sufficient weight, this is the time to consider getting more active. The upside of exercise is that, *over the long term,* it can help you maintain or accelerate your weight loss, as well as contribute significantly to your health, by reducing your risk of heart disease, stroke, diabetes and osteoporosis. Exercise will also help maintain your muscle mass and tone.

Exercise should become an important consideration particularly for those of you moving from being "obese" to "overweight." Most of you are now better able to exercise as you have less weight to carry around, and you should also be experiencing an increase in your energy levels.

Menopause and Exercise

One of the contributors to weight gain during menopause is a general reduction in our level of activity. All the activities associated with the raising of children are past and the pace of life for most has slowed. The accumulation of extra pounds, frequently stemming from pregnancy weight gain, compounded by the onset of menopause, only further reduces the incentive to get off our butts and be active again.

Those of you who decide to do something are frequently lured by the siren song of fitness clubs that promise a dream body if only you'll sign up. Disappointment is the usual outcome. A principle reason for the very high membership turnover in fitness clubs is their failure to deliver on their promises. Those clubs that emphasize diet as a core component of their program are usually the ones that are more successful.

Now you have your diet under control, have fewer pounds to carry around and have more energy, it is time to consider getting more active.

The simplest activity is walking. This doesn't require any special equipment or gym membership, and can be done at virtually any time of the day or year. If you still find it difficult to walk any distance, then a stationary bike is a good investment. The reclining-position bikes are probably easier on your joints as your weight load is spread over a greater area. These are relatively inexpensive and available through many large retail chains such as Wal-Mart or Canadian Tire. Otherwise, join a gym and use the heavy-duty equipment, particularly if your BMI is 30 plus.

My best advice is to incorporate exercise into your daily routine. The easiest way to do this is to follow my "Two Stops Short" program. Simply get off the bus, streetcar, or subway two stops short of the office or workplace, and walk. The same in reverse, coming home. If driving, park the car a few blocks away (1/2 mile/1 km) from the office and walk. Who knows, the parking may be cheaper! This investment of an extra 10 minutes a day each way will certainly pay dividends for your weight and health.

I used to do this and found that far from being a drag or inconvenience, I actually looked forward to my "Two Stops Short" walk each day. It helped get me going in the morning and time to reflect on my day with no phones or people crowding me. In the evening, it was a chance to wind down and relax. It requires some effort for the first week but quickly became routine for my last three years at the Heart and Stroke Foundation. Try it and let me know how it goes.

In summary then, exercise is of more limited value during the relatively short time period when you are actually losing weight. It is, however, a critical factor in maintaining your weight and health for the rest of your life. Believe it or not, exercise can become addictive and I know that I become irritable and edgy if I'm not getting my daily exercise fix—or so Ruth tells me!

Though I have focused on aerobic exercise, the sort of exercise that increases your heart rate, there are some several other important considerations regarding exercise. The most important of these are resistance exercises, which are aimed at strengthening your muscles.

Menopause and Muscle Mass

An insidious and silent change that takes place as we age is the loss or thinning of muscle mass. This is a process that starts in our twenties, and by the time women are fifty, they have lost around 15 percent of their muscle mass. During and post-menopause, the rate of muscle loss escalates quickly. This is due to the decrease in hormone levels and women's increasing inability to convert protein into muscle. Men apparently are able to continue processing protein into muscle, unfair as that might seem.

So why does this loss of muscle mass matter? First, you risk becoming frail as you lack muscle to move and stabilize your body. Without strong muscles in legs and hips, women are at significant risk of a debilitating fall and broken bones or worse. In a recent research report on aging and muscle loss, it was reported "if a woman over the age of 65 has a fall, she has a 50 percent chance of being dead in two years," and that's a frightening statistic.

Second, less muscle means a low metabolic rate. Muscles are the principal consumer of your body's energy (calories); so the less muscle, the fewer calories you burn—and we all know where those surplus calories go. Fat replaces muscle and fat, conversely, burns few calories.

However, all is not lost. There are a couple of things you can do to help offset this decline and raise your metabolic rate.

The first is to make sure you are getting adequate protein in your diet. The best sources of lean protein are chicken/turkey (skinless), fish, eggs (liquid), lean meats, low-fat dairy, soy and legumes (beans). Ideally every snack and certainly every meal should have some protein content. A further benefit of protein is that it slows digestion and therefore effectively lowers the G.I. of the meal.

The second offset is exercise. I do not mean aerobic exercise but, rather, resistance exercises. This is where muscles work against some form of resistance; weights and elastic bands are the two most popular. These are the only resistance exercises that build muscle mass. I'm sure most of you associate weights with an image of over-muscled men sweating and grunting with giant barbells. Don't panic, the reality is far less daunting—even a can of soup can act as a weight.

I don't propose to detail an exact program here, as everyone's needs and budgets are different. Rather, I recommend going to the U.S. Government Center for Disease Control and Prevention site www.CDC.gov/physicalactivity and click on "Growing stronger—Strength Training for Older Adults"; and on that page click "Exercises." This is an excellent site that demonstrates how to do various exercises—and it's free!

Boosting your protein intake and adding a few minutes of simple resistance exercises three times a week will go a long way to stabilizing your muscle loss and, if you are diligent, actually rebuilding some of that loss. You will be less frail and less prone to falling, as well as able to consume more calories. Remember, muscles consume calories even when they are at rest and even when sleeping.

On a personal note, to give you some encouragement about staying slim and active, my ninety-eight-year-old mother who still lives alone in a two-storey house, has always been active to the extent that she sometimes trips over her own feet in her haste to get from A to B. This has resulted in two hip replacements as well as two broken arms in the last five years! However, undeterred, she is still mobile and climbs up to her bedroom every evening, one hand on the stair rail and the other clutching her hot toddy!

E-Clinic Diaries

Last year I underwent a knee replacement and I have really missed my aerobic type activity and can assume that some of my weight gain has been due to the new levels of inactivity. I can't go back to Curves as a lot of the equipment is impossible for me as I don't have the ability to bend my new knee enough. So I just got myself an aerobics video and started the program this week. It focuses on the core with a lot of abdominal tightening. I am using the beginner level and doing the low impact version due to my knee ... I am enjoying it and it makes me feel good. I even find it increases my energy levels. Lynn

They talk about athletes getting high on running, well do you know what it feels like to be two months shy of being 60 years old and keeping up or doing better than, 20, 30 and 40 year olds? That is a high for me. AND NO HOT FLASHES WHILE DOING IT and no aches and pains. The next day [I had] only slight twinges while others were moaning and groaning. Boy it felt good. Linda

Only a one pound loss this week, but slow and steady wins the race. Two years ago for my 50th birthday, I decided to join the gym figuring I would lose weight easily without having to change my eating habits. After a year of exercising regularly I saw very little progress. Certainly, I was a bit more toned than before, but my weight hadn't changed. I started to pay more attention to what I ate and lost 14 pounds, but the holidays came along and some of the pounds crept back on. Your program came at a very good time for me. I was startled when early on you indicated that losing weight is 90 percent diet and 10 percent exercise ... I plan to continue with my exercise regime, but I'll always keep that ratio in mind. Gone are the days when I can eat whatever I want and not gain weight. Your plan is a sound, easy to follow plan that allows one to eat good nutritious food without starving or feeling deprived. Jacinthe

Q: Although my weight is coming down, it is disheartening to see the waist measurement move so slowly. Like 15 pounds and only 3.5 inches. The weight is only a number, and nobody has ever guessed it correctly because except for my belly I carry it well. But the belly is what it is—unattractive and unhealthy. I wish there was a way my 15 pound loss was targeted right to my middle! Lynn

A: Unfortunately it's a myth that we can "spot" remove our weight problems. That said, you might want to think about tightening up those tummy muscles. Check out the U.S. Government Center for Disease Control and Prevention website that I've mentioned for exercises that will help.

Well that's been quite a journey! Some of you will have reached your weight-loss goals or are getting close. Others will be well on their way but are confident they can now stay the course. Either way, next week we will review the top nine lessons from the 13-week e-clinic that will help you stay with the program and make it a permanent part of your new lifestyle.

Week 12 Weight:_____

Week 12 Waist:_____

Week 12 Hips:_____

Week 12 Diary

_____

_____

_____

Week 12 Optional Meal Plan

	BREAKFAST	SNACK	LUNCH	SNACK	DINNER	SNACK
MON	Homey Oatmeal (p. 236) with chopped apple	Whole Wheat Fruit Scone (p. 304)	Open-face lean deli ham sandwich with lettuce, tomato, red pepper and grainy mustard, and Basic G.I. Salad (p. 255)	Laughing Cow Light cheese with crispbread	Fettucine Primavera (p. 273) and Caesar Salad (p. 256)	Mixed berries tossed in lime juice with sour cream
TUES	Mini Breakfast Puffs (p. 240)	Fruit yogurt	Waldorf Chicken and Rice Salad (p. 262)	Hummus with carrot and celery sticks	Tomato and Cheese Catfish (p. 277), serve with leftover Fettuccini Primavera	Orange and almonds
WED	Homemade Muesli (p. 237) with skim milk and fruit yogurt	Whole Wheat Fruit Scone (p. 304)	Cottage cheese with apple and grapes, and Basic G.I. Salad (p. 255)	Babybel Gouda Lite cheese with crispbread	Chicken Schnitzel (p. 286), green beans, carrots and new potatoes	Slice of Strawberry Tea Bread (p. 305) and glass of skim milk
THURS	Homey Oatmeal (p. 236) with blueberries	Small apple and glass of skim milk	Minestrone Soup and Basic G.I. Salad (p. 255)	Crunchy Chickpeas (p. 300)	Meatloaf (p. 294), green beans, carrots and new potatoes	$1/2$ nutrition bar
FRI	All-Bran Buds with skim milk, peach slices and sliced almonds	Fruit yogurt	$1/2$ whole wheat pita with deli turkey, lettuce, tomato and cucumber, and Basic G.I. Salad (p. 255)	Laughing Cow Light cheese with crispbread	Indian Vegetable Curry (p. 291) and Basic G.I. Salad (p. 255)	Fancy Fruit Salad (p. 308)
SAT	Smoked Salmon Scrambled Eggs (p. 244)	$1/2$ nutrition bar	Vegetable Barley Soup au Pistou (p. 249) with Basic G.I. Salad (p. 255)	Hummus with carrot and celery sticks	Roasted Pork Tenderloin with Balsamic Glaze and Gingered Peach Salsa (p. 293) new potatoes, asparagus and Basic G.I. Salad (p. 255)	Slice of Strawberry Tea Bread (p. 305) and glass of skim milk
SUN	Cinnamon French Toast (p. 238) with back bacon	Orange and almonds	Grilled Shrimp and Pear Salad (p. 264)	Babybel Gouda Lite cheese with crispbread	Chicken Stir-Fry with Broccoli (p. 284) and Basic G.I. Salad	Slice of One-Bowl Chocolate Cake (p. 313) with berries

Week 12 Grocery List for Meal Plan

PRODUCE
Almonds (whole and sliced)
Apples
Asparagus
Baby spinach
Bean sprouts
Blackberries
Blueberries (fresh or frozen)
Broccoli
Carrots
Cashews
Celery
Chili pepper
Cucumbers
Dried apricots
Fresh herbs (basil, chives, cilantro, oregano,
   flat-leaf parsley, mint, thyme)
Garlic
Ginger root
Grapes
Green beans
Green onions
Hot pepper
Kiwis
Leeks
Lemons
Lettuce (leaf and Romaine)
Limes
Mushrooms
Onions (red, yellow and Vidalia)
Oranges
Peaches (fresh or canned in juice or water)
Pears
Peppers (green, red and yellow)
Potatoes (new, small)
Strawberries
Sunflower seeds, shelled and unsalted
Tomatoes (large beefsteak and plum)

Walnuts
Zucchini

DELI
Hummus (light)
Lean deli ham
Lean deli turkey
Parmesan cheese, grated

BAKERY
100% stone-ground whole wheat bread
Crispbread (e.g., Wasa Fibre)
Whole wheat breadcrumbs
Whole wheat hamburger buns
Whole wheat pita bread

FISH COUNTER
Catfish fillets
Frozen crab
Shrimp (large raw)
Smoked salmon

MEAT COUNTER
Back bacon
Chicken breasts (boneless, skinless)
Ground beef (extra-lean)
Pork tenderloin

BEANS (LEGUMES) AND CANNED VEGETABLES
Chickpeas
Kidney beans (red)
Plum tomatoes
Tomato paste

PASTA AND SAUCES
Small pasta (e.g., ditali or tubetti)

SOUP AND CANNED SEAFOOD AND MEAT
Anchovy fillets
Chicken stock (low-fat, low-sodium)
Vegetable stock (low-fat, low-sodium)

GRAINS AND SIDE DISHES
Barley
Basmati rice

INTERNATIONAL FOODS
Hoisin sauce
Mild curry paste
Oyster sauce
Rice vinegar
Soy sauce
Tahini

COOKING OIL, VINEGAR, SALAD DRESSINGS AND PICKLES
Balsamic vinegar
Buttermilk salad dressing (low-fat, low-sugar)
Dijon mustard
Grainy mustard
Oil (canola, extra-virgin olive, and sesame)
Red wine vinegar
Worcestershire sauce

SNACKS
Applesauce (unsweetened)
Nutrition bars (e.g., ZonePerfect, Balance Bar)

BAKING
Baking powder
Baking soda
Honey
Oat bran
Spices (cayenne, chili powder, ground cinnamon,
   cumin seeds, ground nutmeg, dried oregano,
   black pepper, red pepper flakes, salt)
Splenda

Vanilla
Wheat bran
Wheat germ
Whole wheat flour

BREAKFAST FOODS
All-Bran Buds cereal
Oatmeal (large-flake oats)

BEVERAGES
Tomato juice

DAIRY CASE
Cottage cheese (low-fat)
Babybel Gouda Lite cheese
Buttermilk
Cheddar cheese (low-fat)
Fruit yogurt (non-fat with sweetener)
Laughing Cow Light cheese
Liquid eggs (e.g., Naturegg, Break Free)
Milk (skim)
Sour cream (low-fat)
Whole omega-3 eggs

FROZEN FOODS
Mixed berries

Week 13

Nine Rules for Success

It's useful to review some of the key lessons that we have learnt over the past thirteen weeks, especially as they are the essential building blocks to your future success. I hope you've enjoyed the last thirteen weeks and are feeling healthier, happier and lighter!

Green-Light Pantry

Clearing red-light foods out of the house and restocking with green-light foods is the single most important step in the program. If those red-light foods aren't there, you won't be tempted. I expect many of you, even after three months, still have those red-light foods around. These are the foods responsible for your weight problem and are poisoning your health. Get them out of your home; they are not your friends.

Portions

Portion distortion, or the doubling or even trebling of portion servings over the past 20 years, is one of the principal reasons you have been putting on the pounds. A simple tip is to substitute a lunch-size plate for the dinner plate and remember the plate should always be 1/2 vegetables (at least 2); 1/4 protein (meat, fish, tofu); and 1/4 rice/potato/pasta. Otherwise use moderation and common sense in your portions. Judging from the results to date, you seem to be doing just that.

Snacks

Snacks are critical to the diet as they keep your tummy busy and stop you from going hungry between meals. Make sure that those snacks are green-light (see Week 3).

Always keep in the fridge a plate of sliced vegetables, such as baby carrots, celery, sliced peppers, broccoli florets, along with a tasty hummus dip. This is a staple in our house and our boys now prefer that to their traditional bag of chips.

Dining Out

Whether it's lunch or evening dining out, you lose some control over what you eat (see Week 7). You are also exposed to greater temptation or choices than at home. However, I've given you the tools to make the right choices, even at McDonald's! Don't be afraid of being assertive. Take control. It's your waistline, your health and your buck. You'll be pleasantly surprised at how cooperative most restaurants will be to reasonable requests. This also may be a chance to show your friends that you are now successfully taking charge of your life.

Emotional Eating

Remember that the original reasons for overeating or using food for comfort may have had origins in our childhood but overeating, negative body image and low self-esteem are the current consequence. And these early psychologically-inspired eating behaviours can become eating habits. We eat not only when hungry but also when tired, bored, frustrated, stressed, sad, angry etc. Stay conscious of your eating habits. Try changing one habit at a time. Work on changing another food-related habit once you feel the first one is under control. Reward yourself with a non-food reward for every successful shift in habits (see Week 6).

Social Occasions

This is clearly a difficult challenge for most of you. You don't want to make yourself stand out by eating differently from others and you're concerned that people will see you setting yourself up for failure, again. By now, all of you have shown a commitment and a determination to stay the course to reach your target weight. You are now setting yourself up for success, not failure. Most of you have now lost sufficient weight that the results are beginning to show. No need to hide your success. Share it with your friends. You may be surprised at how supportive they will be when they see the results and realize your determination to succeed.

Falling off the Wagon

This will happen but it's not the end of the world. The G.I. Diet is not a straitjacket and shooting for 90 percent compliance is quite acceptable. Should the fall be a hard one, then you have the tools and knowledge to get back on. Remember the shopping bag motivator/water bottles (Week 9), which I hope you are keeping alongside your scales. It really works. If you haven't done so already, get a friend—

or partner—to either join you in losing weight or to be your cheerleader. A friend like this can be a great help in those difficult moments.

Exercise

Most of you by now have lost sufficient weight that exercise is starting to become a realistic option (see Week 12). As nearly everyone has let me know that they have experienced an increase in their energy levels—this is because your blood sugar levels have stabilized, and you have fewer pounds to carry around—you can now get off the couch and start exercising. Walking is the most realistic option for most. Start slowly and gradually increase distance and speed. Although it won't contribute greatly to your weight loss, it will help maintain it, make you feel good, and start a healthy habit. Also adding some resistance exercises will help you maintain your muscle mass, which starts declining significantly in your menopause years. Exercise, of course, is essential for your long-term health.

Family and Friends

Family and friends can either be your biggest asset—or your worst nightmare. Either way, they will have a major impact on your success. As most menopausal and post-menopausal women are empty nesters, it's usually your spouse or partner who is your most immediate familial influence. Ensuring your spouse or partner is your principal cheerleader will help immeasurably. Friends, including co-workers, should be co-opted to actively help you achieve your goals even if it sometimes means finding out who your real friends are. I realize that fear of failure is a concern when going public with your plans, but the risk is small and the rewards substantial.

Since this was the final week of the e-clinic program, most diary entries from this week reflected this. Considering the importance of what the members reported, we decided to devote the next chapter to their results and responses rather than report them here. But to end the program on a high note, I have chosen to include a longer than usual "Motivational Minute" that should give you a chuckle—and more inspiration should you need it!

OK Gallop! You've done it now! You and your damn education and teaching me about this—what do you call it—Glycemic Index! You, sir, are expensive! For the last 20 years or so I've had clothes—lots of 'em—that fit me on my ups and downs of dieting (every weight you could imagine) between 260 lbs. and 360 lbs. As a salesman/business owner I had closets full of "Big & Tall" stuff and tailor made suits and shirts. I was croaking because of obesity but at least I had clothes that fit. Now!!! Almost 2 years later, after getting your damn book, I'm down to 245 lbs,(from 345 lbs.) have given away all my shirts and T-shirts, dress shirts, suits, jackets, etc.—the whole works (more than 70 shirts of various sizes alone!) The Salvation Army outlet store thinks I'm a bloody clothes wholesaler and the surrounding clothing stores that sell "regular extra large clothes" where I now shop think several new families have moved in. I think the local "Big & Tall" store may have to close.

I have an annual medical, and now my Doctor phones my house when I'm in her office because she thinks I'm sending my less obese brother in to do my medicals! Who knew that blood pressure of 120 over 80, or whatever, was good? Hell, my numbers for this used to be around my weight!

You've ruined my wardrobe, you've ruined the trust of my Doctor, and now it looks like my wife may be the next to go. She thinks she's got a new man in her life that looks and acts like I used to 20 years ago and keeps suggesting we have little "naps" during the day. Wow—I'm getting tired of this—after all, a guy of 71 SHOULD be able to take it easy.

Tongue out of cheek for a moment, Rick. What a fantastic change in lifestyle—please don't ever call it a diet again! I'm on my way to 200 lbs. over the next year or so and haven't felt this good for many, many years. My wife's encouragement and under-the-table kicks when we're out for dinner have helped us both to just change *what* we eat. It's simply an easy lifestyle change of eating habits that you can stick with. Oh, by the way, my wife (Joann) lost 26 lbs. also—looks (and acts) fantastic.

We can't thank you enough.

Mike and Joann

P.S. Please send money for my new wardrobe, but save some for my next letter's arrival next year. I'll need more for the next 20 or 30 lb. weight loss.

Week 13 Weight: _____

Week 13 Waist: _____

Week 13 Hips: _____

Week 13 Diary

_____

_____

_____

_____

_____

_____

_____

_____

_____

_____

_____

_____

_____

Week 13 Optional Meal Plan

Note: You are *not* required to use these weekly meal plans and shopping lists.
Feel free to pick and choose and make up your own green-light meals.

	BREAKFAST	SNACK	LUNCH	SNACK	DINNER	SNACK
MON	Homey Oatmeal (p. 236) with chopped apple	Cranberry Cinnamon Bran Muffin (p. 301)	Open face chicken sandwich with with lettuce, tomato and onion, and Basic G.I. Salad (p. 255)	Laughing Cow Light cheese with crispbread	Lemon Linguine with Smoked Salmon (p. 266), broccoli and salad	Mixed berries tossed in lime juice with sour cream
TUES	Mini Breakfast Puffs (p. 240)	Fruit yogurt	G.I. Pasta Salad (p. 259)	Hummus with carrot and celery sticks	Cheesy Lentil and Bean Bake (p. 267), basmati rice and salad	Orange and almonds
WED	Homemade Muesli (p. 237) with skim milk and fruit yogurt	Cranberry Cinnamon Bran Muffin (p. 301)	1/2 whole wheat pita with canned light tuna, lettuce, tomato and cucumber, and Basic G.I. Salad (p. 255)	Babybel Gouda Lite cheese with crispbread	Chicken Curry (p. 285) and Raita Salad (p. 252)	Cran-Apple Oatmeal Bars (p. 314) and glass of skim milk
THURS	Homey Oatmeal (p. 236) with blueberries	Small apple and glass of skim milk	Quick and Easy Chicken Noodle Soup (p. 248) and Basic G.I. Salad (p. 255)	Crunchy Chickpeas (p. 300)	Braised Pacific Halibut (p. 278), new or small-potatoes and salad	1/2 nutrition bar
FRI	All-Bran Buds with skim milk, peach slices and sliced almonds	Fruit yogurt	Mixed Bean Salad (p. 261)	Laughing Cow Light cheese with crispbread	Marinated Flank Steak (p. 295), new potatoes, green beans and salad	Mixed berries tossed in lime juice with sour cream
SAT	Smoked Salmon Scrambled Eggs (p. 244)	1/2 nutrition bar	Greek Salad (p. 257)	Hummus with carrot and celery sticks	Orange Chicken with Almonds (p. 287), green beans and basmati rice	Creamy Raspberry Mousse (p. 307)
SUN	Oatmeal Buttermilk Pancakes with strawberries (p. 329)	Orange and almonds	Caesar Salad (p. 256) with canned tuna	Babybel Gouda Lite cheese with crispbread	Vegetarian Moussaka (p. 274), and basmati rice	Piece of Plum Crumble (p. 310)

Week 13 Grocery List for Meal Plan

PRODUCE
Almonds (whole and sliced)
Apples
Asparagus
Baby spinach
Peppers (green, red or yellow)
Blueberries (fresh or frozen)
Broccoli
Carrots
Celery
Cranberries (dried)
Cucumbers (English and field)
Eggplant
Fresh herbs (dill, flat-leaf parsley, thyme)
Garlic
Ginger root
Green beans
Green onions
Kale
Lemons
Lettuce (iceberg, leaf and romaine)
Limes
Onions (yellow and red)
Oranges
Peaches (fresh or canned in juice or water)
Peppers (green, red or yellow)
Potatoes (new, small)
Prune plums (e.g., damson or Italian)
Raisins
Raspberries
Strawberries
Sunflower seeds, shelled and unsalted
Tomatoes (plum)

DELI
Feta cheese (light)
Hummus (light)
Kalamata olives

BAKERY
100% stone-ground whole wheat bread
Crispbread (e.g., Wasa Fibre)
Whole wheat pita bread

FISH COUNTER
Pacific halibut
Smoked salmon

MEAT COUNTER
Chicken breasts (boneless, skinless)
Flank steak

BEANS (LEGUMES) AND CANNED VEGETABLES
Black beans
Chickpeas
Diced tomatoes
Lentils (green)
Mixed beans
Tomato paste

PASTA AND SAUCES
Light tomato sauce (no added sugar)
Rotini or penne (whole wheat)
Small pasta (e.g., ditali or tubetti)

SOUP AND CANNED SEAFOOD AND MEAT
Anchovy fillets
Chicken stock (low-fat, low-sodium)
Tuna (light, in water)

GRAINS AND SIDE DISHES
Basmati rice
Flaxseeds (ground)

INTERNATIONAL FOODS
Soy sauce (low-sodium)
Tahini

COOKING OIL, VINEGAR, SALAD DRESSINGS AND PICKLES
Dijon mustard
Grainy mustard
Mayonnaise (fat-free)
Oil (canola and extra-virgin olive)
Red wine vinegar
Rice vinegar
Vegetable cooking oil spray (canola or olive oil)
Worcestershire sauce

SNACKS
Applesauce (unsweetened)
Nutrition bars (e.g., ZonePerfect, Balance Bar)

BAKING
Amaretto
Baking powder
Baking soda
Cornstarch
Oat bran
Spices (allspice, ground cardamom, Cajun seasoning, ground cinnamon, ground cumin, curry powder, ground ginger, dried oregano, black pepper, red pepper flakes, salt, dried thyme)
Splenda
Vanilla
Wheat bran
Wheat germ
Whole wheat flour

BREAKFAST FOODS
All-Bran Buds or 100% Bran cereal
Oatmeal (large-flake oats)

BEVERAGES
White wine

DAIRY CASE
Babybel Gouda Lite cheese
Buttermilk
Cheddar cheese (low-fat)
Cottage cheese (1%)
Fruit yogurt (non-fat with sweetener)
Laughing Cow Light cheese (extra-low-fat)
Liquid eggs (e.g., Naturegg Break Free)
Milk (skim)
Soft margarine (non-hydrogenated, light)
Sour cream (low-fat)
Whole Omega-3 eggs

FROZEN FOODS
Peas (or fresh)

CHAPTER FIVE

Results of the E-Clinic

Having shared the experiences of the thirty-eight participants for the thirteen weeks of the menopause e-clinic, I'm sure you're wondering how they did. First, we had a remarkably low dropout rate—less than 10 percent—which is quite impressive, given the random selection of participants. Second, for the 90 percent plus who completed the thirteen weeks, they all managed to lose weight and inches from waist and hips. Third, most of the participants who had been suffering particularly from hot flashes and sleeplessness found a distinct improvement in their menopause symptoms.

In this chapter, I will share some of the individual results along with what they learned and experienced with the program. As you will see, those who had more weight to lose generally lost weight at a faster rate than those who were closer to their target weight. Space does not allow for either their complete commentaries or for all thirty-eight of the participants to be included so I've had to make some tough choices. I included these commentaries because I thought they would be most effective at helping you achieve your own goals as they speak to the challenges and the successes that participants experienced and perhaps you will, too!

From Ann (starting BMI 38), who lost 24 pounds and a total of 9 ½ inches from her waist and hips:

Last November, the doctor told my husband he had to go on medication for high blood pressure. My husband refused to ... This clinic diet of green light foods has changed both my husband and my way of eating. My husband no longer has high blood pressure. I had hot flashes so badly before this diet that I was like a teapot boiling over. They are gone! I get a few minor ones now that I can cope with.

The most rewarding thing has been I feel so much better health wise and have more energy and less aches and pains ... we are so thankful you came along at the right time in our lives to help because if you hadn't, I am sure both my husband and I would be in poorer health and going up in weight instead of down ...

This is our "new way" of eating and not a diet. It will be our lifestyle plan forever. It really is truly amazing and it works! Simple too ... it broke our addiction to overeating and we no longer crave junk food. We love our weight loss ... and are enjoying "less" of each other (no pun intended).

From Linda (starting BMI 33), who lost 19 pounds and a total of 11 inches from her waist and hips:
This past weekend I went away to the US shopping. I actually enjoyed it because I got to try on clothes with my sister and sister-in-law and not feel bad about how I looked. It was fun and they had to keep telling me not to choose the big sizes—that part is hard to get past so it was nice to have their encouragement and I loved how the clothes fit. I'm not perfect but I'm very happy and more confident in how I look.

Thirteen weeks was hard to imagine when I first started. I really wanted to do this to change my attitude about food. I think the length of the clinic was perfect because it gave enough time to change your mindset. I focused a lot on food and sometimes it was my only comfort but then I would feel guilty afterwards. Now I enjoy my food and know it is important to eat my 3 meals and 3 snacks a day. I have control over what I choose and I choose the G.I. Diet. I love fresh fruit and veggies and now I love myself enough to make sure I take the time to prepare them.

I should mention that my hot flashes don't happen as often and I find if I have sugar during the day or not enough water, I will have the flashes and they are intense. I can now see what triggers them because I'm not always eating the wrong type of food and my diet is healthier. I know I will still have the odd chocolate or glass of wine or alcohol but not as much as before because I'm aware of what they trigger in me and I don't want that any more.

I will continue on living this way because I feel so much better. I love walking, water running, and moving. It sure helps not having to carry around the extra weight and I want to keep taking it off by continuing the G.I. Diet and exercising. I believe I now have the tools to carry on and ... keep the weekly diary format for myself—that way I'm accountable.

Thanks Rick and Ruth for helping me get closer to my goal of becoming healthier and slimmer.

From Laura (starting BMI 26), who lost 13 pounds and 2 inches from her waist and hips—a significant achievement given her starting BMI was one of the lowest in the group:
I'm thrilled that I've lost weight, although my waist and hip measurement haven't changed much. But I must be losing weight all over, since my clothes are quite a bit looser. Being on the G.I. Diet, I've learned that every time I eat, I have a choice of whether to do the right thing or not. That's what has helped me the most. It's almost like going to an AA meeting, but instead of "one day at a time," for me it's one meal at a time, or one snack at a time. If I make the low-G.I. choice each time, the diet works.

I also find that I'm satisfied with eating much smaller portions. Before the G.I. Diet, the only way I'd stop eating is if I was so full that I started to feel sick. That was my stopping point. Now I eat enough so that I don't feel hungry anymore, and I don't keep eating beyond that point ... If I am tempted to eat something not on the plan, I ask myself, "Do I want that piece of cake, or do I want to be thin?" I know that there will be times when I do give in to that special treat, but I'm going to try and wait until I get to the maintenance phase. All in all, I found the G.I. diet very easy to follow. I'm glad that I'm able to have carbohydrates, and I now actually prefer whole-grain bread to the white bread I used to eat.

My goal is to lose about 20 more pounds, and even though I may not be losing at a fast pace, the fact that I've already gotten down to a weight that I haven't been at for many years is the best motivation I could have.

From Carol Ann (starting BMI 36), who lost 12 pounds and a total of 8 inches from her waist and hips:

For you this has probably been a long and hard 13 weeks, but for me this has been life changing. I have enjoyed the diaries and your knowledge, wisdom and your kindness. No one wants to be big, but we have got out of hand, that is for sure. I cannot change the past but the future is mine, so it is up to me and I will be successful.

I am proud to report to you that I listened at the beginning and there is NO red-light food in our house ... something that I have noticed while shopping for groceries. This country is so concerned with the weight problem we are having ... They should go shopping for healthy food like our green-light food. I watch people shop and it is far less expensive to eat the red-light food. Something in this picture is not right. The red light food should cost more and people would be more likely to buy the green-light food.

I cannot say enough about your books and this clinic that has helped me. (When I started this clinic I shared the story of my son's weight loss[;] to date he has lost 96 pounds since September 2007 ... You have also changed his life). Thank you sounds just too simple, but it is heartfelt and sincere.

From Carol (starting BMI 36), who lost 19 pounds and a total of 14 inches from her waist and hips:

Like the others in this study I too am feeling nervous about not hearing from you weekly, but I know that I really want to succeed over the next nine months and maybe checking in once a month is making me realize that I don't have to be running to diet clubs for weigh-ins as this is not a diet but a new way of eating for the rest of my life.

When I shop I now read labels, which I never did very often before; I cook differently; always looking for ways of making recipes with less calories ... But most of all I just feel better than I have for a long long time. I have given away my clothes that are now too big for me as I know that this time I will not need them again. What a good feeling that is!

I am the youngest of nine and everyone in my family is diabetic except my brother and I, and as I mentioned in my first letter, heart disease is also prevalent in our family, so you can see that the success I have had on this clinic is really a life saver for me ...

From Cindy (starting BMI 29), who lost 14 pounds and a total of 9 inches from her waist and hips:

Although I think I could probably have lost more weight by now, the fact that I didn't is probably why I am still so impressed with this plan/life style and still happily losing weight. Most weight loss plans I have followed in the past have been more rigid, limiting many of the things I like to eat—which leads to the inevitable "sense of failure" and the "I've blown it anyway attitude."

With the G.I. plan, I have never felt like I CAN'T have something. If I want it badly enough, I have it. I do try to keep the portion small, but I still allow myself the option. I also have to admit that when I'm faced with a situation where there are many options (including red, yellow and green choices) I can look over the food choices and arrive at sensible trade-offs ...

The bottom line with this plan is flexibility. I LOVE the flexibility. I don't feel deprived. I don't feel like I'm on a "temporary" diet ... And most important—I DON'T FEEL LIKE I HAD TO CHANGE MY ENTIRE LIFE! I changed my "approach" to how I look at eating ... Rick, I can't thank you enough for allowing me to participate in this project. It truly has been life altering (my boyfriend sends a special thanks as well—not just because I am 15 lbs. lighter but because I'm happier!)! I really couldn't have done it without you!

From Helen (starting BMI 42), who lost 14 pounds and a total of 13 inches from her waist and hips:

I think we all want our weight gone overnight. I know that is never going to happen. I have been on every diet going, lost weight, but could never stick to it. Always felt deprived and would start eating the wrong things and could never get back to the program. The G.I. diet has been easy to follow. Even though my trips and eating out proved a little challenging at times, the program helped me with better choices, watching my portions, and feeling empowered [so] that I was able to keep in control of what I ate and not feel sick, bloated and stuffed after the meal. When I started this program I had just started on Lipitor, it will be interesting to see how that is changed when I go back to the Doctor for the next checkup. I do know that my blood pressure has returned to normal limits, so the Doc will be pleased with that. I am feeling great, lots of energy and know I can continue with the program with no problems

From Kathy (starting BMI 32), who lost 14 pounds and a total of 6 inches from her waist and hips:

My husband gave me a hug this morning and said, "You really are slimming down." In the meantime he is down to his high school weight and we noticed at our son's graduation this weekend that his suit needs to be taken in.

I haven't quite made the 20 pounds I had hoped to lose in these 13 weeks, but I will. I have had less back pain in the last month than usual and my massage therapist told me last week that my tissues feel healthier. Now that may just be coincidence, but I can't help thinking that my change in diet and reduced weight has had an impact. I have had no menopause symptoms to speak of for the last two months and have been sleeping soundly. Again, I can't prove that is diet related but ... I feel very positive about our change in diet and know that we will keep it up. In nine months I hope to be close to my target weight around 160 pounds. I feel privileged to have been chosen to participate in this study and would like to thank you again for getting me started on this journey back to a full and healthy life style.

From Christine (starting BMI 27), who lost 8 pounds and a total of 2 inches from her waist and hips; she had a relatively low starting BMI: I'm pretty sure that I'm not the "biggest loser" on this program, but I feel that I've learned a lot. I had been able to lose an average of 2 lb/week before menopause and was happy with the dependability of those losses. Since menopause things have changed! I not only gain weight [more easily;] it had seemed like I was constantly battling to lose even 1 lb and keep it off! Although I was sceptical because of what I considered to be a tremendous amount of food to eat, the G.I. Diet has come through for me. My weight loss is, at times, painfully slow but it keeps going in the right direction. And my overall feeling of well-being has improved because I'm conscious of my food choices and stay away from too much "junk." I'm satisfied by what I eat and enjoy the tremendous variety of choices. I don't know if anyone else has mentioned this, but one of my menopausal symptoms was difficulty with bowel movements; the focus on high-fibre has eliminated this problem for me.

I continue to use recipes from your G.I. Diet book and am comfortable enough now to make modifications in my own recipes so they are consistent with the basic nutrition guidelines of the plan. Not everything works nor do I want to change everything; if I follow the plan for most of the time an occasional "indulgence" is completely OK with me.

From Linda (starting BMI 34), who lost 16 pounds and a total of 6 inches from her waist and hips:

The thing that saved me on this diet, was to always have your muffins and chicken soup in the freezer to grab for work. Once a week I cooked and baked for a couple of hours and had enough for two weeks for those days that I was too tired to make something different for my lunch. I cleared my cupboards of all red-light foods ... There was many a time in those first weeks, I was hoping to find a piece of chocolate that I knew I would never find ...

The hardest times with this diet was not myself, but other people. When the weight loss became really noticeable, it was like everyone wanted to fatten me up again[;] the worst was at work. Lucky for me the cravings had disappeared by that time and I wasn't tempted. I still get the odd hot flash during the day, but oh boy is it nice to sleep through the night now.

It certainly was tough at the beginning, but of all the diets I have gone on this one didn't seem like I was dieting after awhile. At times it seemed too easy and I was amazed at the one lb a week loss. Sometimes it still boggles my mind when I get on the scale ...

From Louise (starting BMI 27), who lost 14 pounds and a total of 7 inches from her waist and hips:

When I signed up for this clinic, I was excited and hopeful. But I didn't really think I could succeed. I doubted my ability to stay on track, but week after week, I proved myself wrong. I don't feel like a G.I. expert, but I feel competent and in charge when it comes to food choices. I re-read your book and the newsletters. I went from rolling my eyes at some of the members' letters—which I felt were like Catholic confessional in search of absolution—to feeling a kinship with others who were having the same struggles as me. I learned a lot from the people who wrote to you.

I mentioned in one of my early diaries that I rarely if ever weighed myself. Since I was 10, I have been weighed (and looked at the scales when I was doing it) maybe 15 times ... Today, I stepped on the scales consciously, but not fearfully. I know what I weigh and I am proud of it ... My life is less enslaved to cravings and to junk food. I know there are alternatives and can turn to them first. I have never felt this power before and so am completely different than I was 13 weeks ago.

This has been one of the best experiences of my life.

From Lynn (starting BMI 32), who lost 16 pounds and a total of 8 inches from her waist and hips:

After so many attempts at losing weight throughout my adult life, who would have thought that in just 12 weeks I could say "Goodbye 200s, goodbye 190s, hello 180s!" And I am finally seeing an indentation in my middle that most certainly could be referred to as a waist! ... Someday in the not so distant future I will say "Hello 140s." Why would I want to go back to my old way of eating? This is worth every green mouthful just to sleep through the night again, with no more of those horrible night sweats ... I feel as if I have been born again.

From Marlene (starting BMI 37), who lost 12 pounds and a total of 7 inches from her waist and hips:

First—again, I would like to thank you for not only giving me the tools to this new freedom in eating, but for walking me through the rough start, misgivings, and doubt in myself that I could actually be success-ful in this new eating lifestyle. Looking back, the 13 weeks seems to have flown by! I am very pleased with my (almost) 12 pound weight loss, and 7.5 inches lost off my waist and hips. That is huge, not to mention inches lost on other "body parts."

It was just "divine intervention" for me, getting to be included in the study. The new green-light way of eating seems to have reversed the hot flashes, insomnia and mood swings that were part of my daily life. (There have been no other changes in my lifestyle to attribute to the improvement). I had almost resigned myself to living that (horrible) way for the rest of my life. Thankfully, it seems to be gone.

So, with the help from you and Ruth, menopause seems to be a doable part of my life.

I want to be here for a long time, watching my grand kids grow up, and enjoying these retirement years with my husband and family. Thankfully, I have a brand new outlook, an optimism that was missing when I was resigned to being overweight and unhealthy. I can only thank the green-light way of eating for this great new attitude ... Changing one's eating habits can make a dramatic improvement in their quality of life, and when one has tried literally every way they can think of to make changes, without success, hope dims. Now my outlook is great!!

From Mary (starting BMI 44), who lost 15 pounds and a total of 4 inches from her waist and hips:
About 1 ½ ago, I was surfing the internet, feeling depressed again about my weight. I came across your book, the *G. I. Diet*; the reading seemed interesting and held my attention enough for me to buy it ... But, I never could get motivated to start the program. My self-esteem was low, I didn't have any incentive. Well, one day I was reading my email and I received an update from you (Rick Gallop). Also, it said I am looking for women that would like to participate in my program. Without hesitation, I responded ... I was selected! I couldn't believe it ...

The first 3 to 4 weeks was hard. I had to put down sugar, my biggest stronghold. I had to fix breakfast and lunch, which I was not used to doing, because I would skip breakfast and buy lunch at work every day. As the weeks went by, I got better. I saw 2 pounds drop off each week (something I had not seen in a long time). I honestly thought the scale was broken. Then in my 5th or 6th week, I had a busy week and didn't make time to prepare my meals. So, I had a couple of late night meals and ate what was not on the program. Well, when I had to weight in for the end of that week, I was horrified, I had gained some weight ... That uncomfortable feeling was enough for me to know that I didn't ever want to feel like that again ... From that week on, I got back on track because I knew there was someone I was accountable to. I have continued to lose 1–2 pounds a week from the G. I. Diet and I know I have a long way to go. But by God's grace and mercy, He sent me a blessing, Rick Gallop.

PART III

Week 14 and Beyond

CHAPTER SIX

Where to Go from Here

Whether you have reached your weight-loss target by now and are ready to start Phase II of the G.I. Diet (see page 227), or still have some way to go, I would like to offer you what the original participants were offered at the end of the first thirteen weeks of the e-clinic; a nine-month extension of the program, which includes a monthly e-letter. These monthly e-letters will cover issues such as:

- How to stay the course
- Anxiety and fear of failure
- Maintaining motivation
- Dealing with temptation
- Five essentials to permanent weight loss

Whether they wished to maintain their weight, or still had more weight to lose, the original e-clinic members found this extension of the basic thirteen-week program extremely valuable. If you'd like to receive these nine monthly ister at www.gidietclinic.com.

An exclusive website will support you during these nine months through a special members' question-and-answer forum, where I will respond to major issues raised in participants' diaries. In addition, you will receive access to a special Green-Light Forum where you can share experiences with other readers.

Once you register at www.gidietclinic.com, you will receive the first e-letter immediately, as well as access to your personal diary, should you wish to track your results. All of your personal information will be kept strictly confidential. Any use of your questions or comments on the website will refer only to your first name.

The e-clinic is a great opportunity to continue your positive experience with the G.I. Diet. For those of you who do not intend to continue with the nine-month extension, I would be delighted to hear about your experiences. Simply e-mail me at Rick@gidiet.com.

Phase II

Well, you've made it. Congratulations! You've hit your target weight, you're digging out clothes you thought you'd never get into again, and you're finally on good terms with your full-length mirror. I hope you are relishing the new you and making the most of your increased energy. Now that you've graduated from Phase I, you can ease up a bit on limiting portion and serving sizes, and start adding some yellow-light foods to your diet. The idea here is to get comfortable with your G.I. program; this is how you're going to eat for the rest of your life.

The best news for most of us in Phase II is about alcohol and chocolate. While both were considered red-light in the Preliminary Phase and Phase I because of their high calorie content and tendency to spike blood sugar levels, in Phase II, it's time to reintroduce those little pleasures.

Alcohol

Medical research indicates that red wine, which is rich in flavonoids, can help reduce your risk of heart disease and stroke. So, in Phase II, a glass of red wine is allowed with dinner. Just because one glass is beneficial, however, doesn't mean that two or three is even better for you. Immoderate drinking undoes any health benefits, and alcohol contains calories. One glass of wine (5 ounces maximum) provides the optimum benefit.

Apart from red wine, keep your consumption of alcohol to a minimum. I realize that this can be difficult, since drinking is so often a part of social occasions and celebrations. An occasional lapse won't do a lot of harm, but it's easy to get carried away. There are various strategies to combat the social pressure to drink: you can graciously accept that glass of wine or cocktail, raise it in a toast, take a sip, and then discreetly leave it on the nearest buffet table. Faced with a tray of vodka martinis and glasses of red wine, stick with the wine, which lasts longer. Ruth drinks spritzers (wine mixed with soda water) on special occasions. And if you add lots of ice to your spritzer, you can reduce the alcohol even further while still joining in the party spirit. Whatever strategy you choose, always try to eat some food with your drink, even if it has to be a forbidden piece of cheese. The fat will slow the absorption of the alcohol and minimize its impact. (Of course, better to gravitate to the vegetable tray, but an emergency canapé won't be the ruin of you.)

Chocolate

For many of us, living without chocolate is not living. The good news is that in Phase II, some chocolate—the right sort of chocolate in the right amount—is acceptable. You may have heard that chocolate, like red wine, contains natural elements that help keep the arteries clear—but that's probably not your main motive for eating it. Chocolate combines fat, sugar and cocoa, all three of which please the palate. But most chocolate contains too much saturated fat and sugar, which keeps it deep in the red-light zone. Chocolate with a high cocoa content (70 percent or more) delivers more chocolate intensity per ounce, which means that even a square or two is satisfying. A square or two can give chocoholics the fix they need.

Green-Light Servings

PHASE II

Chocolate (at least 70 percent cocoa)	2 squares
Red wine	One 5-ounce glass

Moderation Is Key

Phase II, I must warn you, is a bit of a danger zone, the stage when most diets go off the rails. Most people think that when they reach their weight-loss goal, they can just drop the diet and go back to their old eating habits. And frankly, when I take a close look at what many of these diets expect you to live on, I can understand why people can't stick to them for long.

The reality is that, with some modifications, the G.I. program is your diet for life. But this shouldn't be a hardship, because the G.I. Diet was designed to give you a huge range of healthy choices, so you won't feel hungry, bored or unsatisfied. By now, you will know how to navigate your green-light way through the supermarket, decipher food labels and cook the green-light way. You are probably not even tempted to revert to your old ways. If you should fall prey to a double cheeseburger, you will be dismayed at how heavy, sluggish and ungratified you feel afterward. You will be too attached to your new feeling of lightness and level of energy to abandon them.

Before we look at some of the new options open to you in Phase II, a word of caution: your body can now function on less food than it did before you started. Why? Because you're lighter now, so your body requires fewer calories. Also, your metabolism has become more efficient, and your body has learned to do more with fewer calories. Keeping these two developments in mind, add a few more calories in Phase II, but don't go berserk. Don't make any significant changes in your serving sizes, and remember to make yellow-light foods the exception rather than the rule. This way, you will keep the balance between the calories you're consuming and the calories you're expending—and that is the secret to maintaining your new weight.

As you modestly increase portions of foods that you particularly enjoy and include some yellow-light items as a treat, keep monitoring your weight weekly, and adjust your servings up or down until your weight stays stable. This may take a few weeks of experimentation, but when you've reached the magic balance and can stay there comfortably, that's the formula for the rest of your days.

Here are some ideas of how you might alter the way you eat in Phase II.

Breakfast

- Increase cereal serving size from $1/2$ to $2/3$ of a cup.
- Add a slice of 100% whole-grain toast and a pat of margarine.
- Double the amount of sliced almonds on your cereal.
- Enjoy an extra slice of back bacon.
- Have a glass of unsweetened juice now and then.
- Add one of the yellow-light fruits—a banana or apricot—to your cereal.
- Go caffeinated in the coffee department, if you like, but try to keep it to one cup a day.

Lunch

I suggest you continue to eat lunch as you did in Phase I, as this is the one meal that already contained some compromises in the weight-loss portion of the program.

Dinner

- Add another boiled new potato.
- Increase the pasta serving from $3/4$ cup to 1 cup.
- As a special treat, have a 6-ounce steak instead of a 4-ounce one.
- Eat a few more olives and nuts—but only a few!
- Try a cob of sweet corn with a dab of margarine.
- Add a slice of high-fibre bread or crispbread.
- Enjoy a yellow-light cut of lamb or pork.

Snacks

- Have a maximum of 2 cups of air-popped popcorn.
- Increase your serving size of nuts to 10 or 12.
- Enjoy a square or two of 70 percent dark chocolate.
- Have a banana.
- Indulge in a scoop of low-fat ice cream or frozen yogurt.

Of course, Phase II is not, and shouldn't be, a straitjacket. If you live 90 percent within the guidelines of the diet, you are doing well. The idea that certain foods are completely and forever forbidden would drive you, sooner or later, back into their clutches. With the G.I. Diet, you are in control of what you eat, and that includes (with discipline, moderation and common sense) almost everything.

TO SUM UP

- In Phase II, use moderation and common sense in adjusting portions and servings.
- Don't view Phase II as a straitjacket. Occasional lapses are fine.

PART IV

The Recipes

Breakfast

HOMEY OATMEAL

This hot breakfast is guaranteed to keep you feeling satisfied all morning. You can vary the flavour by topping it with fresh fruit such as berries or chopped apple.

2 cups	skim milk
1 1/2 cups	water
3/4 tsp	ground cinnamon
1/2 tsp	salt
1 1/3 cups	large-flake oats
1/4 cup	wheat germ
1/4 cup	chopped almonds
3 tbsp	Splenda

1. In large pot, bring milk, water, cinnamon and salt to boil. Stir in oats and wheat germ and return to boil. Reduce heat to low and cook, stirring, for about 8 minutes or until thickened. Stir in almonds and Splenda.

Makes 4 servings.

HOMEMADE MUESLI

This cereal makes a delicious and healthy start to the day. Be sure to prepare it the night before so that it's ready to enjoy in the morning. Combine ⅓ cup of the Muesli with ⅓ cup of skim milk or water, and cover and refrigerate overnight. Then, in the morning, combine the mixture with 1 container (175 g) of non-fat, sugar-free fruit yogurt and enjoy it cold, or pop it in the microwave for a hot breakfast.

2 cups	large-flake oats
³/₄ cup	oat bran
³/₄ cup	sliced almonds
¹/₂ cup	shelled unsalted sunflower seeds
2 tbsp	wheat germ
¹/₄ tsp	ground cinnamon

1. In large resealable plastic bag, combine oats, oat bran, almonds, sunflower seeds, wheat germ and cinnamon. Using rolling pin, crush mixture into coarse crumbs. Shake bag to combine mixture.

Makes 3 cups.

CINNAMON FRENCH TOAST

Serve this family favourite with slices of ham or back bacon and extra strawberries for a complete breakfast.

3/4 cup	liquid egg
1/2 cup	skim milk
1 tbsp	Splenda
1 tsp	vanilla
1/2 tsp	ground cinnamon
Pinch	salt
4	slices stone-ground whole wheat bread
1 tsp	canola oil
2 cups	sliced strawberries
1/2 cup	non-fat sugar-free fruit-flavoured yogurt

1. In shallow dish, whisk together liquid egg, milk, Splenda, vanilla, cinnamon and salt. Dip each slice of bread into egg mixture, making sure to coat both sides.

2. Meanwhile, brush oil onto non-stick griddle or large non-stick frying pan over medium-high heat. Cook for about 4 minutes, turning once, or until golden brown. Serve with strawberries and yogurt.

Makes 2 servings.

OATMEAL BUTTERMILK PANCAKES

Make pancake breakfasts a weekend tradition. Serve them with fresh fruit or applesauce.

3/4 cup	large-flake oats
2 cups	buttermilk
1 cup	whole wheat flour
1/4 cup	ground flaxseed
1 tbsp	Splenda
1 tsp	ground cinnamon
1 tsp	baking soda
1 tsp	baking powder
1/4 tsp	salt
1/2 cup	liquid egg
2 tbsp	canola oil
1 tsp	vanilla

1. In bowl, soak oats in buttermilk for 20 minutes.

2. In large bowl, combine flour, flaxseed, Splenda, cinnamon, baking soda, baking powder and salt.

3. In another bowl, whisk together liquid egg, oil and vanilla. Stir in soaked oats and buttermilk. Pour over flour mixture and stir until just mixed.

4. Meanwhile, heat non-stick griddle or large non-stick frying pan over medium heat. Ladle about 1/4 cup batter onto griddle for each pancake. Cook until bubbles appear on top, about 2 minutes.

5. Flip pancakes and cook for another 2 minutes or until golden. Transfer to plate and cover to keep warm. Repeat with remaining batter.

Makes 16 pancakes, 4 to 6 servings.

MINI BREAKFAST PUFFS

Ideal for rushed mornings, these muffin-sized puffs are packed with nutrition.

1 tsp	canola oil
¼ cup	diced onion
1	red pepper, diced
1 cup	chopped broccoli
1 ½ tsp	fresh thyme
¼ tsp	each salt and freshly ground pepper
¾ cup	crumbled light feta cheese
1 ½ cups	liquid egg
1 cup	skim milk
¼ cup	wheat bran
¼ cup	whole wheat flour

1. Preheat oven to 400°F.
2. In non-stick frying pan, heat oil over medium heat. Cook onion and red pepper for about 5 minutes or until softened. Add broccoli, thyme, salt and pepper; cover and steam for about 3 minutes or until broccoli is tender-crisp and bright green. Divide mixture among 12 greased muffin tins.
3. Sprinkle cheese over top of vegetable mixture in each cup.
4. In bowl, whisk together liquid egg, milk, bran and whole wheat flour. Divide evenly over vegetable mixture. Bake for about 20 minutes or until golden, set and puffed. Let cool slightly before serving.

Makes 12 puffs, 6 to 8 servings.

ITALIAN OMELETTE

Omelettes are easy to make, and you can vary them by adding any number of fresh vegetables, a little cheese and/or some meat.

1 tsp	canola oil
1/2 cup	sliced mushrooms
1/2 cup	liquid egg
1/2 cup	tomato purée
1 tbsp	chopped fresh basil or oregano
1 oz	part-skim mozzarella cheese, shredded
Pinch	freshly ground pepper

1. In small non-stick frying pan, heat oil over medium-high heat. Add mushrooms and sauté until tender, about 5 minutes. Transfer mushrooms to a plate and cover to keep warm.

2. In bowl, using fork, stir together liquid egg, tomato purée, basil, cheese and pepper. Pour into frying pan and cook for about 5 minutes, lifting edges to allow uncooked egg to run underneath, until almost set.

3. Sprinkle sautéed mushrooms over half of the omelette. Using spatula, fold over other half and cook for 1 minute.

Makes 1 serving.

BREAKFAST IN A GLASS

This is a great make-and-take breakfast for mornings on the run. It packs protein, fruit and fibre in one glass. Look for whey or soy protein isolate in your local health food store.

¼ cup	flaxseed
2 tbsp	sunflower seeds
2 cups	soy milk
2 cups	fresh or frozen berries
½	banana
½ cup	low-fat yogurt
½ cup	whey or soy protein isolate powder
2 tbsp	soy lecithin granules (optional)

1. In spice or coffee grinder, finely grind flaxseed and sunflower seeds. Set aside.

2. In blender or food processor, blend together soy milk, berries, banana and yogurt until almost smooth.

3. Add seed mixture, protein powder and lecithin, if using, to soy milk mixture. Blend just until mixed, about 5 seconds.

Makes 2 servings.

VEGETARIAN OMELETTE

1 tsp	canola oil
1 cup	broccoli florets
1/2 cup	sliced mushrooms
1/2 cup	chopped red and green pepper
1/2 cup	liquid egg
1 oz	low-fat cheddar cheese, shredded
Pinch	freshly ground pepper

1. In small non-stick frying pan, heat oil over medium-high heat. Add broccoli, mushrooms and pepper, and sauté until tender, about 5 minutes. Transfer vegetables to a plate and cover to keep warm.

2. In bowl, using fork, stir together liquid egg, cheese and pepper. Pour into frying pan and cook for about 5 minutes, lifting edges to allow uncooked egg to run underneath, until almost set.

3. Sprinkle sautéed vegetables over half of the omelette. Using spatula, fold over other half and cook for 1 minute.

Makes 1 serving.

SMOKED SALMON SCRAMBLED EGGS

Smoked salmon makes scrambled eggs elegant and special. Serve with a slice of high-fibre toast.

4	egg whites
2	omega-3 eggs
2 tbsp	skim milk
¼ tsp	freshly ground pepper
1 tsp	canola oil
2 oz	smoked salmon, chopped
1 tbsp	chopped fresh chives or dill

1. In bowl, whisk together egg whites, eggs, milk and pepper.
2. In non-stick frying pan, heat oil over medium heat. Add egg mixture. Using rubber spatula, gently stir eggs until almost set. Stir in salmon and continue to cook, stirring gently, until eggs are set but still slightly creamy. Stir in chives.

Makes 2 servings.

Soups

MINESTRONE SOUP

This soup is one of my favourites because it contains both pasta and spinach. Serve it with a sprinkling of grated Parmesan cheese for extra flavour and a few more red pepper flakes to get your blood pumping.

2 tsp	canola oil
3	slices back bacon, chopped
1	onion, chopped
4	cloves garlic, minced
2	carrots, chopped
1	stalk celery, chopped
1 tbsp	dried oregano
1/2 tsp	red pepper flakes
1/4 tsp	each salt and freshly ground pepper
1	can (796 mL) plum tomatoes
6 cups	chicken stock (low-fat, low-sodium)
1	bag (300 g) baby spinach washed well
1	can (540 mL) each red kidney beans and chickpeas, drained and rinsed
3/4 cup	ditali or tubetti pasta
1/3 cup	chopped fresh flat-leaf parsley
2 tbsp	chopped fresh basil (optional)

1. In large soup pot, heat oil over medium-high heat and cook back bacon for 2 minutes. Reduce heat to medium and add onion, garlic, carrots, celery, oregano, red pepper flakes, salt and pepper. Cook for about 10 minutes or until vegetables are softened and lightly browned.

2. Add tomatoes and crush using potato masher in pot. Pour in chicken stock; bring to boil. Reduce heat to simmer and add spinach, beans, chickpeas and pasta. Simmer for 6–10 minutes or until pasta is tender. Stir in parsley and basil (if using).

Makes 6 servings.

TUSCAN WHITE BEAN SOUP

Serve this soup in deep Italian ceramic soup bowls and dream you're in Tuscany.

1 tbsp	extra-virgin olive oil
1	onion, chopped
4	cloves garlic, minced
1	carrot, chopped
1	stalk celery, chopped
4	fresh sage leaves or ½ tsp dried
6 cups	vegetable or chicken stock (low-fat, low-sodium)
2	cans (540 mL each) cannellini or white kidney beans, drained and rinsed
4 cups	shredded kale
Pinch	each salt and freshly ground pepper

1. In large soup pot, heat oil over medium heat. Add onion, garlic, carrot, celery and sage and cook for 5 minutes or until softened.

2. Add stock, beans, kale, salt and pepper, and cook, stirring occasionally, for about 20 minutes or until kale is tender.

Makes 4 servings.

QUICK AND EASY CHICKEN NOODLE SOUP

Why buy canned soup when you can make this simple homemade version?

2 tsp	extra-virgin olive oil
2	carrots, chopped
2	stalks celery, chopped
3	cloves garlic, chopped
1	onion, chopped
1 tbsp	chopped fresh thyme
6 cups	chicken stock (low-fat, low-sodium)
3	boneless skinless chicken breasts (4 oz each), diced
1 cup	frozen peas
3/4 cup	small pasta (such as ditali or tubetti)
1/4 cup	chopped fresh flat-leaf parsley
1/4 tsp	each salt and freshly ground pepper

1. In large soup pot, heat oil over medium-high heat. Add carrots, celery, garlic, onion and thyme, and cook for 10 minutes or until vegetables are slightly softened.

2. Pour in stock and bring to boil. Reduce heat to simmer and add chicken. Cook for 5 minutes, then add pasta and peas. Cook until pasta is al dente and chicken is no longer pink. Stir in parsley, salt, pepper.

Makes 6 servings.

VEGETABLE BARLEY SOUP AU PISTOU

"Pistou" is just French for pesto, but it makes this soup sound oh so continental. You can used bottled pesto, but why not make your own with the recipe provided?

1 tbsp	olive oil
2	carrots, chopped
2	stalks celery, chopped
1 cup	chopped leeks (well-washed white and light-green parts only)
1 cup	chopped zucchini
1/2	red pepper, seeded and chopped
2	sprigs fresh thyme
6 cups	chicken stock or vegetable-based "chicken" stock (low-fat, low-sodium)
3/4 cup	chopped fresh or frozen green beans
1/2 cup	barley
2 tbsp	tomato paste
1/2 tsp	salt
1/4 tsp	freshly ground pepper
1/3 cup	G.I. Pesto (see recipe, page 250)

1. In large soup pot, heat oil over medium heat; cook carrots, celery, leeks, zucchini, red pepper and thyme for about 8 minutes or until softened.

2. Add stock, green beans, barley, tomato paste, salt and pepper; bring to boil. Reduce heat, cover and simmer for 45 minutes or until barley is tender. Remove thyme sprigs and stir in pesto.

Makes 6 servings.

Variation: Add 1 cup of chopped cooked turkey or chicken to the soup, or try different pestos, such as sun-dried tomato or arugula.

G.I. PESTO

The addition of water along with the oil in this pesto reduces the fat content. It gives the pesto a lighter green colour than traditional pesto, but it still tastes great.

2 cups	packed fresh basil leaves
3	cloves garlic
1/3 cup	sunflower seeds
1/4 cup	grated Parmesan cheese
1 1/2 tbsp	lemon juice
1/4 tsp	each salt and freshly ground pepper
3 tbsp	water
3 tbsp	extra-virgin olive oil

1. In blender or food processor, purée basil, garlic, sunflower seeds, Parmesan, lemon juice, salt and pepper. With motor running, add water and oil in steady stream.

Makes 3/4 cup.

Make Ahead: Refrigerate in airtight container up to 3 days or freeze up to 6 months.

Helpful Hint: When basil is plentiful, make extra batches and freeze in ice-cube trays. When frozen, remove from tray and store in airtight container in freezer. You'll always have a bit of pesto on hand to stir into hot pasta or soups.

Salads

RAITA SALAD

This recipe is based on the refreshing Indian condiment. Try serving this salad with Chicken Curry (see recipe, page 285).

1	bag (300 g) baby spinach washed well
1	medium English cucumber, quartered lengthwise and sliced into 1/2-inch chunks
2	tomatoes, chopped
1/2	red onion, thinly sliced
1 cup	low-fat plain yogurt
1/2 tsp	ground cumin
1/4 tsp	salt

1. In large bowl, toss together spinach, cucumber, tomatoes and red onion.
2. In another bowl, stir together yogurt, cumin and salt. Add to spinach mixture and toss to coat.

Makes 4 servings.

LEMONY GRILLED VEGETABLE PASTA SALAD

This is a lovely side dish for chicken or fish. Toss in some leftover roast chicken or a can of tuna or salmon for a simple lunch.

⅓ cup	chopped shallots
¼ cup	olive oil
¼ cup	lemon juice
2 tbsp	Dijon mustard
2 tbsp	chopped fresh herbs (choose from a mixture of thyme, rosemary, oregano and marjoram)
1 tbsp	grated lemon zest
¼ tsp	each salt and freshly ground pepper
1	small eggplant, quartered, then cut crosswise into ½-inch thick slices
1	each red pepper and yellow pepper, seeded and cut into ½-inch pieces
1	zucchini, halved and cut into ½-inch rounds
1	red onion, cut into wedges
1	carrot, cut into ¼-inch thick rounds
6 oz	shiitake mushrooms (discard stems, cut caps in four)
3 cups	whole wheat penne or other similar-size pasta shape
2 tbsp	chopped fresh basil or parsley

1. Preheat oven to 425°F.

2. In large bowl, whisk together shallots, oil, lemon juice, mustard, herbs, lemon zest, salt and pepper. Add eggplant, peppers, zucchini, onion, carrot and mushrooms and toss with dressing. Place on rimmed baking sheet and roast in oven for 25 to 30 minutes or until vegetables are golden and tender.

3. Meanwhile, in large pot of boiling salted water, cook pasta for 8 minutes or until al dente. Drain and add cooked vegetables and basil, tossing well.

Makes 4 to 6 servings.

Make Ahead: Refrigerate up to 3 days.

TANGY RED AND GREEN COLESLAW

Using a vinaigrette in coleslaw makes it low-fat and really tangy! This is a great keeper salad for the refrigerator or to tote along to a potluck.

4 cups	finely shredded green cabbage
2 cups	finely shredded red cabbage
2	carrots, shredded
1/2 cup	thinly sliced celery
1/4 cup	chopped fresh flat-leaf parsley
1/2 cup	cider vinegar
2 tbsp	canola oil
2 tsp	Splenda
1 tsp	celery seeds
1/2 tsp	salt
Pinch	freshly ground pepper

1. In large bowl, toss together green and red cabbage, carrots, celery and parsley.

2. In small bowl, whisk together vinegar, oil, Splenda, celery seeds, salt and pepper. Pour over cabbage mixture and toss to coat.

Makes 4 to 6 servings.

BASIC G.I. SALAD

1 ½ cups	lettuce (try any type) torn or coarsely chopped
1	small carrot, grated
½	red, yellow or green pepper, diced
1	plum tomato, cut into wedges
½ cup	sliced cucumber
¼ cup	chopped red onion (optional)

Basic G.I. Vinaigrette:

1 tbsp	vinegar (try any type) or lemon juice
1 tsp	extra-virgin olive oil or canola oil
½ tsp	Dijon mustard
1	clove garlic, crushed (optional)
Pinch	each salt and freshly ground pepper
Pinch	finely chopped fresh herb of choice

1. In large bowl, toss together lettuce, carrot, pepper, tomato, cucumber and onion.
2. In small bowl, whisk together vinegar, oil, mustard, garlic, salt, pepper and herb.
3. Pour vinaigrette over greens and toss to coat.

Makes 1 serving.

Variations:
To make a meal out of salad, add protein with 4 oz canned tuna, cooked salmon, tofu, kidney beans, chickpeas, cooked chicken or another lean meat.

Make Ahead: Both the salad and the dressing can be prepared ahead and stored separately, covered, for about 2 days.

CAESAR SALAD

We all need a Caesar salad in our recipe repertoire. No one will guess that tahini is the secret ingredient that makes this green-light version every bit as creamy as Chef Caesar Cardini's original.

3	slices whole-grain bread
2 tsp	extra-virgin olive oil
Pinch	each salt and freshly ground pepper
1	large head romaine lettuce

Dressing:

3	cloves garlic, minced
3	anchovy fillets, finely minced
2 tbsp	tahini
1 tsp	Dijon mustard
1/2 tsp	Worcestershire sauce
1/2 tsp	each salt and freshly ground pepper
3 tbsp	fresh lemon juice
2 tbsp	warm water
1 1/2 tbsp	extra-virgin olive oil

1. Preheat oven to 350°F.
2. Cut bread into 1/2-inch pieces and place in bowl. Add oil, salt and pepper and toss to coat well. Arrange in single layer on rimmed baking sheet. Bake for 20 minutes or until golden and crisp. Let cool.
3. Wash lettuce and tear into bite-size pieces; place in large bowl.
4. In small bowl, stir together garlic, anchovies, tahini, mustard, Worcestershire sauce, salt and pepper. Whisk in lemon juice, water and oil.
5. Pour dressing over lettuce and toss to coat. Sprinkle with croutons.

Makes 4 servings.

GREEK SALAD

2 cups	torn iceberg lettuce
$\frac{1}{2}$	cucumber, chopped
2	tomatoes, chopped
6	kalamata olives
$\frac{1}{2}$	red onion, sliced
$\frac{1}{4}$ cup	crumbled light feta cheese
1 tbsp	red wine vinegar
2 tsp	extra-virgin olive oil
1 tsp	fresh lemon juice
$\frac{3}{4}$ tsp	dried oregano
Pinch	each salt and freshly ground pepper

1. In bowl, toss together lettuce, cucumber, tomatoes, olives, red onion and crumbled feta.

2. In small bowl, whisk together vinegar, oil, lemon juice, oregano, salt and pepper. Pour over lettuce and toss to coat.

Makes 2 servings.

COLD NOODLE SALAD WITH CUCUMBER AND SESAME

These refreshing noodles pair well with Ginger-Wasabi Halibut (see recipe, page 281).

6 oz	thin pasta (vermicelli, capellini or spaghettini)
1 tbsp	rice vinegar
4 tsp	Splenda
2 tsp	soy sauce
1/2	English cucumber, quartered lengthwise and thinly sliced
2 tbsp	toasted sesame seeds

1. In large pot of boiling salted water, cook pasta until al dente, about 4 minutes. Drain and rinse under cold water. Place in large bowl.
2. In small bowl, stir together vinegar, Splenda and soy sauce. Pour over cooked noodles, and stir in cucumber and sesame seeds; toss well to coat.

Makes 6 servings.

G.I. PASTA SALAD

1/2 to 3/4 cup	cooked whole wheat pasta (spirals, shells or similar size)
1 cup	chopped cooked vegetables (such as broccoli, asparagus, peppers or green onions)
1/4 cup	light tomato sauce or other low-fat or non-fat pasta sauce
4 oz	cooked chicken or other lean meat, such as lean ground turkey or lean chicken sausage, chopped

1. Place the pasta, vegetables, tomato sauce and chicken in a bowl and stir to mix well. Refrigerate, covered, until ready to use, then heat in the microwave or serve chilled.

Makes 1 serving.

Variation:

You can use the proportions here as a guide and vary the vegetables, sauce and source of protein to suit your tastes and add variety to your pasta salads.

TUNA SALAD

This mixture is also nice served in endive spears or romaine lettuce leaves.

1	can (19 oz) cannellini (white kidney) beans, drained and rinsed
1	clove garlic, minced
2	cans (6 oz each), chunk light tuna, drained
1	large tomato, chopped
¼ cup	capers
2 tbsp	chopped fresh parsley
1 tbsp	lemon juice
¼ tsp	each salt and freshly ground pepper
4	slices whole-grain bread

1. Using potato masher, in bowl mash half of the cannellini beans with garlic.
2. In another bowl, mix tuna, tomato, capers, parsley and lemon juice. Stir in bean mixture and salt and pepper.
3. Divide mixture evenly among bread slices.

Makes 4 servings.

MIXED BEAN SALAD

1	can (540 mL) mixed beans, drained and rinsed
1/2	cucumber, chopped
1	tomato, chopped
1 cup	cooked whole wheat pasta (small shells, macaroni or similar size)
2 tbsp	chopped fresh flat-leaf parsley
1 tbsp	red wine vinegar
2 tsp	extra-virgin olive oil
1/4 tsp	Dijon mustard
Pinch	each salt and freshly ground pepper
Pinch	finely chopped fresh herbs (such as thyme or oregano)

1. Place beans in large bowl and add cucumber, tomato, pasta and parsley.

2. In small bowl, whisk together vinegar, oil, mustard, salt, pepper and herbs. Pour over salad and toss to coat.

Makes 2 servings.

WALDORF CHICKEN AND RICE SALAD

3/4 cup	cooked basmati or brown rice
1	medium apple, chopped
1 or 2	stalks celery, chopped
1/4 cup	walnuts
4 oz	cooked chicken, chopped
1 tbsp	store-bought light buttermilk dressing

1. Place rice, apple, celery, walnuts and chicken in large bowl. Pour in buttermilk dressing and stir to mix.

Makes 1 serving.

CRAB SALAD IN TOMATO SHELLS

Beefsteak tomatoes are ideal for this dish because their large size will accommodate the filling, and pulp and seeds are easy to scoop out.

2	packages (200 g each) frozen crab, thawed
4	large beefsteak tomatoes
¼ cup	fat-free mayonnaise
2 tbsp	low-fat sour cream
½ tsp	grated lemon zest
1 tbsp	fresh lemon juice
2 tsp	chopped fresh tarragon
Pinch	each salt and freshly ground pepper
1 cup	coarsely chopped cooked chickpeas
½	red pepper, diced
¼ cup	finely diced celery
¼ cup	chopped fresh flat-leaf parsley
2 tbsp	chopped fresh chives
2 tbsp	shredded carrot

1. Place crab in fine-mesh sieve; press out any liquid. Remove and discard any cartilage if necessary; set aside crab.

2. Cut top quarter off tomatoes. Using small spoon, scoop out seeds and pulp, and discard. Place tomatoes cut side down on paper towel–lined plate.

3. In large bowl, stir together mayonnaise, sour cream, lemon zest and juice, tarragon, salt and pepper. Add chickpeas, red pepper, celery, parsley, chives and carrot. Add crab and stir to combine. Divide crab mixture among tomatoes.

Makes 4 servings.

GRILLED SHRIMP AND PEAR SALAD

This light dish from our friend Meryle combines unexpected ingredients to yield delicious results.

4	pears, quartered, cored and sliced
1	red pepper, seeded and chopped
1	red onion, chopped
1/4 cup	chopped cilantro
1 lb	large raw shrimp, peeled and deveined
1 tbsp	canola oil
1 tsp	chopped fresh oregano

Dressing:

2 tbsp	rice vinegar
2 tbsp	orange juice
1 tsp	orange zest
1 tsp	honey or maple syrup

1. Preheat oiled grill or broiler to high.

2. In large bowl, whisk together vinegar, orange juice, orange zest and honey.

3. Add pears, red pepper, red onion and cilantro to dressing; toss to coat. Set aside.

4. In bowl, toss shrimp with oil and oregano. If you plan to grill the shrimp, thread onto bamboo skewers that have been soaked in water for 30 minutes. If you plan to broil them, spread on baking sheet. Grill or broil shrimp, turning once, until pink and firm, about 4 minutes.

5. Divide salad mixture among plates and top with shrimp.

Makes 4 to 6 servings.

Meatless

LEMON LINGUINE WITH SMOKED SALMON

This pasta is good even at room temperature. Try it with different vegetables, such as snow peas, edamame or broccoli florets.

¼ cup	lemon juice
1 tbsp	grated lemon zest
2 tbsp	olive oil
¼ tsp	freshly ground pepper
6 oz	whole wheat linguine
¾ cup	fresh or frozen peas
6 oz	smoked salmon, chopped
2	green onions, chopped
¼ cup	chopped fresh parsley

1. In large bowl, whisk together lemon juice and zest, oil and pepper.

2. In large pot of boiling salted water, cook linguine for 5 minutes. Add peas and continue to cook for another 3 minutes or until pasta is al dente. Drain and add to bowl with lemon mixture. Add salmon, green onions and parsley; toss to combine.

Makes 4 servings.

CHEESY LENTIL AND BEAN BAKE

If you'd like, you can stir in the meat shredded from one smoked turkey drumstick (look in the deli section of the supermarket) before putting the lentil and bean mixture in the baking dish. Serve with basmati rice or pasta.

1 cup	dried green lentils (preferably du Puy), rinsed
1 tbsp	olive oil
1	onion, chopped
4	cloves garlic, chopped
1	can (28 oz) diced tomatoes
4 cups	chopped kale (tough stems removed)
2 tsp	Cajun seasoning*
1/2 tsp	salt
1	can (19 oz) black beans (or pinto beans), drained and rinsed
1 cup	shredded light-style cheddar cheese

1. Preheat oven to 375°F.

2. In saucepan, cook lentils in 3 cups water for 20 to 30 minutes or until soft. Drain and set aside.

3. Meanwhile, in large non-stick frying pan, heat oil over medium-high heat; cook onion and garlic until softened, about 5 minutes. Add diced tomatoes, kale, Cajun seasoning and salt; cook, stirring occasionally, for 10 minutes or just until kale is tender. Stir in lentils and beans.

4. Spread mixture in 13- × 9-inch glass baking dish and sprinkle cheese evenly over top. Bake for 20 minutes or until cheese is melted and mixture is bubbling.

Makes 6 servings.

* If Cajun seasoning is unavailable, make your own by combining 2 tsp each cumin, chili powder, dried basil, dried oregano, dried mustard, paprika, dried thyme, and 1/2 tsp cayenne and salt. Keeps for 3 months in airtight container.

SAVOURY BEANS AND APPLE

This dish was adapted from reader Nadia's recipe. Serve with brown basmati rice and a salad for a comforting vegetarian meal. Leftovers, served in whole wheat tortillas, make a tasty lunch.

1 tbsp	olive oil
1	onion, chopped
2	apples, peeled, cored and grated
2	carrots, grated
1	stalk celery, chopped
2	cloves garlic, minced
1 cup	vegetable or chicken stock (low-fat, low-sodium)
1/4 cup	tomato paste
2 tbsp	sherry or red wine vinegar
4 cups	cooked kidney beans (you can use canned, but it increases the G.I. rating)
2 tsp	each chopped fresh thyme and oregano
2 tsp	dry mustard
1 tsp	ground cumin
1/4 tsp	each salt and freshly ground pepper
	Low-fat sour cream or plain yogurt (optional)

1. In large, non-stick frying pan, heat oil over medium-high heat. Cook onion, apples, carrots, celery and garlic for 10 minutes or until softened.

2. In bowl, whisk together stock, tomato paste and vinegar; add to vegetable mixture in frying pan. Stir in beans, thyme, oregano, mustard, cumin, salt and pepper. Bring to boil. Reduce heat to low, cover and simmer for 45 minutes. Serve with a dollop of sour cream or yogurt, if desired.

Makes 4 to 6 servings.

GRILLED PORTOBELLO MUSHROOM PIZZAS

Look for the largest mushrooms you can find. Use any favourite green-light toppings and add chopped cooked lean ham, chicken or turkey for meat lovers.

8	large portobello mushrooms, stems removed
2 tsp	olive oil
1/2 cup	tomato sauce or G.I. Pesto (see recipe, page 250)
1/2 cup	light-style mozzarella cheese

Optional toppings:

Red or green peppers, seeded and chopped
Olives
Chopped fresh basil or oregano
Chopped tomatoes
Minced garlic

1. Preheat oiled grill to medium-high.
2. Brush both sides of mushrooms with oil. Grill mushrooms, stem side down, for 4 minutes. Turn and grill for another 4 minutes or until slightly softened.
3. Top mushrooms with tomato sauce and desired toppings. Sprinkle cheese over top and grill, covered, for 5 minutes or until cheese is bubbling.

Makes 4 main-course or 8 appetizer servings.

QUINOA, BEAN AND VEGETABLE CHILI

You can use any combination of beans—white, navy, pinto or chickpea—to make this chili attractive.

1 cup	quinoa, rinsed and drained
2 cups	water
¼ tsp	salt
2 tbsp	olive oil
1 cup	chopped leeks (white and light-green parts only)
3	cloves garlic, minced
1 cup	chopped carrots
1 cup	chopped celery
1	each red and green pepper, seeded and chopped
1	hot pepper, seeded and minced
1 tbsp	chili powder
2 tsp	dried oregano
1 tsp	cocoa powder
1 tsp	ground cumin
1 tsp	Hungarian paprika
½ tsp	cinnamon
½ tsp	each salt and freshly ground pepper
2	cans (28 oz each) diced tomatoes
1	can (19 oz) black beans, drained and rinsed
1	can (19 oz) pinto beans, drained and rinsed
4	green onions, chopped
½ cup	low-fat sour cream

1. In frying pan over medium heat, roast quinoa for 5 minutes or until fragrant and beginning to pop. In small saucepan, bring water to boil. Add salt and roasted quinoa; cover and simmer over medium heat for 15 to 20 minutes or until water is absorbed. Remove from heat and stir. Cover and set aside.

2. Meanwhile, in large saucepan, heat oil over medium heat. Cook leeks and garlic for 5 minutes or until softened. Stir in carrots, celery, red and green peppers, hot pepper, chili powder, oregano, cocoa, cumin, paprika, cinnamon, salt and pepper. Cook for 10 minutes, stirring often. Stir in tomatoes and black and pinto beans; simmer, stirring occasionally, for 20 minutes or until vegetables are soft. Stir in quinoa and green onions; cook for 2 minutes or until heated through. Garnish each serving with a dollop of sour cream.

Makes 8 servings.

INDIAN VEGETABLE CURRY

So many wonderful vegetarian dishes come from India. This one has a smooth mild curry flavour, but you can spike up the heat by using a hot curry paste or powder. Serve this with basmati rice.

1 tbsp	canola oil
2	onions, cut in wedges
3	cloves garlic, minced
1 tbsp	chopped fresh ginger
1 tbsp	mild curry paste or powder
1 tsp	cumin seeds, crushed
3 cups	vegetable stock (low-fat, low-sodium)
2	red bell peppers, chopped
2 cups	broccoli florets
8 oz	green beans, cut into 1-inch pieces
1	zucchini, chopped
1	can (540 mL) chickpeas, drained and rinsed
1/4 cup	chopped fresh cilantro

1. In large saucepan, heat oil over medium heat. Cook onions, garlic, ginger, curry paste and cumin seeds for 5 minutes or until softened. Add stock and bring to boil. Add peppers, broccoli, beans, zucchini and chickpeas. Cover and simmer for about 15 minutes or until vegetables are tender-crisp. Sprinkle with coriander.

Makes 4 servings.

FETTUCCINE PRIMAVERA

Primavera means "springtime" in Italian, and you can use your favourite spring vegetables, such as asparagus or fiddleheads, in this pasta. Fortunately, you can get peppers, tomatoes and peas year-round, so you can make this dish any time.

¼ cup	extra-virgin olive oil
2 cups	cubed firm tofu
3	cloves garlic, minced
¼ tsp	red pepper flakes
½ cup	vegetable cocktail juice
2 cups	chopped fresh asparagus or peas
1	red pepper, thinly sliced
1	carrot, thinly sliced
1	yellow zucchini, thinly sliced
6 oz	whole wheat fettuccine or linguine pasta
2	plum tomatoes, chopped
¼ cup	chopped fresh flat-leaf parsley
2 tbsp	grated Parmesan cheese

1. In non-stick frying pan, heat 2 tbsp of the oil over medium-high heat. Brown tofu on all sides for about 2 minutes; remove to plate. Reserve oil.

2. In large shallow saucepan, heat remaining oil and reserved oil over medium heat. Cook garlic and red pepper flakes for 1 minute. Add vegetable cocktail juice; bring to boil. Reduce heat and simmer for 1 minute. Add asparagus, red pepper, carrot and zucchini; cook, stirring, for 10 minutes or until vegetables are tender-crisp.

3. Meanwhile, in large pot of boiling salted water, cook fettuccine for 8 minutes or until al dente. Drain and return to pot. Add vegetables and tofu, and toss to coat. Stir in tomatoes, parsley and Parmesan cheese.

Makes 4 servings.

VEGETARIAN MOUSSAKA

Traditionally made with ground lamb, moussaka can be made green-light by using vegetables.

2	large eggplants (about 3 lbs total)
2 tsp	salt
1 tsp	canola oil
2	large onions, finely chopped
3	cloves garlic, minced
1	each red and green pepper, diced
1 tbsp	dried oregano
1 tsp	ground cinnamon
1/2 tsp	freshly ground pepper
1/4 tsp	ground allspice
1	can (796 mL) diced tomatoes
1/4 cup	tomato paste
1	can (540 mL) chickpeas, drained and rinsed
1/4 cup	chopped fresh flat-leaf parsley

Cheese Sauce:

2 tbsp	canola oil
1/4 cup	whole wheat flour
2 cups	warm skim milk
1/4 tsp	salt
Pinch	each ground nutmeg and freshly ground pepper
2/3 cup	liquid egg
1/2 cup	1% pressed cottage cheese
1 cup	crumbled light feta cheese

1. Preheat oven to 425°F.

2. Cut eggplants into 1/4-inch-thick slices and layer in a colander, sprinkling each layer with some of the salt. Let stand for 30 minutes, then rinse slices

and drain well. Place on baking sheets lined with parchment paper and roast, in batches if necessary, for about 20 minutes or until tender. Set aside. Reduce oven temperature to 350°F.

3. In a large, shallow Dutch oven or deep non-stick frying pan, heat oil over medium heat. Cook onions, garlic, red and green peppers, oregano, cinnamon, pepper and allspice until onions have softened, about 5 minutes. Add tomatoes and tomato paste; bring to boil. Add chickpeas and parsley, reduce heat and simmer for 15 minutes.

4. Cheese Sauce: In a saucepan, heat oil over medium heat. Stir in flour and cook for 1 minute. Whisk in milk and cook, whisking gently, for about 10 minutes or until mixture is thick enough to coat the back of a spoon. Stir in salt, nutmeg and pepper. Let cool slightly and whisk in liquid egg and cottage cheese.

5. Spread one-third of the tomato sauce in the bottom of a 13- × 9-inch baking dish. Top with one-third of the eggplant slices and one-quarter of the feta cheese. Repeat the layers. After the last layer of eggplant, spread the cheese sauce evenly over the top and sprinkle with the remaining feta.

6. Bake for about 1 hour or until top is golden brown. Let stand for 10 minutes before serving.

Makes 8 servings.

Fish and Seafood

TOMATO AND CHEESE CATFISH

An easy weeknight dish. Serve it over pasta with a side salad.

2	medium tomatoes, chopped
1	sweet onion (such as Vidalia), chopped
1	clove garlic, minced
1	small chili pepper, seeded and minced
2 tbsp	lemon juice
1 tbsp	grated lemon zest
2 tsp	olive oil
1/4 tsp	each salt and freshly ground pepper
4	catfish fillets (4 oz each)
1/2 cup	light-style cheddar cheese

1. Preheat oven to 425°F.

2. In bowl, toss together tomatoes, onion, garlic, chili pepper, lemon juice, lemon zest, oil, salt and pepper.

3. Arrange catfish fillets in 13- × 9-inch baking dish; top with tomato mixture and sprinkle with cheese. Bake for 15 to 20 minutes or until fish flakes easily with a fork.

Makes 4 servings.

BRAISED PACIFIC HALIBUT

If you can find them, halibut cheeks have a beautiful dense texture and sweet flavour. You can also use haddock, tilapia or catfish in this dish.

1	pkg (10 oz) frozen chopped spinach
1 lb	Pacific halibut
1 tbsp	grainy mustard
1 tbsp	grated lemon zest
1/2 tsp	freshly ground pepper
2 tsp	olive oil
8	cloves garlic, crushed
1	onion, chopped
1/4 tsp	salt
1 cup	dry white wine

1. Preheat oven to 375°F.
2. In medium saucepan, bring 1/2 cup water to boil. Add frozen spinach, cover and cook for 2 to 3 minutes or until thawed. Drain in colander and squeeze out as much water as possible.
3. Rinse and pat fish dry with paper towel. In small bowl, stir together mustard, lemon zest and pepper. Coat fish on all sides with mixture; set aside.
4. In large ovenproof frying pan, heat oil over medium-high heat. Add garlic and onion and cook for 8 minutes or until softened. Reduce heat to medium and stir in spinach and salt. Pour in wine. Place fish on top of spinach mixture; cover and cook for 15 to 20 minutes or until fish just flakes with a fork.

Makes 4 servings.

THAI RED CURRY SHRIMP PASTA

The combination of curry spices, lime and cilantro are hallmarks of Thai cooking.

1 lb	large raw shrimp, peeled and deveined
1 tsp	Thai red curry paste
1 tbsp	extra-virgin olive oil
4	cloves garlic, minced
2	large tomatoes, peeled, seeded and chopped
3/4 cup	dry white wine
	zest and juice of 1 lime
1/4 tsp	each salt and freshly ground pepper
2 tbsp	chopped fresh cilantro
6 oz	whole wheat spaghettini or linguine
	lime wedges

1. In bowl, toss shrimp with curry paste until well coated. Cover and refrigerate for at least 2 hours or up to 8 hours.

2. In large non-stick frying pan, heat oil over medium heat. Cook garlic just until starting to turn golden, 1 to 2 minutes. Add tomatoes, wine, lime zest and juice, salt and pepper; bring to boil. Reduce heat and simmer until sauce reduces and thickens, about 8 minutes. Add shrimp and cook, stirring, until pink and firm, 3 to 4 minutes. Stir in cilantro.

3. Meanwhile, in large pot of boiling salted water, cook pasta until al dente, about 8 minutes. Drain and add pasta to shrimp mixture. Toss to coat with sauce. Serve with lime wedges.

Makes 4 servings.

G.I. FISH FILLET

You can use virtually any fish in this simple recipe; salmon and trout are favourites in our house. This makes 1 serving, but you can multiply portions as necessary.

4 oz	fish fillet
1 to 2 tsp	fresh lemon juice
pinch	freshly ground pepper

1. Place fish fillet in microwave-safe dish and sprinkle with lemon juice and pepper. Cover dish with microwave-safe plastic wrap, folding back one corner slightly to allow steam to escape.

2. Microwave on High until fish is opaque and easily with a fork, 4 to 5 minutes. Let stand for 2 minutes, then serve.

Makes 1 serving.

GINGER-WASABI HALIBUT

This fish can also be cooked on the barbecue. Serve it with Cold Noodle Salad with Cucumber and Sesame (see recipe, page 258) for a refreshing meal.

2 tbsp	Dijon mustard
2 tsp	wasabi powder
3 tbsp	mirin or sweet sherry
2 tbsp	minced ginger root
2 tbsp	chopped fresh cilantro
1 lb	halibut, cut into 4 pieces

1. Preheat oven to 350°F.

2. In bowl, stir together mustard and wasabi powder. Stir in mirin, ginger and cilantro. Place fish in marinade and turn to coat. Let stand at room temperature for 20 minutes.

3. Place halibut on baking sheet and bake for 8 to 10 minutes or until firm to the touch.

Makes 4 servings.

Poultry

CHICKEN TIKKA

This recipe uses garam masala, an Indian spice mixture with myriad uses.

1/2 cup	Yogurt Cheese
2	cloves garlic, minced
1 tbsp	minced fresh ginger
2 tsp	lemon juice
1 tsp	salt
1/2 tsp	ground cumin
1/2 tsp	chili powder
1/2 tsp	Garam Masala
1/4 tsp	turmeric
1 lb	boneless skinless chicken breasts, cut into bite-size cubes

1. In bowl, stir together Yogurt Cheese, garlic, ginger, lemon juice, salt, cumin, chili powder, garam masala and turmeric. Add chicken and toss to coat thoroughly with mixture. Cover and marinate in refrigerator for 4 to 6 hours.

2. Preheat oiled grill to medium-high or oven to 400°F.

3. Remove chicken from marinade and thread onto 4 bamboo skewers that have been soaked for 30 minutes.

4. Grill, turning occasionally, until chicken is no longer pink inside, about 10 minutes, or place on baking sheet and bake for 10 to 12 minutes.

Makes 4 servings.

CHICKEN STIR-FRY WITH BROCCOLI

This quick chicken stir-fry will get everyone eating their broccoli.

1	egg white
1 tsp	Chinese Spice Mix, optional
1 lb	boneless skinless chicken breasts, cut into bite-size pieces
3 tbsp	orange juice
2 tbsp	soy sauce
1 tbsp	hoisin sauce
1 tbsp	oyster sauce
2 tsp	cornstarch
1 tsp	sesame oil
1 tbsp	canola oil
2	cloves garlic, minced
1	onion, thinly sliced
1	red pepper, seeded and sliced
1 tbsp	minced fresh ginger
1	bunch broccoli, trimmed and cut into 1-inch pieces
¼ cup	water
1 cup	bean sprouts
½ cup	coarsely chopped cashews

1. In medium bowl, whisk egg white and spice mix. Add chicken and toss.

2. In small bowl, stir orange juice, soy sauce, hoisin sauce, oyster sauce, cornstarch and sesame oil until smooth. Set aside.

3. In wok or large non-stick frying pan, heat canola oil over high heat. Add chicken mixture and stir-fry for 5 minutes. Remove to plate or bowl.

4. Add garlic, onion, red pepper and ginger. Stir-fry for 1 minute. Add broccoli and water and bring to boil. Cover and cook for 5 minutes or just until broccoli is tender crisp.

5. Add chicken and sauce, and stir fry for 3 min. Stir in sprouts and cashews.

CHICKEN CURRY

	Vegetable oil cooking spray (preferably canola or olive oil)
1	medium onion, sliced
1 to 2 tbsp	curry powder (or more, to taste)
1 cup	sliced carrots
1 cup	chopped celery
1/2 cup	basmati rice
1	medium apple, chopped
1/4 cup	raisins
1	boneless skinless chicken breast (8 oz), cooked

1. Spray non-stick frying pan with oil, then place over medium heat. Add onion and curry powder, stir to coat onion with curry, then sauté for 1 minute.

2. Add carrots and celery, stir to mix, then sauté for 1 minute.

3. Add rice, apple, raisins and 1 cup of water, and stir to mix. Cover and let simmer until liquid is absorbed.

4. Add cooked chicken and heat through for 2 minutes.

Makes 2 servings.

CHICKEN SCHNITZEL

Kids love this dish. You can substitute more traditional veal scallopine for the chicken.

4	boneless skinless chicken breasts (4 oz each)
$1/2$ cup	whole wheat flour
$1/2$ tsp	each salt and freshly ground pepper
2	omega-3 egg whites
$1/2$ cup	wheat bran
$1/4$ cup	wheat germ
$1/4$ cup	fine dry whole wheat breadcrumbs
1 tsp	grated orange zest
1 tbsp	extra-virgin olive oil
$1/2$ cup	fresh orange juice
$1/2$ cup	chicken stock (low-fat, low-sodium)
$1/2$ cup	thinly sliced dried apricots
$1/4$ cup	chopped green onion

1. Using meat mallet or rolling pin, pound chicken breasts between 2 pieces of plastic wrap until about $1/4$ inch thick.

2. In large, shallow dish or pie plate, combine flour, salt and pepper. In another shallow dish or pie plate, whisk egg whites. In third dish or pie plate, combine bran, wheat germ, breadcrumbs and orange zest.

3. Pat chicken dry and dredge in flour mixture, shaking off excess. Dip in egg whites, letting excess drip off, then dredge in bran mixture, coating completely.

4. In large non-stick frying pan, heat oil over medium-high heat. Fry chicken (in batches, if necessary) for 4 minutes per side or until golden brown and just cooked through. Transfer schnitzel to platter and place in 200°F oven to keep warm.

5. In same frying pan, combine orange juice, stock and apricots. Bring to boil and reduce until slightly thickened and syrupy, about 3 minutes. Stir in green onion. Pour sauce over schnitzel.

Makes 4 servings.

ORANGE CHICKEN WITH ALMONDS

Fans of sweet-and-sour dishes will enjoy this orange-flavoured chicken. The almonds add calcium. Serve over basmati rice.

2	oranges
1 tbsp	canola oil
2	boneless skinless chicken breasts (4 oz each), diced
2 tsp	minced ginger root
1/4 tsp	each salt and freshly ground pepper
2	green onions, chopped
1	each red and green pepper, chopped
Pinch	red pepper flakes
1/4 cup	chicken stock (low-fat, low-sodium)
3 tbsp	soy sauce
2 tsp	cornstarch
1/2 cup	sliced almonds, toasted

1. Using rasp or grater, remove 1 tsp of the orange zest and set aside. Cut away orange zest and pith from 1 of the oranges and discard. Chop orange flesh coarsely. Cut other orange in half and squeeze out juice; set aside, discarding rind.
2. In large non-stick frying pan or wok, heat 1 1/2 tsp of the oil over medium-high heat. Cook chicken, ginger and a pinch each of the salt and pepper for about 6 minutes per side or until chicken is no longer pink inside. Transfer to plate. Add remaining oil to frying pan and cook green onions, red and green pepper, and red pepper flakes, stirring constantly, for about 6 minutes or until tender-crisp.
3. In small bowl, whisk together chicken stock, soy sauce, reserved orange zest and juice, cornstarch and remaining salt and pepper. Add chicken, chopped orange and vegetable mixture to frying pan and cook, stirring, for about 5 minutes or until sauce is thickened and chicken and vegetables are coated. Sprinkle with almonds and serve with rice.

Makes 2 servings.

CHICKEN TARRAGON WITH MUSHROOMS

Tarragon adds a light French flavour. The dish below is great for entertaining.

2 tsp	canola oil
2	boneless skinless chicken breasts (4 oz each)
1/2 tsp	freshly ground pepper
1 tsp	non-hydrogenated soft margarine
1	small onion, chopped
8 oz	mushrooms, sliced
3 tbsp	vermouth or white wine
1 tbsp	chopped fresh tarragon
1/2 cup	chicken stock (low-fat, low-sodium) or water

1. In non-stick frying pan, heat oil over medium-high heat. Sprinkle chicken with pepper and cook for about 6 minutes per side or until no longer pink inside. Transfer to plate and cover to keep warm.

2. Add margarine to frying pan and cook onion and mushrooms, stirring constantly, until soft, about 5 minutes. Add vermouth and tarragon, and simmer for 1 minute. Add stock and simmer for 2 minutes or until reduced by half. Season with pepper.

3. Serve sauce over chicken.

Makes 2 servings.

SPICY ROASTED CHICKEN WITH TOMATOES AND TARRAGON

This recipe is from our friend Meryle. Serve it with basmati rice or quinoa to soak up the sauce.

4 cups	cherry or grape tomatoes, halved
5	cloves garlic, crushed
1/4 cup	extra-virgin olive oil
2 tbsp	chopped fresh tarragon
2 tsp	red pepper flakes
4	boneless skinless chicken breasts (4 oz each)
1 tsp	each salt and freshly ground pepper

1. Preheat oven to 450°F.

2. In large bowl, toss tomatoes with garlic, oil, 1 tbsp of the tarragon, and red pepper flakes.

3. Place chicken on rimmed baking sheet. Arrange tomato mixture in single layer around chicken. Sprinkle chicken and tomato mixture with salt and pepper. Roast for 30 to 35 minutes or until chicken is no longer pink inside. Transfer chicken to platter. Spoon tomatoes and juices over chicken and sprinkle with remaining tarragon.

Makes 4 servings.

ZESTY BARBECUED CHICKEN

The marinade in this recipe helps keep the breasts moist when they are cooked.

¼ cup	lemon juice
2 tsp	chopped fresh rosemary
2 tsp	canola oil
4	boneless skinless chicken breasts (4 oz each)
⅓ cup	Zesty Barbecue Sauce (see below)

1. In bowl, whisk together lemon juice, rosemary and oil. Add chicken breasts; toss to coat. Marinate at room temperature for 30 minutes.

2. Meanwhile, preheat oiled grill to medium-high.

3. Remove chicken from marinade and discard marinade. Brush chicken with Zesty Barbecue Sauce; grill for 6 minutes. Turn, brush with more sauce and grill for another 6 minutes or until chicken is no longer pink inside.

Makes 4 servings.

ZESTY BARBECUED SAUCE

This sauce will keep up to 2 weeks refrigerated in an airtight container.

1	can (398 mL) tomato sauce
2	cloves garlic, minced
¼ cup	frozen apple juice concentrate
¼ cup	tomato paste
2 tbsp	cider vinegar
1 tbsp	Splenda
1 tbsp	Dijon mustard
2 tsp	chili powder
½ tsp	Worcestershire sauce
¼ tsp	each salt and freshly ground pepper

1. In large saucepan, combine tomato sauce, garlic, apple juice concentrate, tomato paste, vinegar, Splenda, mustard, chili powder, Worcestershire sauce, salt and pepper; bring to boil. Reduce heat and simmer, uncovered, for about 20 minutes or until reduced and thickened.

Makes about 1 ½ cups.

Meat

ROASTED PORK TENDERLOIN WITH BALSAMIC GLAZE AND GINGERED PEACH SALSA

This is delicious accompanied by basmati rice, asparagus and a side salad.

½ cup	balsamic vinegar
1 lb	pork tenderloin
2 tsp	olive oil
½ tsp	each salt and freshly ground pepper

Gingered Peach Salsa:

3	medium peaches, peeled and chopped
1	clove garlic, minced
½ cup	finely chopped red pepper
¼ cup	finely chopped green onion
2 tbsp	lime juice
2 tbsp	chopped fresh cilantro
1 tbsp	minced fresh ginger
½ tsp	salt

1. In bowl, stir together peaches, garlic, red pepper, green onion, lime juice, cilantro, ginger and salt. Set aside, refrigerating until needed.

2. Preheat oven to 400°F.

3. In saucepan, bring vinegar to simmer and allow to reduce by half or until thickened and syrupy. Set aside.

4. Using sharp knife, trim any excess fat and silverskin from tenderloin.
Rub pork all over with oil and sprinkle with salt and pepper. In ovenproof frying pan over high heat, brown tenderloin on all sides. Remove from heat and brush tenderloin with reduced vinegar. Place frying pan in oven for about 10 to 15 minutes or until meat thermometer reaches 155°F or pork has only a hint of pink inside. Let stand for 5 minutes before slicing. Serve with Gingered Peach Salsa.

Makes 4 servings.

MEATLOAF

1 ½ lbs	extra-lean ground beef
1 cup	tomato juice
½ cup	old-fashioned rolled oats (uncooked)
1	omega-3 egg, lightly beaten
½ cup	chopped onion
1 tbsp	Worcestershire sauce
½ tsp	salt (optional)
¼ tsp	freshly ground pepper

1. Preheat oven to 350°F.

2. In large bowl, combine beef, tomato juice, oats, egg, onion, Worcestershire sauce, salt (if using) and pepper. Mix lightly but thoroughly.

3. Press meatloaf mixture into an 8- × 4-inch loaf pan. Bake for 1 hour, or until an instant-read meat thermometer inserted into the centre registers 160°F. Let meatloaf stand for 5 minutes before draining off any juices and slicing.

Makes 6 servings.

MARINATED FLANK STEAK

Serve this at your next summer barbecue party, paired with a big green salad.

1/4 cup	soy sauce
1/4 cup	orange juice
3 tbsp	canola oil
3 tbsp	rice vinegar
2	cloves garlic, minced
2 tbsp	minced fresh ginger
1 tbsp	Dijon mustard
1 lb	flank steak

1. In shallow dish, whisk together soy sauce, orange juice, oil, vinegar, garlic, ginger and mustard. Add flank steak and turn to coat evenly. Cover and marinate in refrigerator for at least 4 hours or up to 8 hours, turning meat occasionally.

2. Preheat oiled grill to medium-high.

3. Discarding marinade, place steak on grill; close lid and cook, turning once, for about 8 minutes per side for medium-rare or until desired doneness. Transfer to cutting board and tent with foil; let stand for 5 minutes, then slice thinly across the grain.

Makes 4 servings.

BLUEBERRY BEEF BURGERS

Blueberries help make these burgers moist and juicy.

½ cup	fresh or frozen and thawed wild blueberries
2	cloves garlic, minced
1 tbsp	balsamic vinegar
1 tbsp	Dijon mustard
1 tsp	Worcestershire sauce
½ tsp	salt
¼ tsp	freshly ground pepper
½ cup	ground flaxseed
¼ cup	rolled oats
1 lb	extra-lean ground beef
2	whole wheat buns
4	lettuce leaves
4	tomato slices

1. Preheat oiled grill or broiler to medium-high.

2. Place blueberries in bowl of food processor. Add garlic, vinegar, mustard, Worcestershire sauce, salt and pepper; purée. Scrape into large bowl. Stir in flaxseed and oats. Add ground beef and mix with hands or wooden spoon until well combined.

3. Form meat mixture into 4 patties, each about ½ inch thick. Place on grill or broiler pan and cook, turning once, until no longer pink inside, 4 to 5 minutes per side. Serve each patty on half a whole wheat bun. Top with lettuce and tomato slices.

Makes 4 servings.

BOLOGNESE PASTA SAUCE

This is a great staple sauce to have on hand. Freeze it in 1-cup portions in zip-top plastic freezer bags and place in the fridge overnight to defrost. Use in lasagna, serve with whole wheat pasta combined with cooked kidney beans, or serve over brown basmati rice.

1 tbsp	olive oil
1 lb	extra-lean ground beef
1/2 cup	skim milk
2	cloves garlic, minced
1	onion, chopped
1	red pepper, seeded and chopped
1	green pepper, seeded and chopped
1	stalk celery, chopped
1	carrot, chopped
1 tbsp	dried oregano
1 tsp	salt
1/2 tsp	freshly ground pepper
1 cup	red wine or unsweetened pure grape juice
2	cans (28 oz each) crushed tomatoes
1 tbsp	chopped fresh basil

1. In large pot or deep frying pan, heat oil over medium-high heat. Cook beef for about 8 minutes or until browned. Pour in milk and cook for another 2 to 3 minutes or until milk is absorbed. Reduce heat to medium. Add garlic, onion, red and green peppers, celery, carrot, oregano, salt and pepper; cook, stirring, for about 5 minutes or until vegetables are softened. Pour in wine and cook, stirring and scraping up any brown bits, for about 1 minute or until wine is evaporated.
2. Add tomatoes and basil; bring to boil. Reduce heat and simmer, uncovered, for about 45 minutes or until sauce is thick and flavourful.

Makes about 6 cups.

PORK MEDALLIONS DIJON

Eating the green-light way doesn't mean you have to sacrifice flavour. This pork is fork-tender, and the tasty sauce is rich and creamy.

2	pork tenderloins (about 12 oz each)
5 tbsp	whole wheat flour
3/4 tsp	each salt and freshly ground pepper
2 tbsp	extra-virgin olive oil
2	onions, thinly sliced
1	clove garlic, minced
1/4 cup	Dijon mustard
1 1/4 cups	skim milk
1/2 cup	dry white wine
1 tbsp	chopped fresh tarragon

1. Slice pork into 3/4-inch medallions. Place between 2 pieces of waxed paper; using meat mallet or rolling pin, pound to about 1/4-inch thickness.

2. On dinner plate, combine 3 tbsp of the flour and 1/2 tsp each of the salt and pepper; dredge pork. In large non-stick frying pan, heat 1 tbsp of the oil over medium-high heat. Cook pork until golden brown on both sides, 5 to 7 minutes; transfer to the plate and cover to keep warm.

3. In same frying pan, heat remaining oil over medium heat. Cook onions and garlic, stirring often, for 5 minutes or until softened. Reduce heat to medium-low; cook, stirring occasionally, for 10 minutes or until golden. Add remaining flour and stir to coat onion. Add mustard; cook for 2 minutes. Stir in milk, wine and remaining salt and pepper. Cook, stirring constantly, until thickened. (If mixture is too thick, stir in 1 tbsp warm water.) Stir in tarragon. Return pork to pan and cook until heated through, about 1 minute.

Makes 6 servings.

Snacks

CRUNCHY CHICKPEAS

This is an addictive snack with all the crunch and saltiness of chips and pretzels but without the fat!

2	cans (540 mL each) chickpeas, drained and rinsed
2 tbsp	extra-virgin olive oil or canola oil
1/2 tsp	salt
Pinch	cayenne pepper

1. Preheat oven to 400°F.
2. In large bowl, toss chickpeas with oil, salt and cayenne. Spread on large baking sheet in a single layer.
3. Bake for about 45 minutes or until golden, shaking pan a couple of times during cooking. Let cool completely.

Makes 6 servings.

Helpful Hint: Add more salt or other spices to change the flavour of the chickpeas.

CRANBERRY CINNAMON BRAN MUFFINS

These muffins are very nutritious with a high fibre content and have a great cinnamon flavour.

1 cup	wheat bran
½ cup	All-Bran or 100% Bran cereal
¼ tsp	salt
½ cup	boiling water
1 cup	skim milk
1 cup	dried cranberries
⅓ cup	Splenda
1	omega-3 egg
¼ cup	canola oil
1 ¼ cups	whole wheat flour
1 ¼ tsp	baking soda
1 tsp	ground cinnamon

1. Preheat oven to 375°F. Line a 12-cup muffin tin with paper or foil liners.

2. In bowl, combine bran, cereal and salt. Pour boiling water over and stir to combine. Stir in milk and cranberries and set aside.

3. In another bowl, whisk together Splenda, egg and oil. Stir into bran mixture.

4. In large bowl, stir together flour, baking soda and cinnamon. Pour bran mixture over flour mixture and stir until just combined.

5. Divide batter among muffin cups. Bake for about 20 minutes or until tester inserted in centre of muffin comes out clean.

Makes 12 muffins.

Make Ahead: These muffins can be kept at room temperature for about 2 days or frozen for up to 1 month. (Wrap each muffin individually before freezing to help prevent freezer burn. Then place them in a resealable plastic bag or airtight container.)

CARROT MUFFINS

These healthful muffins are a delightful source of fibre.

1 cup	whole wheat flour
1/2 cup	wheat bran
1/2 cup	ground flaxseed
1/4 cup	Splenda
2 tsp	baking powder
1/2 tsp	baking soda
2 tsp	ground cinnamon
1 tsp	ground ginger
1/4 tsp	salt
1 cup	buttermilk
1/2 cup	liquid egg
1/4 cup	canola oil
1 tsp	vanilla
1 1/2 cups	finely grated carrot
1/2 cup	raisins, softened in hot water for 10 minutes and drained
1/3 cup	chopped pecans

1. Preheat oven to 375°F. Line a 12-cup muffin tin with paper or foil liners.
2. In large bowl, combine flour, bran, flaxseed, Splenda, baking powder, baking soda, cinnamon, ginger and salt.
3. In small bowl, whisk together buttermilk, liquid egg, oil and vanilla. Stir in carrot, raisins and pecans. Add flour mixture and stir just until combined.
4. Divide batter among muffin cups. Bake for 20 to 25 minutes or until tester inserted in centre of muffin comes out clean.

Makes 12 muffins.

APPLE BRAN MUFFINS

Ruth created this recipe several years ago when I was trying to lose weight. We would make large batches and freeze them. Then, whenever I needed a snack, I'd warm one in the microwave. They were so convenient and delicious.

3/4 cup	All-Bran or Bran Buds cereal
1 cup	skim milk
2/3 cup	whole wheat flour
1/3 cup	Splenda
2 tsp	baking powder
1/2 tsp	baking soda
1/4 tsp	salt
1 tsp	ground allspice
1/2 tsp	ground cloves
1 1/4 cups	oat bran
2/3 cup	raisins
1	large apple, peeled and cut into 1/4-inch cubes
1	omega-3 egg, lightly beaten
2 tsp	canola oil
1/2 cup	unsweetened applesauce

1. Preheat oven to 350°F. Line a 12-cup muffin tin with paper or foil liners.

2. In a bowl, combine cereal and milk; let stand for a few minutes.

3. In large bowl, stir together flour, Splenda, baking powder, baking soda, salt, allspice and cloves. Stir in oat bran, raisins and apple.

4. In small bowl, combine egg, oil and applesauce. Stir, along with cereal mixture, into dry ingredients.

5. Divide batter among muffin cups. Bake until lightly browned, about 20 minutes.

Makes 12 muffins.

WHOLE WHEAT FRUIT SCONES

Enjoy these scones with a hot cup of tea. They are even better with a little sugar-free fruit spread.

1 ½ cups	whole wheat flour
½ cup	oat bran
½ cup	chopped dried apricots or dried cranberries
2 tbsp	Splenda
2 tsp	baking powder
½ tsp	salt
¼ tsp	ground nutmeg
¼ cup	non-hydrogenated soft margarine
⅔ cup	skim milk
2 tbsp	liquid egg

1. Preheat oven to 425°F.
2. In large bowl, combine flour, oat bran, dried apricots, Splenda, baking powder, salt and nutmeg. Using your fingers, rub margarine into flour mixture to combine. Add milk and toss with fork to form soft dough.
3. Place dough on floured surface and knead gently about 5 times. Pat dough out to ½-inch thickness. Cut dough into 8 squares, or use cookie or biscuit cutter to cut scones.
4. Place on baking sheet and brush tops with liquid egg. Bake for about 12 minutes or until golden on bottom.

Makes 8 scones.

STRAWBERRY TEA BREAD

This recipe makes two loaves, one for now and one for the freezer. A slice makes a perfect snack or a delicious dessert paired with sliced berries.

1 ½ cups	whole wheat flour
1 ½ cups	rolled oats
½ cup	wheat bran
1 tsp	cinnamon
1 tsp	baking soda
½ tsp	baking powder
½ tsp	salt
3/4 cup	liquid egg
3/4 cup	Splenda
½ cup	canola oil
½ cup	skim milk
1 tsp	vanilla
4 cups	strawberries, fresh or frozen and thawed, mashed

1. Preheat oven to 375°F. Oil two 9- × 5-inch loaf pans.
2. In large bowl, stir together flour, oats, bran, cinnamon, baking soda, baking powder and salt; set aside.
3. In separate bowl, whisk together liquid egg, Splenda, oil, milk and vanilla. Pour over dry ingredients and stir just until moistened. Stir in strawberries.
4. Divide mixture evenly between pans. Bake for 45 to 50 minutes or until cake tester inserted in centre comes out clean. Let cool in pan on rack for 15 minutes. Turn out onto rack and let cool completely.

Makes 2 loaves, 14 to 16 slices each. One serving is 1 slice.

Make Ahead: Wrap in plastic wrap or foil and store at room temperature up to 3 days, or wrap in plastic wrap and heavy-duty foil and freeze up to 1 month.

Desserts

CREAMY RASPBERRY MOUSSE

No one will know this dessert is so easy to make. Serve it as is or dress it up with some fresh fruit or berries.

Makes 4 servings

1 cup	low-fat cottage cheese
1 cup	frozen raspberries
2 tbsp	Splenda
1 tbsp	amaretto or berry-flavoured liqueur (optional)

1. Combine all ingredients in a food processor and process until smooth. Serve immediately or refrigerate in airtight container for up to 3 days.

FANCY FRUIT SALAD

Use pretty glass serving dishes and layer fruit for effect. Vary the fruit combination for colour and taste.

1 pint	strawberries sliced (keep 4 whole for top)
1 pint	fresh berries (blueberries, blackberries)
2 tbsp	orange juice
1/2 tsp	ground cinnamon
1/4 tsp	ground nutmeg
1 tsp	Splenda (or more to taste)
4	kiwi peeled and sliced
4	sprigs of mint (optional)

1. Wash and drain fruit. Sprinkle berries with sugar substitute.

2. Combine together the orange juice and nutmeg in a small bowl. Layer fruits in dish, ending with slices of kiwi on top.

3. Drizzle each dish with a small amount of orange juice mixture. Top with whole strawberry and mint if using. Serve with sweetened strained yogurt on the side.

BERRY CRUMBLE

This is one of Ruth's favourite green-light desserts. Though it's best made with fresh berries during the summer, it's also lovely with frozen fruit.

5 cups	fresh or frozen berries, such as raspberries, blackberries, blueberries and sliced strawberries
1	large apple, cored and chopped
2 tbsp	whole wheat flour
2 tbsp	Splenda
½ tsp	ground cinnamon

Topping:

1 cup	large-flake oats
½ cup	chopped pecans or walnuts
¼ cup	brown Splenda
¼ cup	non-hydrogenated soft margarine, melted
1 tsp	ground cinnamon

1. Preheat oven to 350°F.
2. In 8-inch square baking dish, combine berries and apple.
3. In bowl, combine flour, Splenda and cinnamon. Sprinkle over fruit and toss gently.
4. In medium bowl, combine oats, pecans, brown Splenda, margarine and cinnamon. Sprinkle over fruit mixture. Bake for about 30 minutes or until fruit is tender and top is golden.

Makes 6 servings.

Variation: Prepare as above and microwave on High for about 6 minutes or until fruit is tender. The top won't get golden or crisp in the microwave.

PLUM CRUMBLE

Crumbles are an ideal green-light dessert and can be made with a wide array of fruit. Try using pears instead of the plums, cutting back slightly on the amount of Splenda.

1 ½ lbs	prune plums (such as damson or Italian), halved and pitted
1 tbsp	Splenda
1 tbsp	cornstarch
½ tsp	ground ginger
½ tsp	ground cinnamon

Topping:

3/4 cup	large-flake oats
½ cup	whole wheat flour
½ cup	Splenda
¼ cup	chopped almonds or pecans
¼ cup	non-hydrogenated soft margarine
1 tsp	grated orange zest
½ tsp	ground cinnamon
¼ tsp	ground cardamom

1. Preheat oven to 350°F.

2. In bowl, toss plums with Splenda, cornstarch, ginger and cinnamon. Arrange evenly in deep 9-inch pie plate.

3. In bowl, combine oats, flour, Splenda, almonds, margarine, orange zest, cinnamon and cardamom. Using your fingers, rub ingredients together until crumbly dough forms. Sprinkle evenly over fruit mixture. Bake for 35 to 40 minutes or until topping is golden and fruit mixture is bubbling.

Makes 6 servings.

Make Ahead: Refrigerate up to 2 days.

APPLE RASPBERRY COFFEE CAKE

A piece of this fruit-laden cake makes a delectable light dessert. It can be refrigerated for up to 3 days.

1 cup	whole wheat flour
1/2 cup	wheat bran
1/2 cup	brown Splenda
1 1/2 tsp	baking powder
1/2 tsp	baking soda
1/4 tsp	ground cinnamon
1/4 tsp	ground nutmeg
Pinch	salt
1/2 cup	buttermilk
1/4 cup	non-hydrogenated soft margarine, melted and cooled
1/4 cup	liquid egg
2 tsp	vanilla
1 cup	fresh raspberries
1	apple, cored and diced

Topping:

1/3 cup	large-flake oats
1/4 cup	brown Splenda
2 tbsp	chopped pecans
1 tbsp	non-hydrogenated soft margarine

1. Preheat oven to 350°F. Line an 8-inch square baking pan with parchment paper.

2. In large bowl, stir together flour, bran, brown Splenda, baking powder, baking soda, cinnamon, nutmeg and salt; set aside.

3. In another bowl, whisk together buttermilk, margarine, liquid egg and vanilla. Pour over flour mixture and stir until moistened. Spread two-thirds of the batter in prepared baking pan.

4. Toss raspberries and apple together and sprinkle over batter. Dollop with remaining batter, smoothly gently with wet spatula.

5. In bowl, combine oats, brown Splenda, pecans and margarine. Sprinkle over top of cake; press gently into batter. Bake for about 30 minutes or until tester inserted in centre comes out clean.

Makes 9 servings.

ONE-BOWL CHOCOLATE CAKE

This delicious cake is green-light when served with fresh berries. You can make a yellow-light version with chocolate ganache icing for a special occasion (see Variation below).

1 ¹/₃ cups	whole wheat flour
³/₄ cup	Splenda
¹/₂ cup	unsweetened cocoa powder
1 ¹/₂ tsp	baking soda
1 ¹/₂ tsp	baking powder
¹/₂ tsp	salt
1	omega-3 egg
1	omega-3 egg white
²/₃ cup	buttermilk
¹/₂ cup	unsweetened applesauce
2 tbsp	canola oil
1 tsp	vanilla
	Grated zest of 1 orange

1. Preheat oven to 350°F. Oil an 8-inch round cake pan or springform pan. Cut a round of parchment paper and line bottom of pan.

2. In mixer, food processor or blender, mix flour, Spenda, cocoa, baking soda, baking powder, salt, egg, egg white, buttermilk, applesauce, oil, vanilla and orange zest just until smooth.

3. Pour batter into prepared pan, smoothing top. Bake for 20 to 25 minutes or until top springs back when lightly touched and tester inserted in centre comes out clean.

4. Let cool in pan on rack for 30 minutes. Remove from pan and remove parchment paper; let cool completely on rack.

Makes 8 servings.

Ganache variation: Melt 8 ounces of 70 percent chocolate in a bowl set over barely simmering water. Remove from heat and whisk in 1 ¹/₄ cups low-fat soy milk until smooth. Spread ganache over top and sides of cake.

CRAN-APPLE OATMEAL BARS

Tuck these nutritious treats into packed lunches.

3 cups	large-flake oats
1¹/₂ cups	whole wheat flour
2 tsp	ground cinnamon
1 tsp	baking powder
1 tsp	baking soda
¹/₄ tsp	salt
³/₄ cup	Splenda
¹/₄ cup	non-hydrogenated margarine
1	omega-3 egg
1	egg white
³/₄ cup	unsweetened applesauce
2 tsp	vanilla
1 cup	dried cranberries

1. Preheat oven to 350°F. Lin a 13- × 9-inch baking pan with parchment paper.
2. In large bowl, combine oats, whole wheat flour, cinnamon, baking powder, baking soda and salt.
3. In another bowl, beat together Splenda and margarine until fluffy. Beat in egg, egg white, applesauce and vanilla. Add oat mixture and stir to combine. Stir in cranberries. Scrape dough into prepared baking pan and bake for 20 minutes or until cake tester inserted in centre comes out clean. Let cool completely and cut into bars.

Makes 24 bars.

PECAN BROWNIES

Brownies, you ask? That's right. These are packed with fibre and are absolutely scrumptious, so get baking!

1	can (540 mL) white or red kidney or black beans, drained and rinsed
1/2 cup	skim milk
1/3 cup	liquid egg
1/4 cup	non-hydrogenated soft margarine, melted
1 tbsp	vanilla
3/4 cup	Splenda
1/2 cup	whole wheat flour
1/2 cup	unsweetened cocoa powder
1 tsp	baking powder
Pinch	salt
1/2 cup	chopped toasted pecans

1. Preheat oven to 350°F. Line an 8-inch square baking pan with parchment paper.
2. In food processor, purée beans until coarse. Add milk, liquid egg, margarine and vanilla, and purée until smooth, scraping down sides a few times. Set aside.
3. In large bowl, combine Splenda, flour, cocoa, baking powder and salt. Pour bean mixture over flour mixture and stir to combine. Scrape batter into prepared pan, smoothing top. Sprinkle with pecans.
4. Bake for about 18 minutes or until tester inserted in centre comes out clean. Let cool on rack, then cut into 16 squares.

Makes 16 brownies. One serving is one brownie.

Make Ahead: Wrap brownies in plastic wrap or store in an airtight container for up to 4 days. They can also be frozen for up to 2 weeks.

CREAMY LEMON SQUARES

These tiny treats make an ideal mid-afternoon pick-me-up.

½ cup	whole wheat flour
½ cup	wheat bran
¼ cup	ground almonds
¼ cup	Splenda
¼ cup	non-hydrogenated soft margarine

Filling:

1 cup	Splenda
3/4 cup	liquid egg
2 tsp	grated lemon zest
½ cup	fresh lemon juice
¼ cup	buttermilk
2 tsp	cornstarch
1 tsp	baking powder

1. Preheat oven to 350°F. Oil an 8-inch square baking pan.

2. In mixer or food processor, combine flour, bran, almonds and Splenda. Cut in margarine until mixture is crumbly.

3. Press mixture evenly into bottom of prepared pan. Bake for 20 to 25 minutes or until lightly browned. Set aside to cool, leaving oven on.

4. In bowl, whisk together Splenda and liquid egg. Stir in lemon zest and juice, buttermilk, cornstarch and baking powder. Pour over base. Bake for 15 to 20 minutes or until filling is set. Let cool to room temperature, then refrigerate for at least 2 hours before cutting into squares.

Makes 36 squares. One serving is 2 squares.

Make Ahead: Store in airtight container up to 3 days or freeze up to 1 month.

Appendix

Complete G.I. Diet Food Guide

BEANS		
Baked beans with pork		Baked beans* (low fat)
Broad		Black beans
Refried		Black-eyed peas
		Butter beans
		Chickpeas
		Italian
		Kidney
		Lentils
		Lima
		Mung
		Navy
		Pigeon
		Refried (low fat)
		Romano
		Soybeans
		Split peas

* Limit serving size to 1/2 cup.

BEVERAGES

Alcoholic drinks*	Diet soft drinks (caffeinated)	Bottled water
Coconut milk	Milk (1%)	Club soda
Fruit drinks	Most unsweetened juice	Decaffeinated coffee (with skim milk, no sugar)
Milk (whole or 2%)	Red wine*	Diet soft drinks (no caffeine)
Regular coffee	Vegetable juices	Herbal tea
Regular soft drinks		Light instant chocolate
Rice milk		Milk (skim)
Sweetened juice		Soy milk (plain, low fat)
Watermelon juice		Tea (with skim milk, no sugar)

BREADS

Bagels	Crispbreads (with fibre)*	100% stone-ground whole wheat*
Baguette/Croissants	Pita (whole wheat)	Crispbreads (with high fibre, e.g., Wasa Fibre)*
Cake/Cookies	Tortillas (whole wheat)	
Cornbread	Whole-grain breads	
Crispbreads (regular)		Whole-grain, high-fibre breads (min. 3 g fibre per slice)*
Croutons		
English muffins		
Hamburger buns		
Hot dog buns		
Kaiser rolls		
Melba toast		
Muffins/Doughnuts		
Pancakes/Waffles		
Pizza		
Stuffing		

* Limit serving size (see page 27).

Tortillas

White bread

CEREALS

All cold cereals except those listed as yellow- or green-light	Kashi Go Lean	100% Bran
	Kashi Go Lean Crunch	All-Bran
Cereal/Granola bars	Kashi Good Friends	Bran Buds
Granola	Shredded Wheat Bran	Cold cereals with minimum 10 g fibre per serving
Grits		
Muesli (commercial)		Fibre 1
		Fibre First
		Oat Bran
		Porridge (large flake oats)
		Red River

CEREAL/GRAINS

Amaranth	Cornstarch	Arrowroot flour
Almond flour	Spelt	Barley
Couscous	Whole wheat couscous	Buckwheat
Millet		Bulgur
Polenta		Gram flour
Rice (short-grain, white, instant)		Kamut (not puffed)
		Quinoa
Rice cakes		Rice (basmati, wild, brown, long-grain)
Rice noodles		Wheat berries

CONDIMENTS/SEASONINGS

Croutons	Mayonnaise (light)	Capers
Ketchup		Chili powder
Mayonnaise		Extracts (vanilla, etc.)
Tartar sauce		Garlic

		Gravy mix (maximum 20 calories per ¼ cup serving)
		Herbs
		Horseradish
		Hummus
		Mayonnaise (fat-free)
		Mustard
		Salsa (no added sugar)
		Sauerkraut
		Soy sauce (low sodium)
		Spices
		Teriyaki sauce
		Vinegar
		Worcestershire sauce

DAIRY

Almond milk	Cheese (low fat)	Buttermilk
Cheese	Cream cheese (light)	Cheese (fat-free)
Chocolate milk	Frozen yogurt (low fat, low sugar)	Cottage cheese (1% or fat-free)
Coconut milk	Ice cream (low fat)	Cream cheese (fat-free)
Cottage cheese (whole or 2%)	Milk (1%)	Extra low-fat cheese (e.g., Laughing Cow Light, Boursin Light)
Cream	Sour cream (light)	
Cream cheese	Yogurt (low fat, with sugar)	Fruit yogurt (non-fat with sweetener)
Evaporated milk		
Goat milk		Ice cream (½ cup, low-fat and no added sugar, e.g., Breyers Premium Fat Free, Nestlé Legend)
Ice cream		
Milk (whole or 2%)		
Rice milk		
Sour cream		

Yogurt (whole or 2%)		Milk (skim)
		Sour cream (fat-free)
		Soy milk (plain, low fat)
		Soy cheese (low fat)

FATS AND OILS

Butter	Corn oil	Almonds*
Coconut oil	Mayonnaise (light)	Canola oil*/seed
Hard margarine	Most nuts	Cashews*
Lard	Natural nut butters	Flax seed
Mayonnaise	Natural peanut butter	Hazelnuts*
Palm oil	Peanuts	Macadamia nuts*
Peanut butter (regular and light)	Pecans	Mayonnaise (fat-free)
Salad dressings (regular)	Salad dressings (light)	Olive oil*
	Sesame oil	Pistachios*
Tropical oils	Soft margarine (non-hydrogenated)	Salad dressings (low fat, low sugar)
Vegetable shortening	Soy oil	Soft margarine (non-hydrogenated, light)*
	Sunflower oil	Vegetable oil sprays
	Vegetable oils	
	Walnuts	

FRUITS

FRESH

Cantaloupe	Apricots	Apples
Honeydew melon	Bananas	Avocado* (1/4)
Kumquats	Custard apples	Blackberries
Watermelon	Figs	Blueberries
	Kiwi	Cherries
	Mango	Cranberries
	Papaya	Grapefruit
	Persimmon	Grapes
	Pineapple	Guavas

* Limit serving size (see page 27).

		Pomegranates	Lemons Nectarines Oranges (all varieties) Peaches Plums Pears Raspberries Rhubarb Strawberries
BOTTLED, CANNED, DRIED, FROZEN	All canned fruit in syrup Applesauce containing sugar Most dried fruit** (including dates and raisins)	Canned apricots in juice or water Dried apples Dried apricots** Dried cranberries** Fruit cocktail in juice Peaches/pears in syrup	Applesauce (without sugar) Frozen berries Fruit spreads with fruit, not sugar as the main ingredient Mandarin oranges Peaches/pears in juice or water

JUICES*

	Fruit drinks Prune Sweetened juice Watermelon	Apple (unsweetened) Cranberry (unsweetened) Grapefruit (unsweetened) Orange (unsweetened) Pear (unsweetened) Pineapple (unsweetened) Vegetable	

* Whenever possible, eat the fruit rather than drink its juice.
** For baking, it is OK to use a modest amount of dried apricots or cranberries.

MEAT, POULTRY, FISH, EGGS AND TOFU

Beef (brisket, short ribs)	Beef (sirloin steak, sirloin tip)	All fish and seafood, fresh, frozen or canned (in water)
Bologna	Chicken/Turkey leg (skinless)	Back bacon
Breaded fish and seafood	Corn beef	Beef (top/eye round steak)
Duck	Dried beef	Chicken breast (skinless)
Fish canned in oil	Flank steak	Egg whites
Goose	Ground beef (lean)	
Ground beef (more than 10% fat)	Lamb (fore/leg shank, centre cut loin chop)	Ground beef (extra lean)
Hamburgers	Pork (centre loin, fresh ham, shank, sirloin, top loin)	Lean deli ham
Hot dogs		Liquid eggs (e.g., Break Free)
Lamb (rack)	Turkey bacon	Moose
Organ meats	Whole omega-3 eggs	Pastrami (turkey)
Pastrami (beef)	Tofu	Pork tenderloin
Pâté		Sashimi
Pork (back ribs, blade, spare ribs)		Soy/Whey protein powder
Regular bacon		Soy cheese (low fat)
Salami		Tofu (low fat)
Sausages		Turkey breast (skinless)
Sushi		Turkey roll
Whole regular eggs		TVP (Textured Vegetable Protein)
		Veal
		Veggie burger
		Venison

PASTA

Red	Yellow	Green
All canned pastas		Capellini
Gnocchi		Fettuccine
Macaroni and cheese		Macaroni
Noodles (canned or instant)		Mung bean noodles
		Penne
Pasta filled with cheese or meat		Rigatoni
Rice noodles		Spaghetti/Linguine
		Vermicelli

PASTA SAUCES

Red	Yellow	Green
Alfredo	Sauces with vegetables (no added sugar)	Light sauces with vegetables (no added sugar, e.g., Healthy Choice)
Sauces with added meat or cheese		
Sauces with added sugar or sucrose		

SNACKS

Red	Yellow	Green
Bagels	Bananas	Almonds*
Candy	Dark chocolate* (70% cocoa)	Applesauce (unsweetened)
Cookies	Ice cream (low fat)	Canned peaches/ pears in juice or water
Crackers	Most nuts*	
Doughnuts	Popcorn (air-popped microwaveable)	Cottage cheese (1% or fat-free)
Flavoured gelatin (all varieties)		Extra low-fat cheese (e.g., Laughing Cow Light, Boursin Light)
French fries		
Ice cream		Fruit yogurt (non-fat with sweetener)
Muffins (commercial)		Food bars*
Popcorn (regular)		Hazelnuts**
Potato chips		Ice cream (½ cup, low fat and no added sugar, e.g., Breyers Premium Fat Free)
Pretzels		
Pudding		
Raisins		

* 180–225 calorie bars, e.g., Zone or Balance Bars; ½ bar per serving
** Limit serving size (see page 27).

Rice cakes		Most fresh fruit
Sorbet		Most fresh vegetables
Tortilla chips		Most seeds
Trail mix		Pickles
White bread		Sugar-free hard candies

SOUPS

All cream-based soups	Canned chicken noodle	Chunky bean and vegetable soups (e.g., Campbell's Healthy Request, Healthy Choice)
Canned black bean	Canned lentil	
Canned green pea	Canned tomato	
Canned puréed vegetable		Homemade soups with green-light ingredients
Canned split pea		

SPREADS & PRESERVES

All products that have sugar as the first ingredient listed	Fructose	Fruit spreads (with fruit, not sugar, as the first ingredient)
	Sugar alcohols	Marmite

SUGAR & SWEETENERS

Corn syrup	Fructose	Aspartame
Glucose	Sugar alcohols	Equal
Honey		Splenda
Molasses		Stevia (note: not FDA approved)
Sugar (all types)		Sugar Twin
		Sweet'N Low

VEGETABLES			
Broad beans	Artichokes	Alfalfa sprouts	Cauliflower
French fries	Beets	Asparagus	Celery
Hash browns	Corn	Beans (green/wax)	Collard greens
Parsnips	Potatoes (boiled)	Bell peppers	Cucumbers
Potatoes (instant)	Pumpkin	Bok choy	Eggplant
Potatoes (mashed or baked)	Squash	Broccoli	Fennel
	Sweet potatoes	Brussels sprouts	Hearts of palm
Rutabaga	Yams	Cabbage (all varieties)	Kale
Turnip		Carrots	Kohlrabi
		Mustard greens	Leeks
		Okra	Lettuce
		Olives*	Mushrooms
		Onions	Radicchio
		Peas	Radishes
		Peppers (hot)	Rapini
		Pickles	Snow peas
		Potatoes (boiled, new small)*	Spinach
			Swiss chard
			Tomatoes
			Zucchini

* Limit serving size (see page 27).

Acknowledgements

As my regular Random House Canada editor went on maternity leave, I am eternally grateful to Sarah Brohman for stepping in at the eleventh hour. As we have previously worked together when I was president of the Heart and Stroke Foundation of Ontario in the Lighthearted Cookbook series, I was delighted to have the opportunity to work with her again. She brought a critical sense of focus and organization to the mountain of information generated by the e-clinic. I am deeply in her debt.

I would also like to thank Leah Springate for designing the book's evocative cover. Finally, to Anne Collins, publisher, for her original leap of faith eight years ago in launching the original *G.I. Diet* and for her continuing support for the subsequent seven books in the series.

Index

breakfast
  about, 30
  bacon, 35
  butter, 34
  cereals, 33
  coffee and tea, 32–33
  dairy products, 34
  eggs, 34
  G.I. diet chart, 30–32
  in Phase II, 230
  jams, 34
  skipping, 83
  toast, 34
  while travelling, 139
Breyers Premium Fat-Free ice cream, 45, 320
broccoli, 36, 40, 326
Brown Splenda, 74
Brussels sprouts, 36, 40, 326
buckwheat, 319
buffets, 134, 170
bulgur, 319
buns, hamburger or hot dog, 36, 318
Burger King, 133
butter, 15, 32, 34, 37, 41, 321
buttermilk, 30, 320

C

cabbage, 36, 40, 326
Caesar salads, 137
caffeine
  in coffee and tea, 46–47
  withdrawal from, 65–66
cakes, 36, 40, 137, 318
calories
  balancing intake with expenditure, 60
  and food labels, 52
Campbell's Healthy Request soups, 37, 41, 325
cancers
  and fats, 15
  and menopause, 178
  and overweight, 61, 181–82
  and waist measurement, 180
candies
  regular, 45, 324
  sugar-free hard, 45, 325
canola oil, 15, 27, 32, 37, 41, 73, 321

canola seeds, 321
cantaloupes, 321
capers, 319
carbohydrates
  breakdown measured by glycemic index,
    18–19
  for breakfast, 31–32
  for dinner, 40–41
  for lunch, 37–38
  good vs. bad, 12–13
  how they work, 12
carrots, 36, 40, 326
cashews, 321
cauliflower, 36, 40, 326
celery, 36, 38, 40, 326
cereal bars, 319
cereals
  before eating out, 136
  complete G.I. diet chart, 319
  for breakfast, 31, 33
  made with white flour, 13
  serving sizes, 27, 109
"cheating," 147–51
cheese
  cottage
    1% or fat-free, 30, 39, 45, 320, 324
    low-fat, 34
    whole or 2%, 30, 39, 320
  cream
    1% or fat-free, 30, 320
    light, 30, 320
    regular, 320
  extra low-fat, 31, 45, 320, 324
  fat-free, 39, 320
  light, 39
  low-fat, 320
  regular, 15, 30, 39, 320
  soy, 321, 323
cherries, 31, 36, 40, 321
chicken
  breast, skinless, 35, 39, 323
  leg, skinless, 323
chickpeas, 317
childhood trauma, 118
chili powder, 319
Chinese restaurants, 134–35

chocolate
    dark (70% cocoa), 45, 228, 324
    in Phase II, 228, 229
chocolate drink, 318
chocolate milk, 320
cholesterol, 15
cleaning the plate, 86
clothing, 157, 161
club soda, 318
coconut milk, 318, 320
coconut oil, 321
cod, 42
coffee
    decaffeinated, 137, 318
    increases appetite, 32–33
    regular, 318
collard greens, 326
comfort foods, 118–25
computer use while eating, 85
condiments, 319–20
cookies, 31, 36, 40, 45, 318, 324
cooking
    adjusting recipes to green-light foods, 72–74
    for company, 167
    for family, 89
    green-light sauces, 90
    holiday dinners, 168–69
    in big batches, 74–75
corn, 36, 40, 326
corn beef, 323
cornbread, 318
corn oil, 15, 41, 321
cornstarch, 319
corn syrup, 325
cottage cheese
    1% or fat-free, 30, 39, 45, 320, 324
    low-fat, 34
    whole or 2%, 30, 39, 320
couscous
    regular, 319
    whole wheat, 319
co-workers *see* family and friends
crackers, 45, 324
cranberries
    dried, 31, 322
    fresh, 321

cranberry juice, 322
cranberry sauce, 168
cravings
    and falling off the wagon, 147–51, 203–4
    for sweet or salty foods, 120–21, 137
cream, 30, 320
cream cheese
    1% or fat-free, 30, 320
    light, 30, 320
    regular, 320
crispbreads
    high-fibre, 31, 36, 318
    serving sizes, 27
    with fibre, 31, 36, 318
croissants, 36, 40, 318
croutons, 36, 318, 319
cucumbers, 36, 40, 326
custard apples, 321

D
dairy products
    as protein source, 16
    complete G.I. diet chart, 320–21
    for breakfast, 30–31, 34
    for dessert, 44
    for dinner, 39
    serving sizes, 109
dates, 322
desserts
    about, 44
    at holiday dinners, 169
    at restaurants, 137
diabetes
    and menopause, 178
    and overweight, 61
    risk reduced through weight loss, 180
    and waist measurement, 180
diets
    Mediterranean, 85
    unsuccessful, 2, 62–63
dinner
    about, 38–39
    beans, 42–43
    fish, 42
    G.I. diet chart, 39–41
    in Phase II, 230

and glucose and insulin levels, 18–20
and weight gain or loss, 19
gnocchi, 324
goat milk, 320
goose, 323
grains, *see also* breads
charts, 319
for dinner, 40
for lunch, 36
gram flour, 319
granola, 31, 319
granola bars, 319
grapefruit, 31, 36, 40, 321
grapefruit juice, 322
grapes, 32, 36, 40, 321
gravy mix, 320
grazing, 84, 121
Greek restaurants, 134
green-light foods
adjusting recipes, 72–74
defined, 21
in Phase II, 229
in Preliminary Phase and Phase I, 25–26, 27
preparing your kitchen, 50–51, 202
serving sizes, 27
shopping for, 51
green tea, 33
grills, indoor, 75
grits, 319
guavas, 321

H
habits
cleaning the plate, 86
eating high-sugar, high-fat treats, 87–88
eating too fast, 83–84, 85, 110, 121
grazing, 84, 121
not drinking enough, 85
rewarding exercise, 86
shopping on empty stomach, 87
skipping breakfast, 83
strategies to break, 122–23
unconscious eating, 85, 121
ham, lean deli, 30, 35, 39, 323
hamburger buns, 36, 318

hamburgers
charts, 323
for dinner, 39
for lunch, 35
from fast food restaurants, 132
homemade, 42
hash browns, 32, 326
hazelnuts, 32, 41, 45, 321, 324
headaches, 65–66
health
benefits of weight loss, 60–61
disease risks of excess weight, 48–49, 59, 61, 97
menopause-related issues, 178–84
Healthy Choice
pasta sauce, 324
soups, 37, 41, 325
heart disease
and fats, 15
and menopause, 178
and overweight, 61
risk reduced through healthy eating, 180–81
and waist measurement, 180
hearts of palm, 326
herbal teas, 33
herbs, 320
herring, 15
high blood pressure, 61, 178, 180
hip replacements, 182
holidays, 87, 167–69
honey, 325
honeydew melons, 321
hormones
and glucose, 20
impact on weight, 58–59
and sweet/salty cravings, 137
and weight plateaus, 146
horseradish, 320
hot dog buns, 36, 318
hot dogs, 35, 39, 323
hot flashes, 61, 182–83, 195
hummus, 38, 320
hunger
at start of G.I. Diet, 25
and cleaning the plate, 86

and eating too fast, 85
and other diets, 26
satisfied by protein, 16
hypertension, 61, 178, 180

I
ice cream
low-fat, 45, 320, 324
low-fat, no added sugar, 45, 320, 324
regular, 45, 320, 324
Indian restaurants, 135
insomnia, 182–83
insulin, 19–20
irritability, 120
Italian restaurants, 134

J
jams, 34, 322, 325
Japanese restaurants, 135
Jenkins, David, 18
joint replacements, 182, 195
juices
about, 46
complete G.I. diet chart, 322
for breakfast, 32
sweetened, 32, 318, 322
unsweetened, 32, 318, 322

K
Kaiser rolls, 318
kale, 326
kamut, 319
Kashi
Go Lean cereal, 31, 319
Go Lean Crunch cereal, 31, 319
Good Friends cereal, 31, 319
Kentucky Fried Chicken, 134
ketchup, 319
KFC, 134
kiwis, 32, 36, 40, 321
knee replacements, 182, 195
kohlrabi, 326
kumquats, 321

L
labels, 52–53
lamb
lean cuts, 35, 39, 323
rack, 323
lard, 321
Latin American restaurants, 135
Laughing Cow Light cheese, 45, 320, 324
leeks, 36, 40, 326
lemons, 36, 40, 322
lentils, 317
lettuce, 36, 40, 326
lifestyle in middle age, 59
lunch
about, 35
G.I. diet chart, 35–37
in Phase II, 230
salads, 38
sandwiches, 38

M
macadamia nuts, 321
macaroni and cheese, 36, 40, 324
mackerel, 15
maltitol, 77
mandarin oranges, 322
mangoes, 32, 36, 40, 321
margarine
hard, 32, 37, 41, 321
serving sizes, 27, 109
soft, 32, 37, 41, 321
marmite, 325
mayonnaise
fat-free, 37, 41, 320, 321
in sandwiches, 38
light, 37, 41, 319, 321
regular, 37, 41, 319, 321
McDonald's, 133
meal basics
about, 30
beverages, 46–47
breakfast, 30–35
desserts, 44
dinner, 38–44
how much to eat, 26–27
lunch, 35–38

for dinner, 41
for lunch, 37
for snacks, 45, 324
overall chart, 321
serving sizes, 27

O

Oat Bran cereal, 31, 319
oatmeal, 13, 33, 319
obesity
    defined by BMI, 24
    epidemic of, 11
    and exercise, 190
    health risks, 61, 179–83
oils, *see also specific types of oil*
    complete G.I. diet chart, 321
    sprays, 321
    tropical, 32, 37, 41, 321
    vegetable, 32, 41, 321
okra, 326
olive oil, 15, 27, 32, 37, 41, 73, 321
olives, 15, 27, 37, 40, 326
omega-3 fatty acid, 15
onions, 37, 40, 326
orange juice, unsweetened, 322
oranges, 32, 37, 40, 322
organ meats, 323
overweight
    defined by BMI, 24
    epidemic of, 11
    and exercise, 190
    health risks, 61, 178–83

P

palm oil, 321
pancakes, 31, 36, 318
papayas, 32, 36, 40, 321
parsnips, 36, 40, 326
pasta
    as green-light food, 21
    canned or instant noodles, 36, 40, 324
    complete G.I. diet chart, 324
    dried or fresh, 36, 40, 324
    filled with cheese or meat, 36, 40, 324
    serving sizes, 27, 43, 109
pasta sauces, commercial, 324

pastrami
    beef, 323
    turkey, 323
pâté, 35, 323
peaches
    canned, in juice or water, 45, 322, 324
    canned, in syrup, 322
    fresh, 32, 37, 40, 322
peanut butter
    100% peanuts, 32, 37, 321
    regular or light, 32, 37, 41, 321
peanuts, 321
pear juice, unsweetened, 322
pears
    canned, in juice or water, 45, 322, 324
    canned, in syrup, 322
    fresh, 37, 41, 322
peas
    black-eyed, 317
    green, 37, 41, 326
    split, 317
pecans, 321
peppers
    bell, 36, 40, 326
    hot, 37, 41, 326
persimmons, 321
Phase I
    how much to eat, 26–27
    what to eat, 25–26
    when to eat, 27
Phase II
    alcohol, 227–28, 229
    chocolate, 228, 229
    maintaining the diet, 229–31
physical activity *see* exercise
pickles, 37, 41, 45, 325, 326
pineapple juice, 322
pineapples, 32, 36, 40, 321
pistachios, 41, 321
pita bread, 36, 40, 318
pizza, 36, 40, 318
Pizza Hut, 133
plateaus, 146–47
plums, 32, 37, 41, 322
PMS, 20
polenta, 319

TVP, 43, 323
spelt, 319
spices, 320
spicy foods, 137
spinach, 37, 41, 326
Splenda, 74, 77, 325
spreads, 325
squash, 36, 40, 326
squid, 42
stevia, 325
strawberries, 37, 41, 322
stroke
    and menopause, 178
    and overweight, 61
    risk reduced through healthy eating, 178–81
    and waist measurement, 180
stuffing, 318
Subway, 133
sucralose, 74
sugar
    as "treat," 87–88
    complete G.I. diet chart, 325
    cravings for, 120–21, 137
    and feeling overheated, 172
    and green-light recipes, 73–74
    reading food labels, 52
sugar alcohols, 325
sugar substitutes, 73–74, 77, 325
Sugar Twin, 325
Sugar Twin Brown, 74
sunflower oil, 15, 321
sunflower seeds, 45
sushi, 39, 323
Sweet'N Low, 325
sweet potatoes, 37, 40, 169, 326
Swiss chard, 326

T
Taco Bell, 133
tartar sauce, 319
tea
    about, 32–33, 47
    black, 47
    green, 47
    herbal, 47, 318
    regular, 318

telephoning while eating, 85
television use while eating, 85, 110, 122
tempura, 137
teriyaki sauce, 320
textured vegetable protein (TVP), 43, 323
Thai restaurants, 135
toast, 34
tofu
    as protein source, 16, 74
    complete G.I. diet chart, 323
    for dessert, 44
    for dinner, 39, 43
    for lunch, 35
    low-fat, 35, 323
    regular, 323
tomatoes, 37, 41, 326
tortilla chips, 45, 325
tortillas
    regular, 40, 319
    whole wheat, 36, 318
trail mix, 45, 325
trans fats, 15
travelling, 59, 139
tropical oils, 32, 37, 41, 321
trout, 15
tuna, 15
turkey
    at holiday dinners, 168
    bacon, 30, 35, 323
    breast, skinless, 35, 39, 323
    leg, skinless, 323
    pastrami, 323
    roll, 323
turnips, 326
TVP (textured vegetable protein), 43, 323

V
veal, 35, 39, 42, 323
vegetable juice, 318, 322
vegetable oils, 15, 32, 41, 321
vegetables
    as protein source, 16
    at holiday dinners, 169
    at restaurants, 137
    complete G.I. diet chart, 326
    fibre content, 13

for breakfast, 32
for dinner, 40–41, 44
for lunch, 36–37
fresh, 45, 325
frozen, 76
how to cook, 22
in sandwiches, 38
serving sizes, 109
vegetable shortening, 15, 32, 41, 321
veggie burgers, 323
venison, 323
vinegar, 320

W
waffles, 31, 36, 318
waist measurement
  and disease risk, 97, 179–80
  how to take, 49–50
  tightening stomach muscles through
    exercise, 196
waist-to-hip ratio, 180
walnuts, 15, 41, 321
Wasa Fibre crispbread, 27, 31, 36, 318
water, 46, 85, 136, 318
watermelon juice, 318, 322
watermelons, 321
weight loss
  fears about, 65
  importance of avoiding hunger, 26
  importance of exercise, 64, 189–91, 195,
    204
  importance of sleep, 182
  in spots, 196
  maintaining, 229–31
  plateaus, 146–47
  progress, 50, 72, 101–2
  reasons for, 60–62, 157

recognizing, 157–58
and role of carbohydrates, 20
staying motivated, 157–61
target, 49–50, 57–58
tips to achieve goals, 63–64
Wendy's, 133
wheat berries, 319
whey powder, 323
wine
  red, 227–28, 229, 318
  white, 169, 228
women
  frame size, 24–25
  waist measurement, 49, 179–80
worcestershire sauce, 320
wrist size, 24–25

X
xylitol, 77

Y
yams, 37, 40, 326
yellow-light foods, 21
yogurt
  before eating out, 136
  fat-free, no sugar added, 76
  fat-free, with sugar substitute, 31, 34, 39,
    45, 320, 324
  frozen, low-fat, low-sugar, 320
  low-fat, 39
  low-fat, with sugar, 31, 320
  whole or 2%, 31, 39, 321

Z
ZonePerfect food bar, 44, 324
zucchini, 37, 41, 326

Recipe Index

V

Vegetables, *see also specific vegetable*
    Basic G.I. Salad, 255
    Chicken Stir-Fry with Broccoli, 284
    Fettucine Primavera, 273
    G.I. Pasta Salad, 259
    Indian Vegetable Curry, 272
    Lemony Grilled Vegetable Pasta Salad, 253
    Minestrone Soup, 246
    Mini Breakfast Puffs, 240
    Quinoa, Bean and Vegetable Chili,
      270–71
    Savoury Beans and Apple, 268
    Vegetable Barley Soup au Pistou, 249
    Vegetarian Moussaka, 274–75
    Vegetarian Omelette, 243
Vinaigrettes
    Basic G.I., 255
    for Cold Noodle Salad, 258
    for Greek Salad, 257
    for Grilled Shrimp and Pear Salad, 264
    for Mixed Bean Salad, 261

W

Waldorf Chicken and Rice Salad, 262
Wasabi, Ginger-Wasabi Halibut, 281
Whole Wheat Fruit Scones, 304

Y

Yogurt
    Breakfast in a Glass, 242
    Cinnamon French Toast, 238
    Raita Salad, 252

Z

Zesty Barbecued Chicken, 290–91
Zucchini
    Fettucine Primavera, 273
    Indian Vegetable Curry, 272
    Lemony Grilled Vegetable Pasta Salad, 253